To Stacey &

I hope you find my
brother-in-law's story inspiring.

Eliz y. Lee

Rolling Rabbi

The Power of Perseverance:
The Story of Rabbi Yehuda Simes

SHAINDEL SIMES

Rolling Rabbi

ISRAEL BOOKSHOP
Publications

The Power of Perseverance:

The Story of
Rabbi Yehuda Simes

SHAINDEL SIMES

Copyright © 2022 by Israel Bookshop Publications
ISBN: 978-1-60091-966-4

Book & cover design by:

SRULY PERL | 845.222.1967
srulyperl.com | info@srulyperl.com

Published and distributed by:

Israel Bookshop Publications
501 Prospect Street
Lakewood, NJ 08701
Tel: (732) 901-3009
Fax: (732) 901-4012
www.israelbookshoppublications.com
info@israelbookshoppublications.com

Printed in Bulgaria

Distributed in Israel by:
Tfutza Publications
P.O.B. 50036
Beitar Illit 90500
972-2-650-9400

Distributed in Europe by:
Lehmanns
Unit E Viking Industrial Park
Rolling Mill Road,
Jarrow, Tyne & Wear NE32 3DP
44-191-406-0842

Distributed in Australia by:
Gold's Book and Gift Company
3-13 William Street
Balaclava 3183
613-9527-8775

Distributed in South Africa by:
Kollel Bookshop
Ivy Common
107 William Road, Norwood
Johannesburg 2192
27-11-728-1822

Dedication

Dedicated in everlasting tribute to

Rabbi Yehuda Simes

הרב יהודה פנחס בן ר׳ יצחק אייזיק זצ״ל

To your family and friends, you were Yehuda.

To your children, you were Abba.

To your students, you were Rabbi Simes.

To the world, you were the Rolling Rabbi.

You wore all of these titles with pride,
honor, and distinction.

Ultimately, the title you strove for
the most, you earned as well.

Eved Hashem

When you could not speak, you communicated.

When you could not move, you acted.

When you could not feel, you touched.

You touched our hearts and souls. You moved us to
search deeper inside of ourselves to grow and improve.

We strive to emulate you every day of our lives.

ת.נ.צ.ב.ה.

Table of Contents

Acknowledgments

MY FAMILY, FRIENDS, AND EVEN MY STUDENTS (ONCE THEY get to know me well enough) have all discovered something about me: When my creative juices start flowing, I disappear. I can usually be found roaming the aisles of Michaels for bursts of inspiration. In fact, my state of mind can be measured by the adrenaline rush I feel—or lack thereof. It is never a good sign if I cannot come up with even a single idea for a project. My newly discovered haven is Hobby Lobby. Yes, I did indeed drive twenty miles each way to the franchise nearest me!

My most recent purchase was a plaque. It reads, "Every family has a story; welcome to ours." What you are now holding in your hands is the story of our family. If only I had kept track of all the people who told me, "You should write a book!" Never in my wildest dreams did I think I would have enough adrenaline to do *that*!

Reaching this milestone took many twists and turns. I could not have accomplished it without the countless people behind the scenes. From the people who gave me advice on what it takes to write a book, to the people who directed me and guided me on whom to speak to, and to those who had already published a book and shared their experiences with me…from those who deciphered and typed up my hastily written scribbles and scrawls, as my hand tried to keep up with my mind, to those who read, reread, revamped, and reviewed my work again and again…to all of you, I am extremely appreciative.

I had hundreds of blog posts written by Yehuda, telling his story.

There were hundreds of pages that I had written, portraying my perspective of the story; numerous postings on the CaringBridges website; stacks of newspaper and magazine articles; and piles of CD recordings of Yehuda's speeches. There was even a box of handwritten letters that Yehuda had written to his family over the years. It would take skill, expertise, attention to detail, and a proficiency with words to weave it all together in order to create a book out of it. I am grateful to Mrs. Miriam Zakon for putting me in touch with Mrs. Nina Indig, an editor par excellence. Mrs. Indig took the material I had, and created a masterpiece. When she presented the completed manuscript to me, I was rendered speechless. My dream had become a reality.

Optimistically, I submitted the manuscript to Israel Bookshop Publications, and it was not long before their acceptance email bloomed in my inbox and I was fist-pumping the air, tears running down my cheeks! I am ever so grateful to R' Moshe Kaufman and the entire staff at Israel Bookshop Publications, for seeing meaning in my mission and taking on my book. Thank you to Shaindy Weiss, who edited and polished the manuscript until it shone, and to Esther Malky Sonenblick, who meticulously proofread the entire book, ensuring the accuracy and precision of each detail related and each word written. Thank you as well to Liron Delmar and Malkie Gendelman, who oversaw and facilitated the whole process.

My thanks to Mr. Issie Scarowsky, a dear family friend who is also a talented photographer, for providing us with many of the beautiful pictures that enhance the book. Thanks to Nicola Hamer for her pictures as well.

⚡

Just two words: *Thank you*. How can that expression ever be adequate in giving proper recognition to all those who supported and uplifted our family throughout our journey, never letting us fall for a moment?!

Our dear friends who stayed with us for the ride—it was not a ride for the faint of heart. Did they ever faint? I will never know; they would never tell me. They were always there when we needed them most, so I will have to assume that they did not! Our medical team, who devoted themselves to us for nearly seven years, is included in our friendship circle. We still keep up with many of the people from "Team Simes."

Our *roshei yeshivah* and *rebbeim*. Their Torah perspective and guidance were invaluable even before the accident; afterward, we found them to be life-sustaining. Our *roshei yeshivah* and *rebbeim* provided support, direction, encouragement, and counsel in every way possible. On numerous occasions they gave of their limited time to travel to Ottawa to provide *chizuk* to us, something for which we will always be grateful.

Our family. What a family I am blessed to be part of! My mother *a"h* and *yblch"t* my father laid the foundation that enabled me to weather the storms. May Hashem grant my father *arichas yamim v'shanim* in good health, to enjoy *nachas* from his children, grandchildren, and great-grandchildren. Sadly, I never had the privilege of knowing my in-laws in their prime, but I know that it was they who inculcated in Yehuda the compass that guided his life.

My sisters, brother, sisters-in-law, and brothers-in-law. (Shout-out to my nieces and nephews!) In our family there is no difference between the siblings and the "in-law" siblings. Every single one of you shares the ties that bind. There is no way to measure the extent of what you all did for Yehuda, me, and our kids. If I had a dollar for every mile each of you traveled for us, I would be a billionaire. Maybe I really am one. I would be remiss if I did not include our uncles, aunts, and cousins. Each one provided support in his or her own way. May Hashem enable us all to share in *simchos* for many years to come.

My precious children and grandchildren. You give meaning to my days (and my nights!). You are following in the path paved by Abba's footsteps. Just as Abba used his *kochos*, so, too, each one of you is using your very own tailor-made strengths to serve Hashem. You bear the torch of *kiddush Hashem*. I echo the words of Abba, who so fervently *davened* for all of you every Friday night: יְבָרֶכְךָ ה' וְיִשְׁמְרֶךָ, יָאֵר ה' פָּנָיו אֵלֶיךָ וִיחֻנֶּךָּ, יִשָּׂא ה' פָּנָיו אֵלֶיךָ וְיָשֵׂם לְךָ שָׁלוֹם.

Hashem, the *Kol Yachol* and Source of all good. Even in our darkest hours we turned to You, and You helped us. It is my humble request that You continue to shower Your *brachos* upon us.

Shaindel Simes

Kislev 5782

Foreword

SETTLED INTO MY SEAT IN THE AUDITORIUM, RESIGNED TO A long evening. How on earth had I let Rochel convince me to come out? I had no real interest in being there. In fact, I had no interest in seeing anyone at all that night. I was not in the mood. Enough was going on at home.

The topic of the Chofetz Chaim Heritage Foundation's video presentation was "Coping During Challenging Times." Knowing that I was going through "challenging times" (the understatement of the century!), my friend thought it would be the perfect outing for me. *Rochel*, I thought, *I am* the speech for challenging times! So much so, in fact, that in my "free time" from my challenging times, I did not want to hear about challenging times. No more than I wanted to hear about the masseuse's experience with spinal cord injury when I went for a relaxing massage as a temporary break from my own SCI experience. Yet here I was, surrounded by others who were eager to enjoy their evening hearing about challenging times. What a blast! Party on!

I was in for the shock of my life, a lightning-bolt moment that was completely unexpected.

On screen, the speaker was describing the experience of the soul before it comes down into this world and is placed into a body. The soul is shown a "video" of its life ahead—all its experiences, decisions, milestones, trials, and tribulations from birth until death. As it watches the prophetic proceedings, it nods along. The soul knows that its entire purpose on earth is to achieve its potential, to achieve the perfection for which it was created. It knows that no two people have the same purpose in life; no soul will go through life unscathed. It knows that the world is the soul's laboratory in which to attain these goals. Every situation it experiences, whether positive or negative, happy or sad, joyous or painful, is for its benefit. The soul's inherent desire is to achieve its purpose, so the soul agrees and "signs up" for its role. A child is born.

As I listened to the speaker's words, my spine tingled. I shivered. Before I was born, I had accepted my role. Really? Could it be that I had signed up for this? I sat in my seat, stunned and frozen. I do not recall anything else that was said that evening. At some point, I realized the video had ended, the lights had been turned on, and the other ladies had left. Yet I could not budge.

I had signed up for this! For how many months now had I been telling my family and friends *I didn't sign up for this*? I did NOT sign up for this. This was not the life I expected. This was not the life I wanted. Nobody asked me. Nobody! I had not been in a massive auditorium listening to an authoritative voice challenging the crowd: "We are looking for volunteers. Who here would like to be the wife of a quadriplegic?" I did not hop up and down, making the emphatic ooo-ooo-ooo sound that my students emit when they are eager to sign up for a job or a privilege. I did not call out, "Pick me! Pick me! Please! Pick me!"

I did not. Or so I thought. But the speaker's words were like a bullet piercing my heart. I did. My soul had yelled, "Pick me! Pick me! It is a privilege and an honor that I want. I know that by signing up, I will become the best me I can possibly be."

This was a difficult concept to internalize. I sat for long minutes in deep contemplation until finally, I went home in a daze, muttering under my breath, "I signed up for this." At that point, my competitive nature called out, "By golly! If I signed up for this, I am going to do it right! I will not be a failure."

Slowly, slowly, these words and thoughts seeped into my psyche.

I became empowered: This was something I *chose*. This was not something that "happened" to me. I would need to see how the Divine plan unfolded.

By no means was this an overnight process. It took time, patience— and lack of patience—to internalize.

I was sitting at the table preparing for a Chumash class, reviewing Rashi's commentary. We were studying the portion of Moshe pleading and beseeching over five hundred times for permission to enter Eretz Yisrael. Moshe *davened* again and again and again, not accepting no for an answer.

We have to picture in our minds who and what we are talking about. Moshe was the man called the "servant of Hashem," the highest accolade possible. He was the humblest of all men. He was our leader who ascended Har Sinai three times to receive the Torah and prevent our annihilation. Moshe was in the presence of Hashem in Heaven for a total of one hundred and twenty days and nights without food, water, and sleep. He was the only prophet who could speak to Hashem as a man speaks to his friend, face to face, on his own terms, with no wait time.

How Moshe yearned to go into Eretz Yisrael, the land promised to his forefathers for generations, the climax of the Jewish People's Exodus from Egypt. He would bask in the holiness of the land that flows with milk and honey, where the ultimate spiritual connection to Hashem could take place. Yet Rashi (*Devarim* 3:26) explains: *You have much: [Hashem said,] "More than this is being kept for you; much good is hidden for you."* You may think you know what you need. You may think you know what is good for you. But Hashem knows better. He has something better that awaits you.

I felt a familiar sensation as my spine began to tingle and I began to shiver. I mouthed the words over and over again. "I have something better for you. I have something better for you." I jumped out of my seat and began pacing, round and round the table. I went out of the dining room and into the kitchen, round and round the island, all the time repeating, "I have something better for you."

Shaindel, you thought you knew what your life should look like. You thought you knew how it should proceed. No, Shaindel, I have something better for you, for Yehuda, for your family. You may not see it just yet. You may not understand it ever in This World, but it is better for you. It is to help you fulfill your purpose in This World.

I ran back to the dining room, ripped out a paper from my notebook, and in large letters wrote, "I HAVE SOMETHING BETTER FOR YOU!" I ran back to the kitchen and secured it to my fridge with a magnet, to be seen by all, but most importantly, by me.

I called my sister and several friends to share with them my newfound insight and inspiration. I was so enthusiastic that I had a magnet designed with these words to distribute at my speaking engagements. It serves as a tangible, take-home reminder of how to cope in challenging times.

Over the course of time, I have come to accept that while this is not the life I expected, this is the life I need. It may look different, yet it is very much the same. I am trying to fulfill my purpose.

I invite you to be inspired as well by reading the story of my husband, the Rolling Rabbi.

...Asking "why" and thinking that it's not fair only would make sense if we controlled life. The fact that my mother has Alzheimer's disease proves that we don't. And if we don't, who are we to ask "why"? Do we choose to be born, or to die? Do we choose to be short, or to be tall? Do we choose to be healthy, or to be sick? What right do we have, then, to go looking for answers to why I have brown hair and why Judy has black hair? Do I have any more right to say my mother's illness is unfair than I do to say it's unfair that I'm not a genius?

There are certain givens in this game of life. We didn't make up any rules. Our only job is to make our time here worthwhile and to accomplish the right things as much as is under our power. We must take what we have and use it.

From Yehuda's letter to his aunt and uncle,
May 1986, written in Israel at age eighteen.

Prologue

IT WAS WELL PAST SUNSET. THERE WERE NO LIGHTS ON THE 81 and the road had grown dark. My eyes were adjusting to the transformation of dusk into night. Shadows were everywhere. I blinked several times and squinted. A particular shadow in the road seemed darker. I called out to Yehuda, "Do you see something? Is something there? Is that a deer? I think it's a deer. Help! What should I do? WHAT SHOULD I DO?"

There was no time to process. In the split second I had to make a decision, all I could think of were the horror stories of what happens when a deer comes through a windshield. I could not let that happen. I had to protect my family...

> Suddenly, I awoke with a start. Our faithful blue van began to screech to the left, into the oncoming traffic lane. I sluggishly reached toward the steering wheel to help redirect the van. My wife overcompensated, hurtling the van toward the right. Again, she aggressively pounded the wheel all the way to the left. I don't know how many times we sharply weaved back and forth, screeching loudly and leaving strong black marks on the highway...
>
> I remember saying under my breath, "Oh no oh no." Finally, the van skimmed a post beyond the oncoming traffic lane, causing the van to tumble and roll numerous times. It was during this horrifying somersaulting that I

kept repeating "*Shema Yisrael.*" Looking back, this just poured out of my lips automatically, without thinking to form the words. Eventually, the van ended its death roll in an upright position, giving an appearance of "all is well." But all was not well.

From the Rolling Rabbi blog,
"My Story," August 2013

CHAPTER ONE

From Ellenville to Burns Street

Bubby Country and Bubby Molly

I WAS NAMED AFTER MY GREAT-GREAT-GRANDMOTHER, Shaindel Goodman, affectionately known as Bubby Country. Bubby Country lived in Ellenville, New York.

In the early 1900s, Eliezer Goodman left Russia to escape being drafted to fight the Russo-Japanese War. He was also in search of a better life for his family. His wife, Bubby Country, followed several years later with the children.

Zeide Eliezer was a *rav* and a *shochet*. Bubby Country ran a boarding house on their farm to provide extra income for the family. As the story goes, Zeide Eliezer had a heart attack while preparing to slaughter a sheep and passed away shortly thereafter. Bubby Country was widowed in her forties, left

Bubby Country and Zeide Eliezer Goodman with two of their children, Chaim Zev and Molly, early 1900s.

alone with a young family to raise. Wanting her children to receive a proper Torah education, she bravely sent her young boys off to Yeshiva Rabbeinu Jacob Joseph (RJJ) by train, all by themselves.

People were shocked by her decision. How could she send her sons away to study in yeshivah? Wasn't she crying?

"Of course I'm crying," she would reply. "But I would rather cry now than cry later."

Much of my life mirrors Bubby Country's. She moved and had to acclimate to a new country. She sent her children away to further their Jewish education. Her husband was forty-nine when he passed away, leaving her behind to provide for her family.

Growing up, I was constantly reminded of what a special woman Bubby Country was and how lucky I was to be named after her. A deeply religious woman throughout her life, even when well over eighty she stood the entire Yom Kippur in stocking feet; she never sat down and never stopped *davening*. When Yom Kippur was over, she literally needed to be carried home.

When her granddaughter, my Bubby Eleanor, was a teenager, Bubby Country called her over. She wanted to talk to her privately and had a favor to ask, not one you would expect a grandmother to ask of a fifteen-year-old girl. "G-d willing, you will have children," she said. "Please promise me, if at all possible, to have someone in your family named after me. I know I can count on you. Your children will live by the Torah. They will make me proud!"

When I was born, Bubby Country's request was honored. When I light Shabbos candles every week using Bubby Eleanor's candlesticks, I remember a promise fulfilled.

As a child, however, I would get upset that not a single girl in my whole school was named Shaindel. I threw tantrums and declared that I wanted to be called by my middle name, Sora—or even Suri—a common name like everyone else's! It is quite ironic that when I moved to Ottawa, I taught a girl named Shayndel for five years in a row, and was introduced to several women all named Shelly, who were each proud to say, "My name is Shaindel, too!"

Although I never knew Bubby Country, I was very close to her daughter, my Bubby Molly (Malka). Bubby Molly would share with me in great detail what it was like to grow up on the farm. I heard about the assorted guests and their idiosyncrasies, and how Bubby made sure to accommodate each guest.

L. D. Tel. 240 F. 12 Ellenville, N. Y.

CATSKILL MOUNTAINS

GOODMAN'S FARM HOUSE
MRS. J. GOODMAN, PROP.

ELLENVILLE, ULSTER CO., N. Y.

בשר FIRST CLASS STRICTLY בשר

:: SUMMER RESORT ::

Elegant Summer Garden, Finest Orchard, Hand Ball Courts

— HOT AND COLD WATER IN EVERY ROOM —

EVERYTHING FRESH FROM OUR OWN FARM

Take Cortlandt St or West 42nd St. Ferries, then New York Ontario and Western Railroad or Busses and Stop at Ellenville.

Send postal 2 days before and our Car will await you at depot.

MAIL ADDRESS, ELENVILLE, N. Y. R. F. D, No. 1, BOX 143

Original business card containing information about accommodations on the farm. The farm was purchased November 18, 1913, for $1 and a $450 mortgage.

Neither the farm nor the shul is owned by the family anymore, but they are still up and running. The farm and the adjacent home are located at 164 Frog Hollow Road. The shul is just up the road and around the corner on Briggs Highway. It is a small stone building with a triangular roof. A large, round stained-glass window featuring a Magen David clearly identifies it as a shul. Some years ago, it was shuttered and in a state of disarray. More recently, the shul was once again being used. Camp Ohr Shraga and the Bayit Vegan bungalow colony are keeping Zeide's shul alive.

In the summer of 2017, I brought my children to visit the farm and the shul. The door of the shul was open and we walked right

"The Shul," Ellenville, New York.

in. I immediately noticed an addition to the building that had not been there on my previous visits. We walked around looking at the *siddurim* and *sefarim* on the tables and shelves. We marveled at how beautiful it was that the shul was still in use over a hundred years later.

There were obvious signs that both children and adults used the shul—evident by the empty soda cans and chips bags, and by the type of *sefarim* lying around. We decided to surprise the congregants by tidying up; it would be a mitzvah and a merit to Zeide's *neshamah*.

We felt a deep connection to someone we had never met, but who was directly connected to us. As we rearranged scattered chairs and tables, collected wrappers, and set the books into neat piles, we chuckled. "Can you imagine the reaction of the members when they come back in the afternoon?"

We pictured them, shocked and disbelieving, asking each other, "Did you have anything to do with this?"

"No, did you?"

Oh, to have been a fly on the wall!

After cleaning the shul, we went to say Tehillim at the graves of family members buried in the small old cemetery along Briggs Highway. It was difficult to find their *kevarim*. The headstones in the open area were engraved with recent dates. As we walked to the back, the graveyard seemed to end in bushes and overgrowth. Peering through the foliage, we could see another area. We pushed aside the branches and climbed through into a clearing, where we saw small markers indicating the names and dates of several young children, including a set of twins. These were Bubby Country's children who did not survive infancy or childhood, Bubby Molly's siblings. We said some Tehillim, thankful that we live in an era when life expectancy is considerably longer.

Life on Burns Street

When my parents, Rabbi Dovid and Rochel (Katz) Vinitsky married, it was obvious they would live in Forest Hills, Queens, near Yeshiva Chofetz Chaim, where my father was learning. He was studying under the *rosh yeshivah*, Rav Henoch Leibowitz, and planned on learning full time for several years before obtaining *semichah*.

We lived in an apartment at 68-49 Burns Street, nine blocks from the yeshivah. Many other yeshivah couples lived on the block. When I was old enough to babysit, my mother never let me charge more than $2.50 an hour. She explained that our neighbors were living on very tight budgets. I knew them well and was aware that the wives were working hard to help support their families. Babysitting was never a lucrative career for me.

Shabbos mornings I would go with my father to the yeshivah, mostly to play with my friends, but we did *daven* as well. The highlight for me was standing with my father as all the men lined up to shake the Rosh Yeshivah's hand and wish him a good Shabbos. We would then escort the Rosh Yeshivah home. The walk was not far, but it was slow. Many men used the opportunity to ask Rav Leibowitz for his opinion and advice on a variety of topics. My parents, too, turned to him and his *rebbetzin* for guidance in all facets of their lives and I saw firsthand the importance of seeking guidance from a mentor.

The yeshivah had a strong impact on my life. Rosh Hashanah and Yom Kippur were serious days. Rabbi Hochberg's haunting melodies set the tone for *davening*, and our *tefillos* extended well into the afternoon.[1] The fact that my father was the *ba'al tokei'a* enhanced my feeling of connection to the *tefillah*.

I loved *davening* there on Simchas Torah, watching the Rosh Yeshivah dance with the Torah, a broad, content smile on his face as he sang with his students and community. One of his favorites was "*V'yatzmach*," a song longing for Hashem's redemption. The Rosh Yeshivah would recite a word, and the crowd would repeat it and then burst into a tune.

Shabbos afternoons, twenty minutes after sunset, the Rosh Yeshivah would give a *shmuess* based on the weekly *parshah*. The emphasis was always on the inherent greatness and majesty of man and how we could reach personal perfection. The Rosh Yeshivah imparted advice on how we could tap into inner resources we do not even realize we possess, and about the layers of awareness that can be penetrated.

When I was in high school, my father encouraged me to attend these lectures. Sometimes I did, sometimes I did not. The Rosh Yeshivah's voice was faint, often competing with the hum of the huge overhead ceiling fans and the ancient rattling air conditioners. I managed to pick up key phrases that were common in each lecture.

Teacher in Training

My four younger siblings—Avrohom Dov, Fraidel, Elisheva, and Ahuva—and I experienced the usual sibling camaraderie and rivalry. As eldest, it was my job to boss them around.

I drafted them to be my students when I played school. For as far

---

1. The very first time I ever *davened* in a shul other than the yeshivah was in Ottawa. I was so homesick! After *davening* was over, I told Yehuda that hard as it would be for me to manage fasting and taking care of the kids on my own on Yom Kippur, if he wanted to go back to the yeshivah, I would completely understand. Yehuda looked at me with a puzzled expression. "Why would I want to do that? I put my *tallis* over my head and I *daven*. Why does it matter where I am?" I teased him that *I* would go back to New York on Yom Kippur and *he* could stay home with the kids.

back as I can remember, I always wanted to be a teacher. I would set up my dolls and my siblings with homemade worksheets and give them homework. At the *shivah* for my grandfather, when I was nine, I distributed math tests to the relatives who came for *nichum aveilim*. I loved to be the teacher.

I adored most of my teachers. I still remember their names and which grade they taught. I was a goody-goody in school, afraid of getting into trouble. That does not mean I always received good grades. How hard I studied depended on the subject and how much I liked the teacher.

When I was in college, it was a requirement to take two history courses. History was never one of my favorite subjects; too many names and dates. Give me math any day! I dreaded it and pushed it off until the summer semester. The professor had such an obvious passion for his subject. He was lively and energetic as we made our way through all the Kings Louis and Charles. By the end of the course, I knew who was who and who did what. The professor helped me internalize the importance of teachers loving the subject they taught to be able to pass on that knowledge to others. I wanted to do that!

As I approached marriageable age, I had to decide what I wanted my future to look like. What type of man did I want to marry? What goals did I have? What goals would he have?

After much thought, I came to the realization that I wanted to marry someone who was dedicated to Torah learning and personal growth. I wanted our children to be raised in a home in which Torah was the foundation and the guide. The tone would be set by my future husband spending five to seven years immersed in Torah study and character development, and culminate in his obtaining *semichah*. He would then use all he acquired to teach others. Working on his personal growth during these years would make him mature and better equipped to serve as a role model.

For this to happen I would need to earn my degree and get a "real" job so I could help support my family during those years. I did not want to do anything but teach. It was 1990 and the field of speech pathology was becoming popular. I had taken a course in seminary about speech therapy that I found interesting. I did the math: Speech therapy means teaching people how to speak and I wanted to teach, so… 1+1=2. I registered in Touro College to earn a bachelor's degree in psychology with a concentration in speech pathology, as Touro did not have its own speech program at the time. My plan was to attend college on Sundays and evenings. During the day I would, of course, teach.

In the fall of 1991, I signed a contract for my first teaching job. I was to teach ninth-grade boys at a fairly new high school that catered to recent immigrants, many of whom did not have full command of the English language. I had been hoping to teach Judaic studies. Instead, I began teaching secular subjects until a Judaic studies position opened up a few weeks later. I received all kinds of advice, tips, and warnings from co-teachers and others. Was I crazy to agree to this? I was barely five years older than the students!

I tried not to tremble when I arrived at school the first day. Pulling myself up to my somewhat less-than-imposing full height of five feet and one inch, and assuming as stern an expression as my cherubic freckled face would allow, I strode toward the classroom.

Boys were milling around in the hallway. I did not know who belonged where nor did I know any of their names. I pointed at the tallest, biggest boy in the group and firmly said, "You! Do you belong in that room?" He nervously nodded. "Well, then," I responded, "get in there!" As he walked in, the others followed. I had survived my first minute as a teacher and felt quite pleased with myself.

All seemed to be going well, and soon it was recess time. I took the boys outside to play handball against the side of the building, as the school did not have a gym or a yard. As was to be expected, the ball rolled into the street, under a car. I watched cautiously as the boys went to rescue their ball. On the count of three, they lifted the car and one of them snatched the ball off the ground. I was speechless. I prayed for them to put down the car without dropping it on someone's toe. How would I explain to a student's mother how a car happened to fall on her son's foot?

As autumn slowly turned into winter, my schedule was packed. I was teaching full time and going to college full time. First-year teaching is brutal. I was getting used to the daily grind and preparing lessons from scratch. This, combined with marking papers, preparing reports, and studying for exams, did not leave much time for relaxation.

One day, I saw a travel agency ad offering a trip to Israel for only $550. I had not been to Israel since the summer I was five years old. On a whim, I showed it to my parents, told them I wanted to go, and asked for their opinion. They concurred that it was a great opportunity. I quickly called my friend Mirel to see if she would be interested in joining me. Mirel had spent the prior year in a seminary in Israel, bravely staying put during the Gulf War. She enthusiastically agreed and we excitedly signed up for tours and trips to travel the length and breadth of the country in just one short week. I was also hoping to have the chance to *daven* at the holy sites. Foremost on my mind at this stage in my life was marriage. I wanted to pray that I find my soulmate quickly and easily.

I returned from my trip to Israel on a high, invigorated by the vacation and inspired by the holiness of our homeland.

A few weeks later, the Rebbetzin called. There was a wonderful boy who was fairly new in the Queens branch of Yeshiva Chofetz Chaim. She knew him very well. Yehuda Simes was a close friend of her nephew, Yaakov Trop, and one of the few select students who boarded in her basement. Would I be interested in meeting him?

Yes, I would.

"The boy will call," she said.

And he did.

CHAPTER TWO

From Zhitomer to St. Paul

Yitzchak Isaac Simes

MY HUSBAND YEHUDA'S FATHER ("DAD"), YITZCHAK ISAAC Simes, was born on November 6, 1921. Yitzchak Isaac's mother, Chana Polechenko, immigrated to the United States from Zhitomer, Russia, at the age of nineteen, in 1915, and married Yehuda (after whom my husband was named) that same year. Yehuda had come from Russia in 1908 and was nine years older than his bride. The couple settled in St. Paul, Minnesota's West Side, an area of the city that was home to many immigrants at the time, including a large percentage of Jewish families.

Yehuda passed away in 1945. Although they had grown up in an observant and kosher home, Dad and his siblings did not necessarily follow that path. However, Dad wanted to say Kaddish for his father and went to one of the *shtiebels* on the West Side. Dad always said that he felt he found his place there and connected with the old men in the *minyan*. He became more interested in religion and started to learn with Chaim Asher Weiss,[1] who became Dad's guide in learning

---

1. Chaim Asher Weiss, a *shochet*, would later become his uncle through marriage, as Chaim Asher's wife, Dena, was the sister of Mom's mother. The Weisses had no children of their own.

more about Judaism. There were no institutions at the time for *ba'alei teshuvah*. Chaim Asher presented him with his first siddur. Dad discovered the English translation of the *Kitzur Shulchan Aruch* and began to read it page by page.

Asna Kaplan

Asna ("Mom") Kaplan's father's family originated in Kamenetz-Litovsk.[2] Her maternal grandfather, Efraim Tatelbaum, had studied in the Volozhin yeshivah. He was a yeshivah roommate and lifelong friend of Rabbi Avraham Yitzchak Hakohen Kook, who later became the first Chief Rabbi of Israel. They were buried near each other on Har Hazeisim.

Mom was born on February 21, 1926, in St. Paul. Her parents were Yaakov and Rochel (Tatelbaum) Kaplan. A middle child, she had an older sister, Malcah, and twin brothers born when she was barely two. The family peace-maker, Asna was studious and liked to sing. She belonged to the Young Adult Club, where she and Dad had leadership positions. She attended the University of Minnesota, earned a business degree, and found employment as a bookkeeper.

Mom and Dad Simes

Isaac Simes and Asna Kaplan married in 1953, in an era when not many people were becoming more religious. Asna chose an observant lifestyle unlike most of her contemporaries, who subscribed to the worldview that in order to be successful in the new world, one had to loosen one's ties to the old.

Mom and Dad's wedding was unique for their time in two ways. There was no mixed dancing, as Dad had read in the *Kitzur Shulchan Aruch* that it is prohibited. And the St. Paul community had discontinued the "old-fashioned" custom of the bride circling the groom seven times. Gasps rose from the guests when Mom walked around Dad. They were

---

2. In today's Belarus.

Wedding of Isaac (Dad) and Asna (Mom) Simes, February 15, 1953.

proud to have brought back the custom.

Dad's brother, Uncle Hy, in business with Sam Brenner, owned the St. Paul Barrel and Drum Company. They made barrels for wines and liquors, and were suppliers for a number of companies. The men invited Dad to join them as a partner, but accepting their offer would have required him to work on Shabbos. This was not even a question for Dad—he would not sacrifice his principles! Instead, he worked very hard for the company as their bookkeeper and office manager. Dad and Mom never felt like they had "given up" on something. Working on Shabbos was never an option.

At first, Dad and Mom lived in St. Paul's old Jewish neighborhood on the West Side. Mom's parents, Zeide Yaakov and Bubby Rochel, lived upstairs in the building behind the neighborhood store they owned and operated on Winifred Street. Mom and Dad lived downstairs.

Becky was born in 1955, followed by Judy in 1957. After Bubby Rochel died in July 1958, the young Simes family moved to the Highland Park neighborhood in St. Paul,[3] where they built a house down the street from their cousins Chana and Berel Silverberg.

---

3. Jews began moving out of the West Side in the 1920s and the exodus continued through the 1950s. The pace of urban flight accelerated after the Mississippi River flooded the area.

Life was different in Highland Park. There was no Orthodox shul in the area, there was no *mikveh*, and the day school was in a different city, Minneapolis. Mom and Dad were determined to rise to the challenge. They started a *minyan* in their basement with a proper women's section. The *minyan* was a very vibrant part of their lives. When Rabbi Moshe Feller came from Minneapolis as an emissary of the Lubavitcher Rebbe in 1961 to start a Chabad program, he began with Shabbos activities that took place in the Simes home. When the building for the *minyan* was bought, Rabbi Asher Zeilingold, recommended by Rabbi Feller, was brought in to be the rabbi. The *nusach* was changed from *Sefard* to *Ari* and the shul was named the Adath Israel Congregation.

Even after the shul had its own building, Dad kept up the Yamim Nora'im *minyan* in the house for the older congregants. The shul was a mile and a half away and the elderly members could not walk so far. On Rosh Hashanah, Dad walked several miles to the hospital to blow shofar for the patients.

In later years, when a *minyan* was needed for the shul, Dad would drive around and pick people up. One man had poor hygiene. Dad would pick him up last and give him a private ride, as no one wanted to be in the car with him.

There was no *mikveh* in St. Paul. Dad seized an opportunity to purchase a small storefront and started learning the *mikveh* rules. A visit by a halachic expert soon followed, and before long, the Simeses had the *mikveh* up and running.

Dad served on the boards of the school and the shul and kept the books for the West Side Hebrew Cemetery. He spent every Sunday during the month of Elul at the cemetery, helping people find graves of family members and reciting prayers on their behalf. He would come home sunburned at the end of a long day. It was hard for Mom

---

The city tore down buildings and built an industrial park. By 1962, the Jews were all gone. Archival footage exists of people carrying *sifrei Torah* out of a flooded shul. Dad brought those *sifrei Torah* to Highland Park.

to have him out for so many hours so close to the holidays, but she always supported his work on behalf of the community. In the 1970s, Dad was very involved in the grassroots effort to get a *chevra kaddisha* started. He also did *shemiros* and *taharos*.

Around 1976, a special matzah oven was built in the basement of the *mikveh* building. For several years, the family and community members baked matzos there. As it would be for any Jewish homemaker, it was stressful for Mom to have all her helpers disappear on Erev Pesach as well as some Sundays before. The siblings, however, found it fascinating and received a great education. At some point, though, the group became nervous that they were not proficient enough in the laws of matzah baking. Could it be that they were even eating *chametz*? The matzah baking was discontinued.

Mom and Dad were known for their kindness and generosity. They had a three-bedroom home. Sometimes when a charity collector came for a night or two, Yehuda would share his room. Any organization that sent out a *tzedakah* envelope received five dollars. Dad was often audited by the IRS: How could someone with his modest income be giving away so much money?

Years later at our wedding, while suffering from dementia, Dad was observed gathering loose *siddurim* and Chumashim from the tables of a side room and placing them neatly on the shelves. It seemed fitting, as that is what he dedicated his life to in St. Paul. No task was too big, no chore too small for Dad when it came to the shul and the Jewish community in St. Paul. Our name, Simes, comes from *shamash* in Hebrew—very fitting indeed.

Childhood Years

Rachel and Yehuda were the babies of the family. Rachel was born in 1964, seven years after Judy's birth.

Yehuda was born on Friday, June 16, 1967, the day after Shavuos. Becky remembers sitting and helping fold the family's laundry when they got the phone call. She was so excited that she grabbed all the neatly folded laundry and threw it up in the air, screaming for joy. She was sure Yehuda was her bas mitzvah present. His arrival was quite an event—a boy after three girls!—especially since Mom had suffered the traumatic stillbirth of a son before Becky was born.

The baby was named Yehuda Pinchas, after two grandfathers—Yehuda Simes and Pinchas Polechenko. Poor Judy. She was also named after Zeide Yehuda. On one of her visits to Canada after the accident, she teased Yehuda that she finally "forgave" him for "taking" her name.

At times it seemed as if young Yehuda could do no wrong.

Yehuda learning to walk.

The family had gone on vacation to a cabin in the North Minnesota woods. It was a rainy adventure and the kids were being kids. Rachel was playing with an umbrella and it broke. She had already gotten in trouble and was warned, "If you do one more thing, we are going home to St. Paul." Rachel gave the broken umbrella to Yehuda and said, "Go tell Mommy that you broke the umbrella." Yehuda did. Mom's response? "It's okay, Yehuda. No problem. Thank you for telling me!" The vacation was saved.

Bubby Chana lived with the Simeses for about two years before she was admitted to the Shalom Home. Rachel had to sleep on a cot when Bubby was there, and remembers the time she got caught up in the cot as it folded onto itself! It was not easy for Mom to have her mother-in-law living with her and telling her what her Isaac liked.

Education

When Becky and Judy were younger, they went to Edgecumbe Public School. Later they switched to Torah Academy in Minneapolis.

It was a very long bus ride for little girls. Rachel and Yehuda started in Torah Academy when it was in Golden Valley, a western suburb of Minneapolis. Mom would come with other parents to cook hot lunches for the students once a week. When Rachel was in fourth grade, the school moved to a building it shared with the Talmud Torah. It was much nicer, in a different neighborhood, and closer to the Jewish neighborhood in St. Louis Park, Minneapolis—but still not in St. Paul.

Torah Academy had classes through eighth grade. Depending on demand, they would occasionally open up a ninth-grade class—but not until after Becky and Judy's time. They had to go to public high school, but Rachel was able to continue in Torah Academy through ninth grade.

Simes family, St. Paul, Minnesota, circa 1972.

When Becky finished high school she went to study in Israel together with her cousin Dena. Yehuda was only six years old at the time. He did not know how to write. Mom would ask him what he wanted to say and add it to her letters. Not long afterward, he began to add a joke to every aerogram the family sent. Becky and her roommates would wait for his jokes and have a good laugh. Over the years, the letters developed to include a commentary on what was going on at home, in school, and in sports. Many fond family memories are based on those letters.

In the summer of 1978, when he was eleven years old, Yehuda

heard about a six-week SEED[4] program in Minneapolis and wanted to attend. Although he would be the only attendee from St. Paul, this did not deter him. Judy walked him to the city bus stop, and then he traveled alone, thirty minutes each way, every day. His counselor, nineteen-year-old Zecharya Greenwald, met him at the bus stop in Minneapolis and they biked together to the site of the program.

After the third week, Yehuda invited Zecharya to spend a Shabbos in St. Paul. "My mother sometimes hosts a Shabbos afternoon Torah class in our home," he explained. "Could you give the class this week?" To Yehuda's immense excitement, Zecharya agreed! Approximately twenty women attended the *shiur*. Yehuda sat just outside the room to listen in, beaming from ear to ear. How proud he was that his teacher was giving a class in his house!

Zecharya was impressed by the turnout and expressed his hope that the class would continue on a weekly basis. Judy gave the class the following week, and several years later, she was happy to report, the class was still being given on a consistent basis.

Rabbi Zecharya Greenwald went on to become the founding principal of Me'ohr Bais Yaakov Teacher's Seminary in Yerushalayim, as well as a popular lecturer and consultant on education and parenting. Over the years, he has shared

Yehuda delivering his bar mitzvah *dvar Torah*, June 1980.

---

4.   Under Torah Umesorah's Project SEED, yeshivah students in their teens and early twenties are recruited and sent on two- to six-week summer trips to distant smaller Jewish communities, where they teach classes or supervise children in summer day camps.

this story with others to impart the lesson of how a young child's love for learning Torah can inspire and encourage others.

When Yehuda was in eighth grade, it was time to consider options for high school. Many boys from the community went to yeshivah in Denver or to Telshe in Chicago. His parents were not entirely sold on the idea of sending such a young boy so far from home for ninth grade; they would have preferred a yeshivah closer to home.

3/21/81

Dear Becky,

This letter serves the sole purpose to "fill you in" on the events which are taking place here. Becky, it is imperative that you return the money which you borrowed from me. I (we) desperately need it for yeshivah. Now, you may think it wouldn't be a smart move for me to go to yeshivah next year; after all, there will be a ninth grade in Torah Academy... I feel that the foundation [I received at Torah Academy] is complete and sturdy and that it is time to build on my platform. ...

Before, everybody used to go away right after their bar mitzvah. Why should I now be any different? (Besides, I would be 14.) I am not here on this world to establish any relationship with anyone at this point in my life. Mommy wants to keep me here for her own reasons. She wants me here. She won't let me go because she thinks I'm too young. But I'm not here to be with my mother. The time has come for me to fly away from the nest. I also realize that I am dying (we all are). I mean, who knows how much longer I'll be around? And I wouldn't want to go without a good Jewish education. ...

Yes, a lot is at stake. Who knows? I could crack up under the pressure. Yup, it ain't gonna be easy. I know yeshivah life. Lonely, hard, barely any food, clogged toilets, broken beds, leaky roofs, cold in winter, hot in summer, going to bed so late, waking up so early, and doing nothing but learning in between...unbelievably hard tests, forget about seeing your family and friends for who knows how long, no homey luxuries, etc. But some things are so important that they have to be risked. I also know yeshivah in Israel is very hard and if I don't go this year, I'll be very behind.

There seems no reason why I should not go. All the reasons add up to one thing, going to yeshivah after eighth grade.

—Yehuda

The Wisconsin Institute for Torah Study (WITS) was established in 1980, when Yehuda was in eighth grade. The *rosh yeshivah*, Rabbi Raphael Wachsman, arranged for students to go on "out Shabbosos" to different cities around the Midwest to recruit eighth graders. He arranged for Baruch Lederman to go to Minneapolis/St. Paul and meet with the principal of Torah Academy, Rabbi Heshy Dachs. Rabbi Dachs gave Baruch a list of potential eighth graders and allowed him to speak in the school on Friday. Baruch was invited to stay at the Dachs home in St. Louis Park, Minneapolis, for Shabbos. All the boys lived within walking distance of the Dachses except Yehuda, who lived in St. Paul. They all got together on Motza'ei Shabbos for bowling and a *melaveh malkah*. This was the first of many such trips to Minneapolis. Baruch would always stay at the Dachses for Shabbos, but he was a guest at the Simes home for the last days of Pesach.

Despite Baruch's best efforts, the two boys who were considered most likely to go to WITS—one of whom was Yehuda Simes—seemed disinclined to attend. Yehuda was leaning toward Toras Chaim of Denver because he felt that was where he would learn the most. It seemed that Baruch had spent a great deal of time for a whole school year for nothing.

Baruch and Yehuda had developed somewhat of a relationship during that year. They spoke about Yehuda going to Milwaukee to learn with Baruch in the summer of 1981 to hone his still-limited Gemara-reading skills. That summer in Milwaukee, Yehuda and Baruch learned every morning for about four hours and for an hour or two every evening. As an additional bonus, Yehuda learned *Mishnah Berurah* every morning with Rabbi Wachsman for about twenty to forty minutes. He liked the style of learning he experienced over the summer and decided to enroll in WITS after all.

Simes family, St. Paul, Minnesota, circa 1981.

He joined the yeshivah in 1981, the second year it was in existence, and never looked back. There were ten boys in his fabulous ninth-grade class, and he grew close to many of them. He also became good friends with several students in the grade above, and eventually with boys who were a grade or two below him. Some of them remained lifelong friends. Some time later, Yehuda's mother told Baruch Lederman how thrilled she was that Yehuda was going to Milwaukee, as it was so much closer than Denver to St. Paul.

For its first four years, the yeshivah rented a wing in a defunct public school. The dorms were one mile away, on Mohawk Street. The *rebbeim* and their families lived nearby. The "Mean Green Machine Van" would transport the boys from the dorm to the yeshivah. If you missed the van, it was a long walk in the freezing cold. In order to avoid that, the students would scramble to make sure they did not miss the ride. One evening, some of them decided to pull a prank. They changed the clocks in the dorm and convinced one of the boys that his alarm had not rung and he was about to miss the van. He went running out—only to discover that it was the middle of the night!

Yehuda knew how to have a good time. He instigated "The Great Snowball Attack," an epic battle during which the high-schoolers pelted their older *beis midrash* friends with snowballs from the yeshivah's roof.

A level of responsibility was instilled in the boys as well. Yehuda was in charge of cooking eggs every morning for breakfast. This was part of a work-study program where students received a government stipend for services they provided to the school.

While Yehuda was away in yeshivah, his mother was diagnosed with Alzheimer's disease. In 1983 this was a new term. No one really knew or understood the illness. Becky came in from Israel to accompany Mom and Dad to the various diagnostic tests. These were very upsetting to Mom as they pointed out her deficiencies. She did not complete the round of tests. It was decided that the family would wait one and a half years for Yehuda to finish high school and then move to Israel, where everyone could help take care of Mom.

The years of Mom's illness were very hard for Yehuda. When he arrived home from yeshivah for Pesach, he assumed the house would be completely ready. Far from it. Yehuda had to get to work immediately in order to be ready for Yom Tov. He did not discuss his situation with anyone, preferring to keep it private as it was embarrassing to him. He could not understand what was happening to his super-confident and capable mother. However, he did keep in close touch with his sisters and wrote them frequent letters describing what was happening at home and in his heart.

4/2/85

Dear Family,

Here is a report. Today is Tuesday. First Seder is Friday night. The house should be ready to go tomorrow afternoon. This means all rooms will be cleaned of chametz. Chametz does not equal dirt. The downstairs refrigerator/freezer will be Pesachdig. This means we can start baking & cooking. Oh, we also need an order, I guess.

Daddy is still out of town. As soon as he comes back, he has to clean the shul for Pesach in three days. Oh well. ...

It's not that hard (yet). Just lonely and sort of sad.

–Yehuda

Move to Israel

The move to Israel finally took place in 1985. Although it was Dad and Mom's life-long dream, it was not easy for Dad as it uprooted him from everything familiar. The support systems to which he was accustomed were no longer in place and new ones needed to be established.

Yehuda wrote to his Aunt Malcah (Mom's sister) and Uncle Irving in St. Paul, updating them on the situation.

5/22/86

I guess it is pretty much an accepted thing. Day-to-day life goes on. It is no longer a shock. I think that everybody in this world needs help from others in one way or another. And I believe that those who are able to must help their neighbors any way they can. It could mean a cheery "good morning," teaching a child manners, helping your friend with his homework, or helping a blind man along his way. It makes no difference, really. It's the way the world runs.

It's the same thing with my mother. At the beginning, she may have needed help cooking up a Shabbos meal. And although it may have been frustrating at first, you get used to it. Because why should helping her make a cholent be any more unnatural than doing a favor for my father, or for one of my sisters? And if she needs help to eat an ice cream, or to wash her hands–why should that be any different from loaning my roommate ten bucks? The point is, the initial shock, pain, and frustration dissipates with every advanced stage in the disease–not because it hurts any less, but because you learn to understand that this also is part of Hashem's way of running this world.

As you know, I love my mother very much. It's simply unbelievable how great of a mother she was when I was growing up (that is not to say that I am done!). You just cannot imagine. As much as you know, as much as you have seen, as much as you have heard—it's nothing compared to what she has been to me, and what she has done for me. I know that my mother is a real tzaddekes.

So how can I say it's difficult to help her? How can I say she "interferes"? How can I say that helping her is hard and unhappy work? No way! Now, I can really give to her. I once heard that parents love their children more than children love their parents, because of how much more parents give to their kids, since that's the whole basis of love (giving). Well, maybe this is an exception to the rule. ...

One of the interesting things is how her talent and love for music were unharmed by the disease. She easily recalls and sings old songs and picks up new ones quickly. Listening to music is one of her favorite things. She (unknowingly) claps her hands and stamps her feet along with the beat—keeping perfect time. Listening to music makes her extremely happy.

There's just one more thing I want to touch on. And that's the subject of asking "why." I really think that although that may be naturally the first thing we do, it really is pretty ridiculous. Asking "why" and thinking that it's not fair only would make sense if we controlled life. The fact that my mother has Alzheimer's disease proves that we don't. And if we don't, who are we to ask "why"? Do we choose to be born, or to die? Do we choose to be short, or to be tall? Do we choose to be healthy, or to be sick? What right do we have, then, to go looking for answers to why I have brown hair and why Judy has black hair? Do I have any more right to say my mother's illness is unfair than I do to say it's unfair that I'm not a genius?

There are certain givens in this game of life. We didn't make up any rules. Our only job is to make our time here worthwhile and to accomplish the right things as much as is under our power. We must take what we have and use it.

—Yehuda

As the whole family was now living in Israel, Yehuda thought it would make sense to attend an Israeli yeshivah and joined Yeshiva

Kerem B'Yavneh. After one year, though, he missed his friends and the style of learning he was used to in WITS. He therefore transferred to the Chofetz Chaim yeshivah in Yerushalayim. There, when night *seder* was over at 10:30 p.m., only two sets of *chavrusas* remained to learn until midnight—one of which was Yehuda and his study partner.

Mom passed away in 1987. Yehuda sat *shivah* in Israel with his family and then transferred to the main branch of Chofetz Chaim in Forest Hills, New York.

> *8/18/88*
>
> *Did I tell you that another one of my roommates got engaged? ... Becky, you would probably be pretty pleased to know that the tendency here at Chofetz Chaim is to wed late. No, not twenty-two or twenty-three, but twenty-five to twenty-seven is not at all unusual. So, don't worry about my peers influencing me.*
>
> *–Yehuda*

> *9/88*
>
> *I can only hope that when I get engaged, I'm still in yeshivah. I think that being in a setup that the yeshivah provides is the greatest when you have a simchah. The atmosphere is just really special. Especially weddings. And sheva brachos. The yeshivah is really a sort of closely-knit community with strong comradeship. At least it should be. It really depends on the chevrah. B"H the chevrah here are decent fellows. ...*
>
> *Anyways, it's Elul around here. That's also another thing I like about yeshivah. The Yamim Tovim. You can really get into the different seasons. ... I love it!*
>
> *–Yehuda*

Yehuda remained in New York for one year and then went back to Israel. He was in Israel during the Persian Gulf War in January 1991. The following fall, he returned to the States, to learn in Chofetz Chaim—and to seek his *bashert*.

CHAPTER THREE

Dating Chronicles

I PREPARED FOR MY FIRST DATE WITH A MIXTURE OF EXCITEMENT and nerves. I had heard a lot about Yehuda. He was known to be honest, sincere, and kind. One of his friends described him as the life of the party. Others described him as quiet and reserved. How could one be the quiet life of the party? I did not want to marry a wallflower. I wanted someone with personality—but not the boisterous, calling-too-much-attention-to-himself type; serious—but not too serious; smart and knowledgeable—but not geeky. I would have to meet him to find out.

Our first date, planned around my college schedule, was on a Wednesday, two days after our first phone call. When Yehuda came to pick me up, I noticed his smile right away. He made a genuine and friendly impression.

Yehuda took me to the Rainbow Room lounge where, over cold Cokes and Sprites, we began to get acquainted. The conversation centered mostly on the one thing we had in common at that point—our connection to Yeshiva Chofetz Chaim, the Rosh Yeshivah, and the Rebbetzin. Nothing too exciting, but it gave us what to talk about.

We both agreed to another date. There was no reason to say no at that point. Though there were no guarantees that things would progress, I definitely thought there was potential. We went on several more dates, enjoying each other's company. Now it was I who was the quiet, reserved one. I was too nervous to open up and discuss "real" topics.

 On our fifth date, Yehuda told me he had something important to say. It was about us. I felt a knot forming in my stomach. Was he about to dump me? I did not want the relationship to end. I wanted to learn more about him and get to know him better.

Yehuda gingerly asked that I try to get past my reservations and be more open with him. We went on a "fun" date rather than a "sit-and-talk" date. As we walked around Roosevelt Island, I realized that this was a turning point. I knew that I did not want to give up the opportunity to spend the rest of my life with Yehuda. It took our dating to the next level.

We had some more personal discussions about our hopes and dreams and life aspirations. Walking along the cobblestoned roads of South Street Seaport, Yehuda shared with me that he was considering becoming a teacher, but was having mixed thoughts. Some people to whom he was close were discouraging him. They said he was too quiet and it would be a disaster. He could never stand in front of a class; he would be mincemeat within seconds.

By then I knew Yehuda and his personality well enough to vehemently disagree with the naysayers. Yehuda was not a pushover. He did not let others walk all over him. True, he was quiet and reserved, yet I recognized that it was a sign of his inner strength, his innocence and sincerity. Yehuda recognized the good in others and encouraged their good behavior. All of these were great qualities for a teacher to possess.

We had a long discussion about teaching. Having taught for six months already, I was a pro! We discussed various classroom scenarios and how to handle them. In my mind, Yehuda's temperament and sincerity were strengths that would serve as assets in the classroom.

That Shabbos, I went to the yeshivah to *daven*. As I opened the back door of the *beis midrash*, I glimpsed Yehuda with his siddur. Something about his mannerism and countenance assured me that my judgment of his character was correct.

Purim was around the corner. By this point, I was nearly certain that I wanted to marry Yehuda. On Purim day, Yehuda called to wish me a happy Purim. On that call, he opened up and shared with me the story of his mother's struggle with Alzheimer's and how he had struggled with it and her untimely passing. When my friends came to deliver *mishloach manos*, I was on the phone with Yehuda. When they came back hours later, we were still on the phone. My reaction to Yehuda's story passed his litmus test and was the final proof he needed.

Eleven days later, on April 1, 1992, Yehuda asked me to marry him. On June 29th, I did.

The Rosh Yeshivah was *mesader kiddushin* at our wedding, June 29, 1992.

CHAPTER FOUR

Back to Burns Street

The Early Years

IT WAS EXCITING TO SET UP OUR FOURTH-FLOOR, ONE-BEDROOM apartment on Burns Street which, after a hiatus of many years, was once again home to young yeshivah couples and families.

We slowly settled into a routine. Yehuda went to yeshivah every day. I taught and went to college. I tried to take as many courses as I could on Sundays so that I would only have to be out of the house one night a week. It was a juggling act—teaching until 4:00 p.m. every day, preparing lessons, and keeping up with college assignments. I felt fulfilled.

Life on Burns Street was like living in a village; all of us felt like we were "in it" together. Our neighbors became our friends. Our friends became our family. We knew we had support when we wanted and needed it, but at the same time we gave each other space and privacy. Most of the husbands were on the same schedule, coming home for lunch break from 1:15 to 2:45 p.m. and supper from 7:30 to 9:00 p.m. The wives were either working or in school or juggling some combination of both. We shared the same goal of helping to provide financially for our families to enable our husbands to focus on their learning.

When one of us had a baby, a meal train was set up for two weeks. On

Shabbos mornings, we would walk together to pick up our husbands after *davening* in yeshivah. On long Shabbos afternoons, we would trek to the park with snacks and suppers packed for the kids. On Sundays we would strap the kids into their strollers laden with diapers, changes of clothes, bottles, snacks, lunches, bathing suits for going under the sprinkler, and bicycles hooked over the handlebars. Sundays were a short break from the rush-rush schedule of the week.

Yehuda and I were thrilled to find out that we were expecting in August. I was determined to finish school as soon as possible. As we imagined what our baby would look like, we thought of names. If the baby was a girl, we would name her Asna, after Yehuda's mother, and if a boy, Shmuel Meir, after my Zeide Vinitsky.

Shmuly Simes arrived on August 8, 1993, and quickly earned the reputation of being the loudest baby in the nursery. We brought him home from the hospital several days later, and my parents and siblings were there to welcome us and share in the excitement. When they left, Yehuda and I looked at each other, looked at the baby, and I said, "Now what do we do?"

You know that feeling when you are babysitting? The parents say they will be home at a certain time, the time has passed, and you wonder if they will actually come home or not. Well, here was the baby, and the parents were not coming home! *We were the parents*!

It was an adjustment. I did not attend summer school that semester. Fortunately, I was able to delay my return to teaching until October. At that point, I shortened my hours from full time to three quarters of the day. My mother was kind enough to babysit every morning until Yehuda came home for his lunch break from yeshivah. At 2:35 p.m., Yehuda would stand on the street corner with Shmuly in the carriage. I would come running down the block from the other direction as Yehuda would run off to be back in yeshivah by 2:45. On college nights, we had a babysitter come to the house.

At one point, Yehuda purchased an old used bicycle from a friend. He figured it would shave off five minutes from each trip to or from yeshivah. At three round trips a day, the shorter traveling time would allow him an extra half hour at home.

We most certainly did not have room for a bicycle in our one-bedroom apartment, so he kept it chained to a No Parking sign in front of our building. Sadly, a bus hit the sign while trying to avoid a double-parked car. Both pole and bike were sent flying down the street.

Meanwhile, in Israel, Dad was having a difficult year medically. Becky and Judy bore the brunt of the responsibility for him as they were the closest. We felt bad. Living so far away, with such a busy schedule and the baby, we were unable to help out. By the time summer was over, it was clear that Becky and Judy needed a break.

Yehuda offered to go to Israel for Sukkos. He would take care of Dad for the week—put up his sukkah, purchase meals, and spend time with him. As much as I wanted to join, it really did not make sense. The three of us had just been there for Pesach, which was beautiful. The trip would not be a vacation. Shmuly was more active and I was expecting again. I stayed behind. It was a very intense week for Yehuda, physically and emotionally. Yehuda was happy that he was able to go and only gave me the details after he returned.

It came as a huge shock when, just one week after Yehuda's return home, we received a telephone call from Becky. It was early Friday morning and we were getting ready to start our day. Dad had passed away! In Yerushalayim, funerals are held the very same day. As it was Friday, the preparations were made quickly. Both Yehuda and Rachel missed the funeral. Rachel flew from Chicago to Queens and traveled with Yehuda on Sunday to sit *shivah* in Israel. The time Yehuda had spent with his father became even more meaningful. Again we knew what our baby's name would be—either Asna for Mom or Yitzchak for Dad.

As my due date drew closer, the final semester of my undergraduate studies came to a close. I was nervous the baby would be born before finals and I would have to make up the exams postpartum. All three of my professors agreed to allow me to take their final on the second-to-last day of class. I sat for two exams, and on the appointed date I waddled into class, prepared to take the third. My professor took one look at me and slapped his forehead. He had forgotten the exam at home! This was 1995, before flash drives, email, laptops, or smartphones. Absolutely nothing could be done. As it was Thursday night, he gave me his phone number and told me to call him on Sunday to remind him to bring the test on Monday. Monday night was not usually a college night for me, but he did not want to make me wait until Thursday. He took full responsibility for his mistake.

Asna was born on Shabbos. I called the professor to "remind him" about the test I would not be able to take on Monday night.

I had the choice of applying for graduate school for February or the following September. I did not want to go back to work and school with a newborn and a toddler, so I deferred until September. It turned out to be an ongoing deferment.

Meanwhile, Yehuda was very busy.

> During those years [in Chofetz Chaim] I toiled in Torah learning (as well as completing a bachelor's degree in computer science and a master's degree in education) and I grew in my passion for spreading Torah wherever it may be most appreciated. I took side jobs in tutoring, bar mitzvah lessons, leading youth groups, becoming a chaplain at a nursing home, substituting at yeshivah elementary schools, and teaching a bit in the Chofetz Chaim high school. I also took part in teacher training programs offered by excellent hands-on yeshivah training colleges.
>
> From the Rolling Rabbi blog,
> "My Story," August 2013

As our family grew, I reduced my teaching hours. To compensate for the loss in income, Yehuda took on small jobs, which added up.

Most of them were on Shabbos, such as tutoring and bar mitzvah lessons. He would also work in the evenings and during lunch breaks.

There was a shul about a twenty-minute walk away, Machane Chodosh, which had a JEP *minyan* club. Yehuda was the group leader, leading the teenagers in their own *davening* service. Another twenty-minute walk from Machane Chodosh was Scharf Manor, a nursing home. Yehuda would go there after the JEP *minyan* and serve as chaplain, singing Jewish songs and making Kiddush for the residents. Sometimes the kids and I would accompany him, bringing along homemade banana cake. It was hysterical to hear the residents talk about how young the rabbi and *rebbetzin* were. Yes, we were very young, and no, we did not feel like a rabbi or a *rebbetzin* at all. We felt like a couple of kids playing grown-up.

Yehuda's close friend, Rabbi Hillel Waxman, gave a Chumash class for ladies at the Queens Jewish Center every Shabbos afternoon. When Hillel could not go, Yehuda filled in for him. He prepared long and hard for those classes. When the Waxmans moved to Israel, Yehuda took over on a permanent basis.

After one of these classes Yehuda came home bursting with news. Rabbi Zecharya Greenwald, with whom he had learned back in 1978 and who now lived in Israel, was in town collecting for his organization. It was the first time they had seen each other since that summer! Naturally, Yehuda invited him over to reminisce. I was excited to meet the man I had heard so much about. Besides, his sister Morah Basi was my beloved first-grade teacher.

Yehuda also taught ninth-grade Hebrew language in the yeshivah's high school. All these jobs were great opportunities for him to practice his skills and have what to put on his résumé.

Having already earned his bachelor's degree before we were married, Yehuda tossed around the idea of getting a master's as well. A group was being formed to earn an M.A. in reading through

Adelphi University. The coursework was estimated to take one year to complete.[1] The timing was perfect. Yehuda and his friend signed up.

On the last night, an actual class was not being taught. The professor was planning to collect the term papers and then dismiss the students. The group decided it would be a shame and a waste of a night for all of them to drive to Manhattan, hand in their papers, and drive home. How about if only one of them went and submitted all the papers? Well, guess who was "volunteered" to go? Of course, it was Yehuda. I was somehow not surprised that he was chosen and agreed. But I was due any day and had visions of Yehuda getting stuck in Manhattan traffic and not being able to get in touch with him if I needed him. (Remember, we did not have cell phones in 1996!) I warned him that if I needed him and could not get in touch with him, I would never let him talk to his so-called friends again. Luckily, he made it home in record time. Malka was born that night.

Malka was named after Bubby Molly, who had passed away just a few weeks apart from Zeide Sam, when I was in seminary. Bubby Molly outlived her daughter Bubby Eleanor by eight years. Despite her pain, she became even closer to us.

I remember telling her that I loved the name Malka. "One day when I have a daughter, I will name her Malka," I said.

"You can't," she replied. "My Hebrew name is Malka—and I am still alive."[2]

Apartment Life

Neither our first nor our second apartment was equipped with a washing machine. When we were first married, we lived in a building with coin-operated units in the basement. It seemed simple enough: Load the laundry bags into a granny cart, wheel it to the elevator, and

---

1.   I would think of that course every month as I paid the student loan. August 2020 was the final $103.56 payment.

2.   Ashkenazi Jews do not name after the living.

go downstairs. I would pray that a machine was available and that I had enough quarters. If I returned too late to catch the end of the final spin cycle and transfer my load into the dryer, our clean wet clothes would be in a heap on a dirty table. As our family grew, going down to the basement became more cumbersome.

Just before Malka, our third, was born, we moved down the block. A two-bedroom apartment—also sans washer and dryer—on the fifth floor had become available. There was no laundry room in the building. Instead, we walked around the corner to the laundromat.

Doing laundry became a field trip. We packed up the stroller with kids, snacks, and bikes, and of course took the granny cart loaded with laundry bags. If we let go of the cart, it tipped over from the weight. We tried to avoid doing laundry too often, as it was such an ordeal. We had many changes of clothes, especially for the kids—enough to last a week or two.

A kindly woman frequented the same laundromat. "I notice how long it takes you to do laundry," she commented. "Perhaps if you were to do it more often, it would take less time?"

In a way, she was correct. It would take less time, but I could not tolerate doing it more often.

Grocery shopping also had to be done according to a well-thought-out plan. We would pile the full bags into the stroller basket and swing a couple from the handles. If it was a really big order, the granny cart came along. With one hand I would push the stroller and with the other I pulled the granny cart from behind.

At times, we were able to use my parents' station wagon. Having a car made shopping easier. We would stop the vehicle in front of our building, hazard lights flashing, as parking was not allowed on our side of the street. Burns Street is a busy two-way thoroughfare for cars, buses, trucks, and emergency vehicles. The threat of getting a parking ticket was ever present; it was the price we paid to live in New York City. We would unload the packages as quickly as we could and leave them by the front door of the building, where they would sit while we went to park the car.

The chance of being able to park on the other side of the street was slim and bordered on miraculous. Sheer desperation taught me how to parallel park into the tiniest of spots. It was realistic to park as far as four blocks away, especially on days of alternate-side parking. It seemed there was always at least one child who had fallen asleep in the car and had to be woken up.

Once back at our building, we carried the packages up three steps to another door that had to be unlocked and held open to pass through. We then waited for the elevator. When it arrived, we loaded in the packages, ascended to our floor, and unloaded the elevator. With the door of our apartment held open, we brought in all of the packages and shopping paraphernalia. Our shopping expedition was finally complete—except for putting away the groceries!

Life with three kids under three years and three months was triple the fun and triple the work. Between school, yeshivah, and babies, we were busy. We were slowly getting closer to the end of Yehuda's program in yeshivah. Over the next couple of years, he would have to fulfill certain criteria, prerequisites, and requirements before being allowed to proceed to the next step—studying for *semichah*. Because he had spent time learning in Israel on two separate occasions, he had to make up that amount of time in Queens. He also had to give a mandated number of *chaburos*—peer-presented Talmudic theses that had to be pre-approved by the *hanhalah*. It was exciting to see that we were nearing our goal. Our hard work together as a team was really paying off.

My plan was to go on maternity leave shortly after the beginning of the new school year—my eighth year of teaching. I managed to make it through the first week of school. Our third daughter was born in the wee hours of the morning on the second Sunday in September 1998. We named her Rivka Bayla after Mom's grandmother, Rivka Bayla Tatelbaum.

When Bayla was born, about two years after Malka, Yehuda was finally eligible to begin the *semichah* program. I was eager to see him succeed and wanted to make things as easy for him as possible. I bought a huge bag of note-taking and study aids, various colored pens, highlighters, index cards, sticky notes—whatever I thought might be useful to help him retain all the information he would be tested on.

I knew that once he began studying for *semichah*, Yehuda would be less available to help out with the kids. I was okay with that. It certainly helped that my parents and siblings lived up the street and could almost always be counted on to take care of the cutest grandchildren, nieces, and nephew ever to have been born. Life was going according to plan.

Temporary Derailment

On Sunday of Chanukah 1999, Yehuda and I took the children to a playground in Staten Island. I was looking forward to some relaxing family time. Usually I took the kids to the local park on Sundays together with my friends and their kids. My husband's company was a real treat for me.

Yehuda complained that he was not feeling well. He stretched out on a park bench.

"Are you able to get up and be more involved with the kids?" I asked.

"I absolutely cannot. I feel like I've been run over by a truck."

"You look okay to me. Nothing unusual. You don't have any fever."

No matter what I said, he just could not get up. We chalked it up to exhaustion from his busy schedule and assumed it was all catching up with him. Surely, by taking it easy over the next few days, he would snap back to himself.

By Tuesday there was no change; he was simply too tired to do anything. We decided that a call to the doctor was in order. Dr. Raymond Feinberg, the Rosh Yeshivah's personal doctor, was an excellent diagnostician and a real friend to all of the yeshivah members. He rose above and beyond the call of duty to help anyone who approached him. When Yehuda described his symptoms, Dr. Feinberg ordered him to go immediately to Parkway Hospital for a chest CT scan. Innocent and clueless, I called one of my siblings to come babysit as I drove Yehuda to the hospital. Dr. Feinberg was on staff there and told the CT department to expect us. We were seen without delay. As one technician set Yehuda up for the scan, I waited in the booth with another technician. He turned to me.

"How are you related?"

"He is my husband."

"Do you have children?"

"Yes. Four."

"Oh, G-d!"

My heart dropped. Things were apparently more serious than I thought. Before we arrived, I thought that maybe Yehuda had pneumonia and would get some antibiotics. At worst, he would have to remain in the hospital overnight and then come home. But no. Things were very serious. The CT scan showed a huge mass in Yehuda's chest. The doctor ordered a biopsy to confirm his suspicion: Hodgkin's lymphoma.

Cancer.

It was December 14, 1999. My birthday.

Yehuda remained in the hospital for the biopsy. I went home—and the floodgates opened. I curled up on the couch, sobbing uncontrollably. I was twenty-seven years old. I had four children under the age of six. My husband was thirty-two. He could not die. I could not become a widow. My children could not become orphans. Could not. Could not. Could not. I cried all night long as I thought of Yehuda, myself, and our four precious children.

The biopsy results confirmed the cancer diagnosis. I knew that news of Yehuda's illness would travel fast. My sister Fraidel offered to pick up Shmuly at the bus stop. This seemed like a good way to avoid the comments, questions, and stares from the other moms, but I knew

I would have to deal with them eventually. So, squaring my shoulders and taking deep breaths, I walked down the street and into my new role as wife of a cancer patient.

We arranged for Yehuda to be transferred to New York-Presbyterian Hospital to be seen by Dr. Kohane, an exceptional oncologist, and set up a treatment plan. Becky and Rachel came to provide us with support and help us to navigate the healthcare system.

Dr. Kohane told us that if someone "had" to get cancer, Hodgkin's was the "best" one to have. It had a pretty standard treatment plan—six months of chemotherapy followed by one month of radiation. Every person reacts differently and there may or may not be complications along the way. All in all, the prognosis was excellent.

However, dealing with six months of chemo was definitely not excellent. We braced ourselves for the worst six months of our lives. Yehuda was so sick—in a constant state of nausea and lacking an appetite. Even going with Rachel to an upscale Manhattan restaurant—a treat normally way beyond our budget—was too nauseating.

He lost his hair soon after.

We were newbies to the healthcare system. We called the doctor multiple times a day for the smallest of questions. It got to the point where we thought they changed the message on the answering machine because of us. "If this is a true medical emergency, you may call the doctor's beeper. Otherwise, please leave a message." For us, everything was a medical emergency. After all, this was cancer.

Our family and friends were extremely helpful and supportive. Meal trains, babysitting, and cleaning help were all arranged. I continued to go to work, but was given leeway due to the circumstances.

As New Year's Eve 2000 approached, the world was predicting a catastrophe of epic proportions. Y2K. It was unclear how all the computers would react to the change in millennium. Would everything electronic cease to function? Would it create one huge blackout?

Everyone was advised to set up several days' worth of emergency supplies—water for each family member, canned goods, flashlights, a radio with batteries—to tide us over until systems were back in working order.

I could not be bothered with all of that. As far as I was concerned, a catastrophe of epic proportions had already occurred. We were fighting a battle against cancer.

On January 1, 2000, I woke up to discover that the world around us was still intact. There was no emergency on the outside, but our personal emergency was still there.

A few weeks before Purim, Yehuda was hospitalized with complications. He was diagnosed with neutropenia. His neutrophil (a type of white blood cell) count was very low and down to dangerous numbers. Needless to say, Purim was not looking very joyous at all. I left the children with my parents and went to visit my ailing husband.

I walked into Yehuda's room, greeted him with a wimpy "Happy Purim," and went to the sink to wash my hands with soap. To my absolute horror, my engagement ring and wedding band were gone. I started yelling, "My rings are gone! My rings are gone!"

I wanted to cry, and I did. How could this have happened? As the only son, Yehuda inherited the diamond ring Dad gave Mom, a valuable antique. Soon after our engagement, he traveled to Israel to spend Pesach with his family. When he returned to New York, he had the ring with him. He had carefully wrapped it up and kept it in his pocket for the duration of his journey, unwilling to pack it in his suitcase or carry-on luggage. He wanted to be sure he could check on it at regular intervals to be sure it was still there.

This could not have happened! It was impossible. I never take off my rings. Except when I wash for bread, they never leave my finger. I had not eaten bread. Where could they be? They could not have fallen off. They were not loose. I knew for certain that I had them on the night before. I had gone to hear the Megillah reading at a friend's house and was twirling them around my finger as I waited for the reading to begin. I was not feeling sociable. My husband had cancer. He was in the hospital. I just wanted to go home.

As I sat in the hospital bemoaning my loss, I tried to make a mental list of places to check. Then I turned to look at my sick husband, and caught myself. *All I want is for Yehuda to get better. Are rings more significant than my husband?* Obviously not. But I still had a problem on my hands. Or, rather, *not* on my hand.

How would I tell Becky, Judy, and Rachel that I lost Mom's diamond? Although the ring was insured (if not found, it could be replaced), its sentimental value was high.[3]

We searched everywhere, but the rings never turned up. We notified our insurance agent, who advised us on how to proceed. I went down to the jewelry shop that had appraised the ring and arranged to get a replacement. The new ring was hideous—and it was not the one Yehuda gave me when we were engaged. I cried some more.

After some more careful research I went back to the jewelry store and tried again. I told them that I did not like the replacement ring and described what I wanted. A short time later, my new ring was ready. It was beautiful, but I felt no sentimental attachment toward it.

Yehuda and I had decided that when the six months of chemotherapy and the month of radiation were up, we would go as a family to Israel to celebrate. Budget or no budget, we would be buying six round-trip tickets to the Holy Land! Such a trip would be meaningful in so many ways; spending time with Yehuda's sisters and their families, *davening* at the holy sites to thank Hashem for listening to our prayers, and rejuvenating our family who had been through so much. This was the carrot at the end of the stick, the dream that helped us get through the brutal treatments.

---

3.   I need not have worried. Yehuda's sisters were not angry with me; they were only concerned about their brother's recovery.

As the months passed, the dream trip to Israel was always on our minds. At one point, I told Yehuda that I had made a decision. I was going to sell the diamond and replace it with a cubic zirconia. We would use the money for our trip. At first, Yehuda would not even entertain the notion. He wanted me to have a real diamond. After I insisted that I did not need a real gem—it was not the one we were engaged with and had no meaning to me—he finally agreed.[4] We sold the diamond and began anticipating our trip for real.

Treatment was coming to an end. Scans and blood work were looking good. Other than having to come back yearly for monitoring, Yehuda was given the all-clear to get on with his life. However, he would not be considered fully cured until five healthy years had passed.

We rejoiced and celebrated, eager to put the ordeal behind us. We looked at the calendar and called the travel agent to book our tickets. We knew we had a story to tell when, a few days after purchasing tickets, the travel agent called us back. If we were to change our reservations to just one day later, the price would go down considerably. Would we be interested? The price of the tickets was now—to the dollar!—the value of the ring. Yes, we were interested!

That summer trip to Israel was a dream come true. We spent quality time with our children and extended family, and got together with friends

Our family trip to Israel. One ring, six tickets!

4.   Later on, Yehuda would occasionally ask me what I would want my ring to look like if I were to ever get a new one. Several years later, he presented me with a brand-new authentic diamond ring. Unbeknownst to me, he had been saving up for this gift. He was so proud to once again ask me if I would marry him. Of course I said yes!

whom we had not seen in years. All of them had been praying for Yehuda's recovery.

We had beaten the demon. Yehuda built up his stamina and was feeling more and more like himself. He was ready to reapply himself to studying for *semichah*. Heroically, even in the hospital when he was feeling sick and not up to visitors, he studied on his own. But he had to make up for lost time. His peers were now ahead of him. He needed to catch up.

Rabbi Yehuda Simes

When it was time to schedule Yehuda's exam, two significant changes were made. First, he would be taking the test by himself. Usually it was given orally in groups. There was "safety in numbers," as the men could discuss the rationale behind their answers. These discussions would make obvious how much each person knew and understood the material. Second, since he was taking it alone, Yehuda would be able to have two shorter sessions instead of a single long one. Rabbi Paltiel Friend,[5] who had been giving the test for many years, was suffering from diminished eyesight. It was difficult for him to read the cards with the test questions printed on them. His daughter Dvora meticulously copied the cards in a more legible font. The two-part exam would give Rabbi Friend a reprieve and take pressure off Yehuda. He would not have to go solo for so many hours.

As the date of the first session drew closer, we were filled with anticipation. I held my figurative breath the day of part one, waiting for Yehuda to call and tell me that everything had gone well. I need not have worried. He did very well—once he got past the first question. There had been a rumor in yeshivah that a certain chapter on the study list was never actually included in the test, and Yehuda skipped it. When the first question was asked, Yehuda was flabbergasted. "That's never on the test!" he blurted. Rabbi Friend replied that there was no

---

5. Rabbi Friend passed away a few years later, in 2003.

such thing and advised him to study that chapter for the second half of the test.

I celebrated Yehuda's semi-*semichah* with half a poster on the door of our apartment. Within a few days, the second half of the sign was hanging there too.

We made it! Yehuda Simes had joined the ranks of rabbis despite life-threatening obstacles!

Life began its return to normal. I was teaching half days and Yehuda had three part-time jobs. His résumé was looking fuller and more rounded. In the mornings, he taught boys with special needs in a self-contained

Rabbi Yehuda Simes receiving *semichah* at the Yeshiva Chofetz Chaim 68th Annual Dinner and Chag Hasemichah. With the Rosh Yeshivah and Rabbi Paltiel Friend.

classroom. In the afternoons, he taught Chumash to eighth-grade boys, and in the evenings, he studied with college-age men.

We celebrated our ninth wedding anniversary—June 29, 2001— with the birth of Elisheva, named after my Bubby Eleanor. We now had five children living in a two-bedroom apartment on the fifth floor of an apartment building. It was time to get serious about seeking long-term employment options.

Yehuda took on a full-time job teaching fifth-grade boys in Yeshiva Tiferes Moshe in addition to his eighth-grade Chumash class. Rabbi Yaakov May, the principal, had been his principal when he was a student in Minnesota. Tiferes Moshe, Yehuda's new place of employment, was the school Shmuly attended. Asna and Malka were attending Bnos Malka Academy, where I was teaching. Life seemed to be a series of circles within circles.

CHAPTER FIVE

Oh, Canada!

Armed with a deep commitment to teach Torah, and willing and ready to carry out this lofty ideal, I taught for two years in the New York area, gaining priceless experience and proficiency at touching the souls of young people. Meanwhile, my wife and I were looking to relocate to a smaller Jewish community where we might be "big fish in a small pond," hoping that our entire family of seven would become integrated within the community and integral to its functioning. After exploring various opportunities, we fell in love with Ottawa, Canada. We knew at once that this was our home. The Jewish community was extremely warm and abundantly helpful in making us feel at home and truly valued. The year was 2002, my wife and I immediately became entrenched in teaching and changing the lives of our new community that drew us close, and we never looked back.

From the Rolling Rabbi blog,
"My Story," August 2013

Exploring Options

WE BOTH AGREED THAT STAYING IN NEW YORK WAS NOT IN our long-term plans. In New York, teachers are a dime a dozen. The farther away from New York that we went, the less likely there would be an abundance of teachers. Yehuda wanted to be able to make a difference where no one else would.

Over the course of the school year, we considered several job offers in cities other than New York. For various reasons, these options were not applicable. We had really hoped something exciting would come our way. By April, we were painted into a corner; Rabbi May, the principal, needed a commitment from Yehuda: Would he be returning for the upcoming school year or not? Positions were being locked in and the school had to make plans. With nothing else on the horizon, I gave Yehuda an ultimatum—he could say yes to Rabbi May, but that would be our last year on Burns Street. Regardless of where he would be teaching the following year, I would not be living in a two-bedroom apartment. I resigned myself to managing for just one more year. Knowing it was temporary made it a little easier to tolerate.

In May, Micah Shotkin, Yehuda's very close friend, called. He had just returned from an interview in Ottawa, Canada, and was enthralled with the city. It was beautiful. The people were lovely and there were several *chinuch* and *kiruv* positions available in the community. Micah was planning to accept his job offer and thought Yehuda would be a perfect fit for another position. A few other Chofetz Chaim families were already living there—Rabbi Zischa and Lauren Shaps and Rabbi Dovid and Suzanne Burger. We knew both families well; in fact, Rabbi Shaps had been Yehuda's dorm counselor in high school! It sounded intriguing, but there was one catch: Yehuda had already committed to Rabbi May and was not one to go back on his word. Micah suggested we go up to Ottawa on a pilot trip and check out the schools and community. If it was what we were looking for, we could then discuss the situation with Rabbi May.

Memorial Day weekend 2002 found us loading up our van with

enough snacks to keep five kids occupied during an eight-hour car ride. Yehuda met with the principals of Hillel Academy, a board member, and others. We also toured Torah Academy Day School; in theory, I could teach there and our children would attend. We met with Rabbi Howard and Rivka Finkelstein, the rabbi and *rebbetzin* of Beth Shalom West.[1] All these people made a positive impression on us. Their dedication and desire to grow their community was praiseworthy. We were sold on Ottawa!

With trepidation, Yehuda called Rabbi May to discuss our dilemma. Rabbi May completely understood Yehuda's perspective. He himself had the same ideals of wanting to reach and teach others and had also lived in smaller communities. He did not want Yehuda to have to turn down this opportunity. It was also to Yehuda's benefit that there were some scheduling and staffing issues for the coming year. Having one less teacher in the mix would help resolve the problem.

When Yehuda got off the phone and repeated the conversation to me, I was in disbelief. It was that simple. Rabbi May agreed. We would be moving to Ottawa! I could not believe it. We were going out into the big, wide world!

The Move

Talk about down to the wire! Now we had to find a house, give up our apartment, and pack. Moving to a different country entailed dealing with issues such as work visas and socialized health benefits, to name but a few. Hillel Academy took care of the legal aspects and gave us a stipend for moving expenses.

We had no idea that moving the contents of a two-bedroom apartment would cost so much—more than our allotted stipend. In order to stay within budget, we decided to self-move. Knowing what I do now, I would definitely do things differently. At the time, though,

---

1.   The shul's name was later changed to Congregation Beit Tikvah Ottawa.

we were young, inexperienced, and completely clueless. Did I mention naïve?

We found a nice house that accommodated our needs—not gorgeous or fancy, but very practical. It was behind the field next to the shul, thereby fulfilling our requirement of being in close proximity to the shul. It was impossible to get any closer than that! Once we moved in, our backyard became the shortcut to shul.

Ideally, we wanted to move in July and have enough time to unpack and get settled before school started. Although the owner of the house was very aware of how important this was to us, he insisted he could not move out before December. He finally agreed to a closing date of Friday, August 30th—with no deduction in the asking price. School was set to start Tuesday, September 3rd, the day following Labor Day. Labor Day is a true holiday in Ontario; all businesses, including supermarkets, are closed. We had no choice but to agree to these inconvenient arrangements.

The Shotkins were moving in July. Micah told us that if all our paraphernalia was packed by then, our truck could follow along with them. We could enter the country at the same time and clear customs together at the border. He offered to let us stash our belongings in the garage of their new home until we arrived. It sounded like a good plan. Yehuda would rent a U-Haul truck and drive up with Shmuly. We collected boxes from grocery stores and started packing and purging.

We hired packers to carry the boxes from the apartment and load them onto the truck. They were a crew of five. One assigned himself the role of overseer and another took the role of feet dangler on the ramp of the truck. That left three workers shuffling back and forth. It became immediately obvious that they were not experienced. They had to unload and reload the boxes several times to make things fit. It was a long, long day. No matter how many times the movers left the apartment, there seemed to be the same number of boxes left inside.

Our bookcases were a real challenge. They were taller than the door frame. Every time the mover walked with a bookcase to the door, it hit the top of the frame. He backed up, walked forward, and hit the frame again. After several unsuccessful attempts to get through the door, he had a brainstorm and turned the bookcase on its side. Magical. It fit! Now, on to bookcase number two. Walk to the door frame, hit the top, back up, walk forward, hit the top again. And again. And again. Could this really be happening?

It was well after nightfall when the truck was fully loaded—but the apartment was not yet empty. There was not enough room on the truck for everything. Professional movers would have done a better job.

Yehuda paid and dismissed the packers and took off with Shmuly in the U-Haul to catch up with Micah and his truck, who had left hours earlier. Just before reaching the George Washington Bridge, Yehuda realized he did not have any cash on him. It had all gone to the packers. Our debit card was maxed out for the day. My parents went to bail him out with money for the journey. Yehuda and Shmuly eventually caught up with Micah and they entered Canada together. After unloading the contents of the U-Haul into Micah's garage, Yehuda and Shmuly returned to New York. Later, Yehuda regaled us with stories of the road trip; drinking cup after cup of coffee to stay awake, changing the route to accommodate the height of the truck, and driving around the parking areas of rest stops to find a spot big enough to park the U-Haul.

Over the next few weeks, we stayed in other people's apartments for several days at a time. Every morning when I awoke, I had to get my bearings anew. *Where am I today?*

On Wednesday, August 28, 2002, we strapped the kids into the car with our belongings stuffed around them. The hard drive of Yehuda's computer was on my lap; it was my job to protect it. The plan was to stay in a motel for two nights and tour Ottawa during the day. We enjoyed a mini-vacation in our new country.

When Friday dawned bright and clear, we were awaiting a call from our lawyer to inform us that the sale had gone through. We would pick up the keys and spend Shabbos in our new home. Micah and his wife Shani tried to convince us that that was an absolutely ridiculous idea. The house was completely empty. However, having lived in an apartment my whole life, I was excited at the prospect of owning a house. I wanted to spend our first Shabbos as homeowners in our own home. Shani insisted that at the very least we should take food from them. She also said that if at any time we wanted to back out of our plan, we could sleep in their house.

As the hours ticked by on Friday, it was looking like there would be less and less time to get ready for Shabbos in our new home. I do not remember what the holdup was, but we finally got the call: 28 Ardell Grove belonged to Yehuda and Shaindel Simes! It was Bayla's fourth birthday according to the Jewish calendar. We teased her that we had just bought her the most expensive gift ever and she would have to share it with the rest of us.

We let ourselves into the house and dropped our belongings wherever they fell. The kids ran around exploring. They were certain we had just purchased a palace. When they discovered the basement, they were giddy with excitement. Exhausted, I just wanted to sit down and relax for a few minutes. But there was a slight problem: There was not a single chair in the house.

How on earth would we spend Shabbos here? What were we thinking? As Yehuda used to say, who says we were thinking? Sheepishly, we rang the bell at the Shotkins' house. Without even an "I told you so," they welcomed us inside.

Sunday morning found us waiting for the movers. When we finished waiting, we waited some more. They finally arrived, offered a nonsensical excuse for their tardiness, and got to work quickly and efficiently—or so it seemed. As they carefully maneuvered our boxes from the Shotkins' garage into the truck, it seemed this service was better than that in Queens. Looks, though, can be deceiving. Once we left the Shotkins' house and arrived at 28 Ardell Grove, things slowed down considerably. There were lunch breaks, coffee breaks, smoke breaks, and dangling-feet-off-the-edge-of-the-truck breaks. I was getting impatient and just wanted them to be done and out of my way.

Only a few boxes were left on the truck. The end was in sight. It would only be a few more minutes. But then, as if on cue, all the workers grabbed their backs and started moaning. They began poking and prodding each other. Who would be the one to call the boss on their behalf? They were all "sick" and there was no way they could possibly go to work the next day. I, on the other hand, was not at all concerned with the next day. Just finish today!

As the sun set, the last box was carried into the house. I looked at Yehuda. "I sure hope you like it here," I said, "because I am never moving again."

Beginnings and Milestones

Somehow, we had to unpack at least enough to get the kids and Yehuda ready for school on Tuesday. Rosh Hashanah would be that

Putting up the *mezuzah* on our new home, 28 Ardell Grove, Ottawa, Canada, September 2002.

Friday night. I had my hands full with the move and planned to start teaching after Sukkos.

That Monday, we met many neighbors and community members. The children almost instantly acquired a surrogate local *zeide* and *bubby*, Arthur and Maxine Rabinovitch. The Burger girls came by with a grocery order to stock up our fridge, and another neighbor dropped off a delicious hot supper. We certainly felt welcomed!

My parents and siblings drove up to see our new home and help us unpack. Monday morning, my father came home from shul with a group of high school boys to help us. They were a delightful bunch and we hit it off with them right away. Soon we became very close to "our boys." They would come to our house every Shabbos afternoon for a Shabbos party, enjoying licorice, pretzels, and other treats while sprawled on our couches. Yehuda began bringing them home after Minchah on Shabbos afternoon and they would join us for *seudah shlishis*. Nothing too fancy—challah, hard-boiled eggs, chips and salsa and the like. Over time, our group grew as our boys brought their friends, and younger boys became teenagers. We just added more chairs around the table and moved closer together to accommodate them all. Everyone chatted freely and often used the time to ask Yehuda for his opinions and insights.

But I am getting ahead of myself.

Tuesday morning, I drove Yehuda to his first day of work at Hillel Academy. The school is centrally located on a beautiful campus with large fields and playgrounds, along with the Soloway Jewish Community Center and Hillel Lodge (a home for the elderly). One can meet community members of every age and background at this location. I wished Yehuda good luck and success. I am not sure which of us was more nervous.

I drove on and dropped off our four eldest children at Torah Academy of Ottawa, which was located at the time in the basement of Temple Israel. In some ways it resembled a one-room schoolhouse. There was a *bayit katan*, a "small house," for the preschool. The other grades were combined in several classrooms. A large multi-purpose room in the center served as the lunchroom. When it was time for recess or lunch, the bell monitor would run out of a classroom, pick up a small hammer, hit the fire alarm, and yell, "Recess!" Students would come running from all directions and race to be the first one outside. A year and a half later, Torah Academy moved to a proper building with a proper bell system.

I took Elisheva home and spent the day unpacking. Later in the afternoon, we picked up Yehuda and the kids. Everyone was eager to share stories of their first day.

We lived in the West End of the city, home to the neighborhoods of Craig Henry and Centre Point. The majority of Hillel students lived in those neighborhoods; we had wished to live within walking distance of them. Yehuda wanted to be a fully involved teacher in and out of the classroom. He wanted to be able to invite his students for all kinds of extracurricular activities.

The first of these was what became our annual sukkah party. We had a beautiful large deck that was perfect for building our very own sukkah. On each of the four nights of Chol Hamoed, a different class of Yehuda's was invited. It was a family affair. The kids and I, and even members of our extended family who had come to us for Sukkos, would participate. We had ice cream and toppings, chips, and other treats. Yehuda planned several games and a story. The students were intrigued by our children and our children were excited to meet Abba's students. A fun time was had by all.

As the year progressed, groups of students were invited to spend Shabbos with us. Our Shabbos meals were very friendly and all guests contributed to the wholesome atmosphere.

Yehuda loved to sing at the Shabbos table. He sang traditional Shabbos songs, traditional Jewish songs, and random made-up-on-the-spot songs. The made-up ones, silly as they were, got the most attention. How he managed to get grown men dancing around the table to a ditty about their name is beyond me.

A special jar called the "*parshah* bean jar" graced our table. Everyone was invited to share an insight from that week's *parshah* or any Jewish-related topic. Alternatively, they could pick a topic on which Yehuda would ask them a question. Whoever offered an insight or answered correctly received a jelly bean. Yehuda always made sure that everyone got the correct response. The respondents were allowed to poll the audience, ask a friend, or employ any other creative method of arriving at the correct answer. Yehuda used jelly beans as a classroom incentive as well. We had cases of jelly beans stockpiled at all times. *Parshah* beans were not only for our children and Yehuda's students; adult guests were encouraged to participate as well. They did—and loved it.

Guests were also asked to share stories or jokes. We will never forget Elliot and the joke he told about a man going to Miami on a bus. The man was excited to be traveling and kept singing, "Nah ni nah nah, I'm going to Miami." The passengers were yelling at him to stop. He kept singing. Finally, they had had enough. They warned him that if he kept singing, they would take his suitcase and throw it off the bus. He continued to sing. (Of course, as Elliot told the story, there were lots of "Nah ni nah nah, I'm going to Miami" chants thrown in for good measure.) The passengers were furious. They grabbed a suitcase from the luggage rack directly over his head and threw it out the window. At which point, the man changed his lyrics. "Nah ni nah nah. That was not my suitcase." To this day, when we go on a family trip, we sing, "Nah ni nah nah, I'm going to Miami."

Elliot became very close to Yehuda and the two of them grappled over deep philosophical questions. He kept in touch after the accident. One summer, Elliot started a window washing service. As a courtesy to Yehuda, he offered to wash our windows for free. They sparkled. Elliot's father offered to take care of our lawn and landscaping every summer for several years in a row.

Everyone liked Yehuda; they knew he cared about them. His sincerity was obvious. He exuded warmth, compassion, and enjoyment of life. Judaism was real to him. There were no pretenses, no shows. What you saw was what you got. Never one to get caught up in a disagreement, he had a way of seeing things from the other's perspective.

Fall slowly turned into winter. We were told that snow begins to fall in Ottawa as early as November 1st and that Ottawa winters are freezing, with tons of snow. We had no idea what to expect so we expected the worst.

One Sunday, we went on a major winter shopping spree. We had learned that boots come with a weather rating and it is important to check that they are guaranteed warm to -20^0 C (-4^0 F). In

Ottawa, schools have outdoor recess throughout the winter until the temperature hits -24⁰ C (-11⁰ F). We outfitted each member of the family with extra-warm boots, gloves, hats, and scarves. A long coat with a big furry hood completed the outfit.

There was one more important accessory on the "must have" list—ice skates. Everyone in Ottawa skates. Local parks put up boards in a huge oval, hose down the surface to create an outdoor ice rink, and maintain it throughout the winter. We were ready to brave the elements.

Sure enough, on November 1st, a Friday afternoon, the snow began to fall. I called my mother in New York to tell her that this was It. Winter was coming and I was in for it. I was relieved when the snow stopped almost as quickly as it had started without leaving much of an accumulation.

That was not the case a few weeks later. The snow began to fall with no sign of letting up. We had been planning to attend Arts Alive, a pre-Chanukah boutique and sale at the JCC, that afternoon. We thought it would be a great way to meet more people in the community. Due to the snowstorm we changed our minds. How could we navigate our car through all that snow?

Susan was a new friend from shul whose daughters, the same ages as Asna and Malka, were Yehuda's students. That day, she called to invite me and the kids to go sledding with her and the girls. Up on the hill, Susan asked, "Are you planning to go to Arts Alive?"

"We had been planning on it, but now with the snowstorm we reconsidered. I was surprised to hear that it wasn't canceled."

"Why would it be canceled?"

"Um, because of all the snow?"

Susan smiled. "The snowplows are out and will clear the snow immediately. The highway and main road will be completely passable. Side streets will take a little longer, but not much."

Feeling like true Canadians in the Great White North, we went to Arts Alive.

With Chanukah coming, Yehuda had more great plans in store. He invited a different class for each night of Chanukah. The program included menorah lighting, a pasta dinner, dreidel and other games. There was an added surprise. One plate at the table had a sticker on the bottom. Whoever sat at that place would win a prize. We had to make sure our children would not leak the secret or sit in that spot.

Our kids would set the table and help run the program. They were so proud to be Rabbi Simes's kids. By now, we had already met a lot of the students and knew their names. At drop-off and pick-up, we spoke with their parents, all of whom sang Yehuda's praises. They were so touched that we opened our home to their children. They shared with me some of the special things Yehuda was doing in the classroom: how he tailor-made worksheets and tests for those who needed it, even giving oral tests to those who could benefit from that method. Different students were given different incentives to improve—hockey cards, extra recess, even having lunch with Rabbi Simes. Yehuda had become very popular very quickly.

In the spring, Hillel Academy had their annual sports day. Having been warned by his colleagues that there would be a staff-versus-students baseball game, Yehuda began a regimen of running on the treadmill and jumping rope to improve his stamina.

The day of the much-anticipated game finally arrived. Yehuda was up at bat. The pitcher threw the ball and Yehuda hit it with all his might. Home run! He was a hero! The students were in an uproar. It was the talk of the town. Rabbi Simes hit a home run! For his birthday in June, some students bought him a baseball jersey with his name on it and the number eighteen for *chai*. They also gave him a Minnesota Twins baseball cap, for his home team. Every year on sports day, he would wear that uniform proudly, ready for another homer. Nathan Cantor, a member of the Hillel graduating class of 2010, recalled: "He was incredible. They always saved a grapefruit to be disguised as a softball to avoid him getting a grand slam."

The following September, Yehuda began teaching at the Ottawa Talmud Torah program. Classes were held on Sunday mornings and twice a week after school. When his class had their Chumash party and presentation of their first Chumash, the kids and I made special crowns for each student. We attended the ceremony and applauded them. We loved being part of Yehuda's success and developing relationships with his students and their families.

I was teaching grades six through eight at Torah Academy for ten hours a week. Lauren Shaps asked if I could give a Chumash class for women one evening a week. I agreed right away. The class was held in Kathi Kovacs's house. This was the start of a very close friendship between Kathi and me. Eight other women attended, some of whom were nearly old enough to be my mother. I learned that age is not a barrier to friendship. These women became my very close friends and their support was limitless.

Our lives were busy, full, and meaningful. We joked that our home should have a revolving door for the many guests we hosted. With a front door, a side door, and a back door, we never knew from where guests would enter.

In February 2004, shortly before Purim, our first Canadian, Chan, was born. Her full name is Chana Esther and she is named for Yehuda's grandmother. Asna had a friend who was my student who had the same name. Elisheva was troubled. "But there already is a Chana Esther. Why did you pick that name?" In a community where you know everyone, there is a lot of overlap. My students were my children's friends. My friends were my children's teachers. We learned very quickly to separate life from school. There would be no parent-teacher conferences in the produce aisle.

In 2005, Yehuda was approached by Bram Bregman, director of NCSY Ottawa, to partner in creating something new in the city. There was a highly successful program operating in Toronto and he wanted to bring it to Ottawa. Torah High was an after-school program for Jewish students who attended public high schools. Students received high school credits by taking Ministry of Education–approved Judaic courses. Would Yehuda agree to be the principal of this program? His role would be to design and teach the courses.

At the time, around 80 percent of Jewish students in Ottawa attended public high schools, including the majority of Yehuda's elementary-school students who graduated from Hillel Academy. Yehuda jumped at the opportunity to continue to teach his former students and others. His reputation preceded him, and under his guidance, the program grew to over one hundred students. Of course, these students were also invited to our home. There were *Shabbatons*, barbecues, and Friday night dinners. One of the highlights was the Calabogie Lodge Resort *Shabbaton* in Calabogie, Ontario—with skiing on Friday afternoon and Motza'ei Shabbos.

Another new beginning was on the way. For many months, Shmuly had good-naturedly put up with ribbing: "So, hoping for a brother this time?" To which he would reply, "Nah, it's too late for that—we'll be thirteen years apart. I won't be able to play with him anyway."

In March 2006, three weeks before Pesach, Yitzchak was born. Finally, Yehuda had a son to name after his father. It seemed as if the entire community came to his *bris*. Yehuda recounted how he had longed for a son to carry his father's name, but he kept on having girls. We all chuckled as he recited the names of each of his daughters, whom he loved so much, who were born after his father passed away— five in all. He thanked the community for embracing us and becoming our extended family.

Yitzchak became the community mascot, especially during his year-long fireman phase when he did not go anywhere without his signature red plastic fire hat. In fact, it was not long before he started answering to the name "Chief."

It certainly was a year of milestones, as we would be celebrating Shmuly's bar mitzvah in August. Our eldest son was becoming a man. As with everything else we did, we wanted to include the entire community. We anticipated a large contingency of family coming in for the weekend festivities from New York, Chicago, Minnesota, and Israel. We would have to feed an army! As there were no hotels within walking distance of our shul, we would have to house them as well.

Our friends were eager to help and be part of the *simchah*. After getting the all-clear from the shul board, I put together a kitchen team. Together, we would be providing in-house catering for three hundred or so people. As far as I could recall, this would be a first for our shul. We were a team of eight, armed and ready with homemade personalized aprons designed on Shmuly's behalf. The words, "Thanks for making my bar mitzvah incrEDIBLE," were ironed on. We got to work, ready to cook practically everything from soup to nuts (minus the nuts; the shul is a nut-free zone, as is most of Canada, due to allergy concerns): fluffy challah; tri-colored gefilte fish rolls; dozens of kugels both savory and sweet; varieties of chicken; bright, flavorful salads; and a sweet table that nearly caved in under its own weight. We shopped and chopped, cut and measured, filling up industrial-sized freezers. We schmoozed, we sang, we shared the stories of our lives. We each chose the chores we enjoyed and passed on the ones we least liked.

Other friends took on the job of hoteliers. They made lists of available accommodations which they matched up to guests who needed them. They determined which host families would be the right fit for each of our guests. Some friends took on the role of tour guides. As the bar mitzvah was in the summer, many of our guests decided to take advantage of their summer vacation. They made plans to extend their trip to tour and explore Canada's capital. Rabbi David and Aviva Rotenberg put together a comprehensive welcome packet which included places of interest and a short list of kosher eateries.

While I took care of the physical side, Yehuda worked on the spiritual. He had already ordered *tefillin* several months in advance. He was now teaching Shmuly how to read his *parshah* and preparing a *dvar Torah* to present to the congregants. It was certainly gearing up to be the bar mitzvah of the century!

The weekend of August 19, 2006, was glorious. Friday night we hosted our immediate family and out-of-town guests. We were so proud to show off our community to them.

I thought I had made it very clear to Yehuda that I did not want him to thank me publicly for everything I had done for the bar mitzvah. Sure enough, as he went through all the thank yous, I heard my name being mentioned. I was hoping he would stop right there. Instead, he continued to elaborate on seemingly all of my virtues, not only bar mitzvah-related. At home, he apologized and said there was no way he could not thank me. It would have been wrong. He had intentionally left this section of his remarks out of the handwritten notes I had looked over before the meal.

Shabbos morning, I anxiously took my seat in the sanctuary, my stomach doing flip-flops as I waited for Shmuly to read his *parshah*. As tears flowed freely down my face, Shmuly read flawlessly. I was proud as a peacock. Family and friends came over to embrace me and congratulate me on a job well done. Following the Torah reading, Shmuly delivered his *dvar Torah*. With poise and confidence, he compared the Torah to a map, a guidebook for living a proper way of life. His message was clear and relatable.

Rabbi Finkelstein spoke as well. He marveled at the depth of Shmuly's discourse and commended him on growing up into such an outstanding individual. We were touched and honored when Rabbi Finkelstein commented that our family, as a whole, was a *"mishpachah l'dugmah"*—a model family of what it means to live by the ideals of the Torah and what it represents. It was validating to hear that we were on the right path, that we were meeting our goals and fulfilling our purpose in life.

Following *davening*, the entire congregation was invited to join us downstairs in the social hall to partake of a delicious luncheon. As we joyfully mingled with our guests, we relished every moment. I teased my kitchen comrades that they were already hired to cook with me for Yitzchak's bar mitzvah in twelve-and-a-half-years' time.

Master Educator

Yehuda had many principles when it came to teaching. In order for him to be a truly effective educator, it had to be clear and evident that he had only the best interests of the students in mind. It was

not about him. He did not take things personally. He always spoke to our children and his students in a low tone, never raising his voice. Elisheva once said, "I knew I was in trouble, the lower Abba's voice got." He never used sarcasm or criticism to convey his point but focused on the positive, on what good had been or could be done. He caught children doing good and praised them for that. If there was something to correct, he waited until the right time and used the appropriate method to deal with it.

Yehuda doing what he loved! Interacting and engaging with his students.

Sometimes, while sharing my day with Yehuda at the supper table, I noticed that his eyes were glazed over. When I asked if he had heard anything I had said, he would apologize for having gotten lost in thought; he was contemplating a situation with a student and trying to figure out how to best resolve it.

Yehuda was constantly reading books about teaching. He always felt he could learn more, that maybe there was another technique out there to utilize. What would be the best way to deal with a specific challenge involving a specific student? The way he dealt with one child's situation was not necessarily the way he would deal with a similar scenario involving another. He always took their personalities and abilities into account.

Mrs. Jacquie Levy[2] was a board member of Hillel Academy whose children were Yehuda's students. As she recalled:

> One of our sons has had many health challenges, and at times, we did not understand how much this impacted his schoolwork. In a parent-teacher conference one term, Rabbi [Simes] was telling us that our son was not handing in assignments. I suggested tough love. "Just fail him, Rabbi, and then he will get the message." Rabbi put down the paper he had in his hand and looked at me, perplexed. He said, "Mrs. Levy, no one ever fails Judaism." It embodies to me who he was and how he thought. Each student was a treasure to be nurtured, a valuable member of our community, a sacred duty to teach, however they came to him, however they performed.
>
> I once asked him why he never seemed to have classroom management issues, even with some of the more "challenging classes." He said, "I offer respect and I hope to receive it in return. So far it has never failed me." Rabbi went on to teach our son his bar

Yehuda was able to relate to his students on all levels. Shown here with the National Hockey League (NHL) Stanley Cup at Hillel Academy.

---

2. Later, as a neuro-physiotherapist, she would work closely with Yehuda on his rehab.

mitzvah portion, was there for us when we had to postpone the bar mitzvah when our son was too ill, and guided us in our decision to do a quiet, early morning *aliyah*. He understood so much without us ever having to explain. Rabbi went on to teach all of our children. I asked them what their memories of Rabbi are… All three said a man who lived his beliefs. A man who found great joy in his Judaism. A man whose faith was deep even in the face of great suffering.

Yehuda at the front of the classroom, a rare occurrence, as he was not a frontal teacher.

Yehuda with his students visiting Hillel Lodge, the Ottawa Jewish Home for the Aged.

Teachers often requested that the most challenging students be placed in Yehuda's class and not theirs. Yehuda was not afraid of these children. They thrived in his classes. When Yehuda arrived at school in the morning or if he had recess duty, they would run to spend time with him.

The school ran an auction with teachers donating prizes. Yehuda's donation? Eat a Shabbos dinner at our home! Parents paid for the experience of seeing how Yehuda conducted himself at home.

His students could earn a can of Coke for their accomplishments. A co-worker once complained, "It's not fair you're giving out Cokes to the kids. It makes me look bad because I don't do that." Yehuda smiled and said, "No worries.

No problem. I don't mind. You could also give out Cokes if you want." That was not the answer she was expecting. She never complained again.

Yehuda was a master storyteller, often turning a ten-second story into ten chapters, keeping everyone hooked. The stories were ways of imparting lessons for life in a meaningful way.

When I was teaching in the classroom, I did not impose rules. I actually elicited from my students what they would need to help them learn effectively. After reaching a full class consensus, we reduced the list of procedures to five or six. We also determined consequences for failure to comply with what the students and teacher agreed upon. To be expected, every one of my classes had their own tailor-made lists of what was important to them.

However, I did impose one incredibly harsh rule.

You see, at times young and healthy students tend to become loud and rambunctious. Surprised? Well, you shouldn't be! To be on the offensive against this scourge, I devised the most strict and merciless rule in my arsenal. When they heard this terrifying rule, they shivered in fright in their boots.

Now that you have an inkling of the severity of this spine-tingling rule, I will proceed to share the rule in the hope you can withstand it. When I tell a story, if there dares to be any preventable interruptions, I will stop the story in the middle. And, I will NEVER EVER finish the story. They may be in high school or beyond, and they may beg and plead to hear the climax of the story, but I will never tell it, for the rest of their lives. An adjunct of this rule was that nobody was allowed to yell at or otherwise embarrass the unfortunate soul who disturbed the story.

This rule was a sure-fire way of quieting down a too loud class.

From the Rolling Rabbi blog, "My Signature Boat Story," April 14, 2015

One morning, Yehuda had to be late and called the school to let them know. The principal was concerned that the students would take advantage of being without a teacher and went to check up on them. The students were not running around or making noise. They had formed groups and were reviewing the material Rabbi Simes had taught them. The students' respect for their *rebbi* and his for them were immeasurable. He provided them with an environment that fostered their love of learning.

Yehuda's students wanted to please him. One time, some students were missing at recess. He found them hiding in the bathroom. They

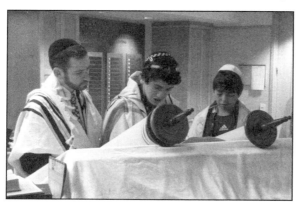

were not trying to cut recess and stay warm indoors— they were studying for the Chumash test he was giving them the next period.

Yehuda leading *tefillah* at Hillel Academy.

He made his lessons come alive. He would sing the *pesukim* with them.

When he met up with his students years after teaching them, they would sing to him the Chumash he had taught them in fourth or fifth grade. It was their first exposure to singing in learning Judaic subjects. When one student called his grandfather to sing the *pesukim* to him, his grandfather cried with emotion. It was the very tune he had chanted when he went to *cheder* before the Holocaust.

Yehuda spent hours preparing his lessons. There were no shortcuts for him. No matter if he had taught a subject one time or ten, he always made sure to review the material and refresh the presentation. If he taught two classes, he introduced different nuances to each lesson.

I dreaded report card time. With hundreds of students and numerous subjects, it would take Yehuda days to finish filling them out. Every student needed a mark and a comment in *every* subject. No two students received the same comment and no student received the same comment for different subjects. When the report cards went digital, he would spend hours on the computer in school or at Torah High. We finally got Wi-Fi at home so that we could at least see him at the dining room table as he worked.

At times, after spending hours creating worksheets, he left them home in the morning rush. Sometimes he left a carefully prepared lunch in the fridge. Yehuda would call and ask me if I could please, please come drop it off at school. I would go to Hillel with a child or two in tow and make a stop in the office to explain why I was there. The secretaries were always excited to see me and sing Yehuda's praises. They would call up to Yehuda's classroom to announce my arrival. After the child(ren) and I climbed all the stairs to his room, Yehuda would greet us with a huge grin and introduce us to his class. With a reception like that, it was hard to be annoyed at him.

In recognition of his dedication to his students, Yehuda was honored with the 2007 North American Grinspoon–Steinhardt Award for Excellence in Jewish Education. Every year, winners are invited to attend a dinner and award celebration hosted by a different city. Yehuda was invited to receive his award at the Gaylord Opryland Resort and Convention Center in Nashville, Tennessee.

Awardees received a stipend toward furthering their professional development. Yehuda used his to spend a week in Israel learning and touring during his spring break. I stayed behind with the children. In true Yehuda fashion, he did not come home empty-handed. He bought me a new pair of earrings as a token of his appreciation for helping him with his achievement, and beautiful Purim costumes for the children.

"A token of appreciation" was one of Yehuda's favorite expressions and lessons. When he wanted to reward or recognize one of our children or one of his students, he would explain his philosophy to them: "As a human, I cannot possibly reward you to the full extent that you deserve, but I can express my appreciation and recognition in a symbolic way. This reward is a symbol that you have accomplished a goal."

Proud Canadians

Home and school were closely intertwined. Shortly before Devorah was born, Yehuda rented a beeper so I could be in touch with him if I needed him during school hours. He was so excited imagining the scenario: I would beep him and he would make a dramatic exit, explaining that his wife was having a baby and he needed to leave. I made it quite clear to him that no matter what, that would not be happening. I could only imagine all of his students and their parents camping out in the lobby of the hospital, waiting to hear the good news. Luckily, Devorah's entrance to the world in February 2008 did not necessitate using the beeper. Poor Yehuda, he was so disappointed.

By this time, we had been living in Ottawa for about six years. When we originally moved, we came on work permits. These documents, valid for three years, made it legal for us to reside and work in Canada and allowed the children to attend school. After three years, they needed to be renewed, a process entailing paperwork and time at a border crossing. Legal benefits such as health insurance or child tax credits were based on this document. At a certain point, the Canadian government can deny your right to reapply for this permit, in essence asking you to make a decision: Do you want to be a Canadian, or not? If yes, go through the process. If not, go back to where you came from. Upon becoming a citizen, there is no longer a need for permits or other documents.

We began the citizenship process, a process which was to take about two years. First we became permanent residents, which awarded us certain benefits. However, if permanent residents leave Canada for an extended period of time, they lose those benefits. Upon their return, they must begin the whole process again by applying for a work permit.

There is a required number of days that applicants for citizenship must reside in Canada each calendar year. Every trip out of the country has to be recorded, as well as its duration and purpose. We had to list every address we ever lived at and for how long. We were asked to document the names and addresses of our siblings and obtain proof of a clean police record from every jurisdiction in which we had resided.

Once that was all submitted and approved, we had to study for the citizenship test. The children were young enough to be exempt from this requirement. Yehuda and I memorized the national anthem, names of the political parties, names of the provinces and territories, and other details of historical significance. We went to take the exam with butterflies in our stomachs. We were not used to being on the other side of the desk. I breezed through the test and went to hand it in.

The proctor looked at me. "Are you a teacher?"

"Yes. How did you know?"

"The teachers always finish first."

The kids, who had been testing us and cheering us on, were thrilled when we passed. The official ceremony, attended by the new citizens and their family members, took place in a room filled to capacity with representatives of every nationality, race, and religion. We listened to the judge explain the significance of becoming a Canadian citizen. He listed the names of every country represented and the trials and tribulations that people faced in their native lands. He cited their hopes and dreams for freedom—freedom of speech and religion, the right to vote, and other democratic privileges. It was humbling to realize how much the others had risked to achieve a better life for themselves,

Yehuda sharing the pride of his citizenship status with his students.

while we risked nothing at all. All we were saved from was the annoyance of completing a form every couple of years.

When the ceremony was over, Yehuda went straight back to school. He had prepared a bag full of red and white Canada–motif accessories to wear as he walked into the building—a proud new Canadian carrying celebratory cookies to share with his colleagues and students.

I was now a proud Canadian... with a secret. We would be having a new Canadian in a few months' time.

CHAPTER SIX

A Deer in the Headlights

> A glorious decade went by, constantly feeling enriched as we enriched the lives of others. Our family grew with the birth of three Canadians, we continually became influential in the educational fabric of the Ottawa community, and all we knew was success, achievement, and blessing. I remember thinking that all of this was almost too good to be true. Alas, prophetic thinking.
>
> *From the Rolling Rabbi blog,*
> *"My Story," August 2013*

The Last Weekend "Before"

IT STARTED OFF AS A ROUTINE FAMILY WEEKEND. THE SCHOOL year was drawing to a close. Torah Academy had finished on Thursday and Yehuda had another week to go. We were all looking forward to the start of summer and a break in routine.

We decided to visit my sister Fraidel and her family in Rochester, New York, and spend a relaxing weekend with them. There was another reason we wanted to travel to Rochester. Fraidel's husband, Rabbi Eliezer Lehrer, was the headmaster at Ora Academy, the girls' high school. Their graduation was scheduled for Sunday. Since our daughter Malka was enrolled as a ninth-grade student for the upcoming

September, we felt it would be good for her to visit with the Ora girls, see the school, and attend the graduation.

Shmuly wanted to remain in Ottawa with his friends. I felt it was a family vacation and the whole family should go. Yehuda felt it was not a "real" vacation—there was a purpose to it. Shmuly should be free to choose. We discussed it, and in the end I agreed.

Asna was finishing grade nine at Bais Yaakov of Montreal.[1] She had a matriculation exam, a standardized government test, on the morning of Friday, June 18, 2010, after which she was free to leave.

The kids and I picked up Yehuda after dismissal at Hillel on Thursday. We drove the two hours to Montreal, and went out with Asna for dinner. When we dropped her off at the Biegeleisens, where she was boarding, we chatted for a while before heading to the motel.

It was fun catching up with the Biegeleisens. We had become friends over the course of the year and our families are very similar. We are the same age and their daughters line up with ours. We were both expecting. Chana Ita was due in July and I in September.

Well, what do pregnant women talk about when they get together? Pregnancy aches and fatigue and birth plans. As her due date was closer than mine, I asked what her plan was.

She absolutely threw me for a loop. Never in my wildest dreams would I consider what she was considering! Rabbi Biegeleisen was the director of a sleepaway camp in the Midwest. In years past, the whole family went together and enjoyed the benefits of the camp experience. This year, however, due to the imminent birth of their child, he would go alone and she was planning to stay home. I was absolutely flabbergasted and appalled.

---

1.   One of my requirements for moving out of town was that there had to be a girls' high school in the community. We were relocating with four daughters and did not want to send them away after eighth grade. (I was less concerned about sending Shmuly away for yeshivah, as Yehuda had done it at his age.) But man plans and G-d laughs. When Asna was in seventh grade, the local girls' high school shut down.

"How on earth will your husband make it back in time?"

"He can't."

"What do you mean, 'He can't'?"

"Well, there is no direct flight and it's a fourteen-and-a-half-hour drive."

"What about the delivery?"

"Oh, it's okay. My mother will come with me and he will come after."

I could not process that at all! Have our baby alone, without my husband—no way would I ever do that! NEVER! For each of our eight births, Yehuda was with me the entire time. I counted on him for support. There was no one else I would want to take his place!

We exchanged goodbyes and we headed to the motel.

The next morning, after Asna's exam, we picked her up and drove to Rochester. Sunset that week was at 8:53 p.m., so we had plenty of time to travel and make it for Shabbos.

Over the weekend, I made sure to remind Yehuda that he was coming with me when our baby would be born—just in case he was getting any "smart ideas" after our discussion with the Biegeleisens. I even spoke to Fraidel about it. "Could you imagine letting your husband go away when you are due to have a baby?"

We enjoyed a pleasant weekend, relaxing and spending quality time with our family. Yehuda, who was often distracted with his lesson plans and figuring out ways to challenge his students, was especially present. I do not recall him speaking about work at all.

The Ora graduation took place in the late afternoon of Sunday, June 20. Every girl was given special mention highlighting her qualities and achievements. In addition, each had the opportunity to share the experiences that helped mold and shape her growth throughout high school.

One student's words were extremely personal. She had lost her mother a year earlier and described what it was like for her. She thanked her mother for the life lessons she had taught her.

Tears flowed down my cheeks. When I could no longer hold back full-blown, heaving sobs, I ran out of the room and tried to find someplace to compose myself. I stumbled into the washroom and completely broke down. How horrible, painful, and sad to lose a parent at the age of seventeen! My heart ached for the girl and her mother. I wondered about my own beloved children and my precious unborn child. What would their lives be like without me or my husband? It was too difficult to imagine and I kept on crying.

I had to pull myself together. I washed my face and tried to look presentable, but there was no denying that I had been weeping. Pregnancy hormones, I supposed.

At the collation, we mingled over refreshments and congratulated everyone on a job well done. Yehuda and Eliezer went off to the side. Yehuda asked Eliezer if he would be interested in attending the annual *yarchei kallah* in Queens the following week and learning together. Eliezer enthusiastically agreed.

As unrushed and relaxed as we were, we still had a four-hour drive back to Ottawa. Yehuda wanted to get home at a somewhat decent hour so as not to be too exhausted for the upcoming week. I, on the other hand, was officially on vacation and was in no rush at all. In fact, not only was I looking forward to summer vacation, but, in addition, I had worked the required number of hours the previous year to make me eligible for a full year of paid maternity leave.

Obviously, I was excited for the birth of our child. But a year of maternity leave? That was a luxury. In the US, six weeks is customary. With luck, you might get eight. Often it is unpaid leave. Becky and Judy would try to convince me to move to Israel, where I could get three months' leave. I teased that I moved to Canada instead so I could get twelve. The joke was on me, though, since with our first three Canadian kids, I never ended up working enough hours to qualify.

With this pregnancy, however, I increased my hours to max out my benefits.

With baby number nine, I was going to be spoiled. Very spoiled. I would get to spend time with my baby, and be paid for it! Imagine— we could go to a mom and baby program, the park, the library... I would spend endless moments staring into my baby's eyes as we bonded. I would prepare gourmet meals for my family. Without a work schedule to tie me down, I could go with the flow. I had so much to look forward to.

As we piled into the van, we said our goodbyes and promised to keep in touch. We already had plans for another weekend get-together later in the summer. Yehuda wanted to take the kids on a road trip "home" to St. Paul after the *yarchei kallah*. He wanted to retrace the steps of his childhood with them and get together with some relatives who still lived there. My obstetrician did not like the idea of a trip at all. Under no condition would he allow me to travel so far at that late stage of pregnancy. I was disappointed, yet at the same time a little relieved at the prospect of having some time alone. I was going to stay home with Devorah and possibly Yitzchak, and meet up with the rest of them back in Rochester when they returned. At least, those were the plans.

The Accident

Yehuda took his seat behind the steering wheel and I climbed into the front passenger seat. All the children were strapped into their appropriate car seats and boosters and seat belts. With a final wave, we were off, driving along the route that would soon become very familiar to us: 590N–490E–90E–81N to the Canadian border at Thousand Islands.

We had traveled about an hour and a half when we passed Mattydale, New York, near the exit for the Syracuse airport.

> We were happily chatting, singing, and playing road games. As the sun began to set, I exited at a turnoff to

pray Minchah. Looking back, those moments spent in prayer were to be the last moments I would ever spend standing on my own two feet.

Feeling a bit fatigued, I asked my wife if she wouldn't mind taking over the driving for a couple of hours. As always, she graciously agreed. So we switched spots, she taking the driver's seat with me occupying the passenger position.

This would end up being the way we would drive for the rest of our lives. Funny how things repeat themselves without our realizing...

From the Rolling Rabbi blog,
"My Story," August 2013

We were back on the road. Soon we passed Watertown. Shmuly called to check up on us and our estimated time of arrival. All we knew was that the last sign we passed said "Canada 20"—twenty miles to the border. We estimated we would be home in about two hours. The kids continued to talk, laugh, and snack on pretzels as the phone was passed around. They filled in their brother about the trip and he, in turn, shared his weekend experiences with us. He said that he decided not to stay over at his friend's house but rather to wait at home for our arrival.

It was well past sunset. There were no lights on the 81 and the road had grown dark. My eyes were adjusting to the transformation of dusk into night. Shadows were everywhere. I blinked several times and squinted. A particular shadow in the road seemed darker. I called out to Yehuda, "Do you see something? Is something there? Is that a deer? I think it's a deer. Help! What should I do? WHAT SHOULD I DO?"

There was no time to process. In the split second I had to make a decision, all I could think of were the horror stories of what happens when a deer comes through a windshield. I could not let that happen. I had to protect my family.

Suddenly, I awoke with a start. Our faithful blue van began to screech to the left, into the oncoming traffic lane. I sluggishly reached toward the steering wheel to help redirect the van. My wife overcompensated, hurtling the van toward the right. Again, she aggressively pounded the wheel all the way to the left. I don't know how many times we sharply weaved back and forth, screeching loudly and leaving strong black marks on the highway...

I remember saying under my breath, "Oh no oh no." Finally, the van skimmed a post beyond the oncoming traffic lane, causing the van to tumble and roll numerous times. It was during this horrifying somersaulting that I kept repeating *"Shema Yisrael."* Looking back, this just poured out of my lips automatically, without thinking to form the words. Eventually, the van ended its death roll in an upright position, giving an appearance of "all is well." But all was not well.

From the Rolling Rabbi blog,
"My Story," August 2013

I have a vague recollection of spinning sensations. My eyes opened and closed. Time stood still yet moved quickly. When I finally opened my eyes, the car was right side up. I was so relieved. We had not flipped after all.

Yehuda was yelling, "The keys! The keys! The keys!"

I could not understand what he wanted. "What about the keys?"

"Turn off the motor and take the keys out of the ignition so the car doesn't explode!"

I did not know what the keys in the ignition had to do with the car exploding, but I sure knew that the car exploding would not be a good idea.

In the brief moments this exchange was taking place, the kids were unbuckling themselves and each other and clambering out of the smashed vehicle. The van was in a ditch on the left side, facing the two-lane highway, perpendicular to the road.

At this point I was confused: Did we or did we not flip? Apparently, we had flipped multiple times. I let myself out of the car feeling quite dazed and trying to understand what had happened. I was wearing only one shoe. Malka realized I was no longer wearing my head covering. As an Orthodox married woman, I keep my hair concealed in public at all times. Malka was wearing a short-sleeved T-shirt over a long-sleeved one. She pulled off the top layer and helped me fasten the shirt around my head like a scarf. I promptly forgot it was there, as I was accustomed to having something on my head. In retrospect, it must have looked strange. Bayla, dressed in two layers like her sister, stripped off her brand-new, favorite T-shirt and wrapped it around her father's bleeding head.

Thankfully, the eight others in the vehicle escaped with no [injuries] or minor scratches and bruises, with my seven-months-pregnant wife sustaining the most worrisome injuries. But it was I, sitting in my wife's original seat, who absorbed the brunt of the fury that night. The roof of the van was crushed above my head, effectively breaking my neck and trapping me in the van.

The rest of my family unbuckled each other and climbed out through the bashed-out windows. They huddled together on the side of the highway. Amidst sobbing and crying out, they tearfully realized that they no longer had a working cell phone; they felt hopeless and helpless.

A man suddenly appeared, having stopped his car to see how he could help. It was he who called 911, and within fifteen minutes, a multitude of fire engines, ambulances, and police cars quickly descended all around us.

From the Rolling Rabbi blog,
"My Story," August 2013

The highway was ablaze with flashing lights and loud sirens. Emergency personnel were everywhere. I walked over to Yehuda on the passenger side, vaguely aware of the shattered window. He told me he was in pain and could not get out of the car. I responded nonchalantly, "That's okay. The paramedics are here. They'll get you out and take care of you."

A car had been traveling behind us. The driver witnessed the whole event. As our van rolled, he called 911, fearing the worst. The children were thanking him and asking his name. He did not want to say. Later, they would refer to him as Eliyahu Hanavi. Tradition is replete with stories of Eliyahu Hanavi saving people from disaster.

"Mommy! Mommy! It's a miracle!" Malka was yelling. "We're all okay!"

I agreed with my daughter wholeheartedly, without even knowing any details.

"We'll have to make a *seudas hoda'ah* to celebrate!"

I assured the children that one day we would.

I was in a fog, not really comprehending what had happened between the time I saw the deer and the present moment. In fact, I was not even sure—had I seen a deer? Was there a deer? Someone confirmed for me that there had been a deer. No, I had not hit it. It dashed off into the woods.

Are Deer Bad Animals?

Some time after the accident, Yitzchak, who was four, asked me, "Mommy, are deer bad animals?" It was an out-of-the-blue question, but not really. Yitzchak's life had changed dramatically as the result of a deer.

Indeed, are deer bad animals? After processing briefly, I said, "No. Deer are not bad animals. Being bad means you had a choice to do something and you made a wrong choice on purpose. A deer is an animal. It can't make choices. It can only do what its brain is programmed to do. It can't think things through. It can't say to itself, 'Um, should I cross the road now? I better check for cars. I might get hit. I might hurt someone.' The deer went out onto the road to get to the other side."

Yitzchak seemed satisfied with my answer.

I feel like that deer was the catalyst that changed my life forever. Life is not unlike a play. Everyone stands in their places, and, on cue, they step out in front of the curtain and into the limelight to perform their part. That deer was put onto this world to serve a purpose. When the time was right, not a moment too soon or too late, it stepped out onto that road and retreated when its part was done.

"Ma'am, When Are You Due?"

By now the paramedics were assessing us and determining our injuries. A paramedic came over to me. "Ma'am, are you pregnant?"

I stared at him. *Excuse me*, I thought, *now that is a personal question. How dare you ask me that? Why does it even matter if I am or not?*

"No. I am not pregnant."

"Are you sure?"

"Of course I'm sure. No, I am not."

Bayla started screaming. "Mommy! Mommy! Yes, you are! Don't you remember? Please, Mommy, don't you remember? You told us we are having a baby!"

I was so puzzled. *A baby? We're having a baby? I'm pregnant?*

I started to pat down my body, feeling my clothes, trying desperately to remember what I was wearing. Maybe that would jog my memory.

Oh, yes, I'm wearing my brown skirt with the cute T-shirt. I like that outfit. It's my favorite weekday maternity one. Well, then, I guess I'm pregnant.

"Ma'am, when are you due?"

"Due? I don't know!"

"How many weeks are you?"

"I don't know!"

I heard Bayla again. "Mommy! Mommy! Don't you remember? In September. Rosh Hashanah time!"

The poor girl was terrified I had lost my mind.

I was in shock.

Slowly it began to make sense. "Yes, I'm pregnant. I'm due in September."

"Ma'am, we are going to take you with us in the ambulance. We are going to bring you to the hospital to get you checked out. Does anything hurt?"

"No. I mean, yes. My neck. My shoulder."

"Come with us."

I looked at him.

"No! I will not come with you. I can't come with you. I will not leave my children on the side of the highway in the middle of the night. I am not going. I am staying right here with them."

The paramedic bent down and looked me straight in the eye, as you would when dealing with a non-compliant toddler. Firmly and clearly, he stated, "You need to come with us. You need to get checked out. We have to make sure that you and your baby are okay. We will take care of your children. We will be responsible for them. They are going to join you at the hospital. We will divide them up into a few ambulances. There will be an older child with each of the younger ones."

With that, they proceeded to lay me down on the stretcher and strap me to a board to prevent further injury to my neck and shoulders.

After a bumpy ride I arrived at Samaritan Hospital, anxious to hear news about Yehuda. As far as I could tell, he seemed totally fine. I had been talking with him and he responded. How hurt could he be? There was no news on his condition.

"Is Abba Going to Die?"

As promised, the children arrived soon after. I was offered the choice of having them come in to see me all at once or one by one. I felt that one at a time was best. They ranged in age from two to fifteen; they could not all get the same information. They could not all hear the same thing the same way. I wanted to be able to address the needs of the child who was in front of me. The younger kids just wanted to kiss their mommy and get a hug. The older ones had more questions.

When Asna came in, she kept asking, "Is Abba going to die?"

I was shocked. "Die? No. Of course not. Why would he die? He is just as alive as the rest of us. We were talking to him. He just needed help to get out of the car."

She kept asking. She did not believe me.

Aside from Asna, who needed four staples for a head laceration, the children were unharmed. Yehuda's injuries, however, were very serious. He had been airlifted to the nearest level one trauma center at Upstate University Hospital in Syracuse. It was decided that I would be transported there as well, to be in the same hospital.

"Whom Shall We Call?"

A firm but gentle voice penetrated my fog. "Ma'am, whom shall we call to come take responsibility for the children?"

Instinctively, I told the nurse to contact Eliezer and Fraidel in Rochester. They were the closest in terms of distance and we had just come from their home. I stipulated that whoever calls should only speak with Eliezer, definitely not with Fraidel. Ever the protective older sister, I did not want her to panic.

Eliezer was at *minyan* when the hospital rang. As instructed, the caller refused to tell Fraidel the reason for the call and insisted that Eliezer call back as soon as possible. This set off alarm bells in my sister's mind. She did not recognize the name or number of the hospital and wondered if it could be a hoax or a scam. Why would a representative from a random hospital be calling her husband in the middle of the night and not be willing to speak to her?

When Eliezer walked through the door, Fraidel handed him the phone. Eliezer called the number she had written down and was connected.

"Your family was in a rollover. The children are all fine but both parents are seriously injured. Your sister-in-law is signing custody of the children to you and we need you to come pick them up right away."

Stunned, but trying to keep his wits about him, he asked, "What happened to my brother-in-law? Is he alive?"

"I can't tell you. HIPAA."

"Let me put it this way. It is close to eleven o'clock at night. It will take me at least two and a half hours to get to Watertown. I need to know if the family needs to make funeral arrangements. You need to figure out some legal way to answer my question."

"All I can say is he was alive at the scene of the accident and he was airlifted to Syracuse. I do not have any further information."

"Fair enough. I'll be over as soon as I can."

Fraidel called a babysitter to stay with their four children, including a six-month-old baby, grabbed a change of clothes and some provisions, and sped off toward Watertown. Driving along the Thruway, Eliezer called his brother Moshe—who was a hospitalist at New York-Presbyterian/Columbia University Medical Center and internist at Ezra Medical Center in Brooklyn at the time—and apprised him of the situation. "I don't have details yet," he concluded. "Please leave your phone on. We don't know what the night is going to bring and I'm afraid we may need your medical advice and expertise."

After an hour on the Thruway, they chose to make a quick detour to

Upstate University Hospital where Yehuda had been airlifted. Eliezer and Fraidel knew the children were safe and they wanted to see what was happening with Yehuda. He was alone, they figured, without family members or an advocate.

Fortunately, Yehuda was not entirely alone. Upon realizing the severity of his injuries, the hospital had called the chaplain, Rabbi Yaakov Rapoport, to come be with him. Rabbi Rapoport met the Lehrers as they entered the ER and informed them that the situation was very precarious. The hospital team wanted to speak with them in the family room before they could see Yehuda.

Two attending doctors summed up what they knew so far.

"Your brother-in-law suffered the brunt of the damage of the rollover and had his neck snapped. He needs immediate surgery. Right now, he is in trauma bay one awaiting an MRI. He seems to be awake but is in tremendous pain. The family should start planning and preparing themselves. His injuries are presenting as total quadriplegia, which means he has suffered the loss of function to all four major limbs.

"We cannot predict what his recovery will be. Likely, the way you see him now is how he will be for the rest of his life. Once we see the results of surgery and his swelling recedes, we may have a better idea."

Eliezer went in to see Yehuda briefly and reassured him that he was getting the help he needed.

A social worker handed Eliezer a small, zippered, bio-hazard bag containing Yehuda's glasses, bloodstained watch, and wallet. I still have that bag in my drawer. For months after the accident, the watch would beep at the times Yehuda had set for his teaching schedule.

After getting directions to Samaritan, Eliezer continued on to Watertown to claim the children while Fraidel stayed behind to await my transfer.

"Can He Walk?"

I kept prying for information about Yehuda and being told none was available. After a while, I began to sense they were keeping something from me. I asked again, "Is my husband all right? What is happening with my husband?"

"We were told he suffered a spinal cord injury."

My brain froze. A spinal cord injury? I knew practically nothing at all about spinal cord injuries, but what I did know was enough to shake me.

"Can he walk?"

A soft and somber "no" was the immediate reply.

I took a deep breath.

I had two options—I could galvanize myself to hold it together or completely collapse. Frankly, shutting down and hiding was the more appealing option. The problem with that choice was that I had seven children waiting on the other side of the curtain (plus Shmuly at home) who were counting on me. There was no choice. I had to stay strong. I had to be there for them. We were going to have to figure this out together. Whatever was going to happen was going to affect them as well. This was to be a family journey. I promised myself I would hold up the fort—but only temporarily. When Yehuda recovered, he would get his role back.

Our very close friends, the Burgers, were driving down from Ottawa to be with the children until Eliezer arrived. I did not know when they would arrive or when I would be leaving. I feared for my children to be left alone. The nurses were kind and thoughtful. They contacted one of the Jewish doctors on staff who lived nearby. He came with kosher food and offered to stay.

Around 3:00 a.m., I was finally transported. As I was being wheeled into the ambulance that would transfer me to Syracuse, the nurses brought me forms to sign, temporarily releasing the children into Eliezer's custody.

Syracuse is little more than an hour's drive from Watertown. The ambulance driver promised to go slowly as the ride would be very bumpy. He meant well, but it did not help. I felt every shake and turn. My neck ached. My shoulder ached. I could not move my arm without wincing or holding my breath.

I had no idea what was awaiting me. Luckily, my imagination was shut down. I thought I only needed some painkillers. I was worried about Yehuda.

Thankfully, by the time I arrived in Syracuse, some of my family members were already there. My sister Fraidel was waiting, and my father, apprised of the news by Eliezer, had made the five-hour drive from Queens with my siblings Avrohom Dov and Ahuva. By then, Eliezer was on his way to Watertown to pick up the kids. My mother contacted Yehuda's sisters.

Fraidel accompanied me to the various tests I needed. They do not routinely perform nuclear tests on pregnant women, but all sorts of CT scans and MRIs were necessary. An ophthalmologist spent a long time examining my eyes. I could see just fine. I was not sure why I was being subjected to his thorough examination. Apparently, due to the force of the airbag, numerous blood vessels had popped. The whites of my eyes were completely red. They wanted to be sure it was just a cosmetic issue and not a medical one. I did not get a chance to look at myself in a mirror for several days. By then, it had improved somewhat.

I was diagnosed with broken ribs, a broken collarbone, and pneumothorax (punctured lungs). Since I was now at risk for premature labor, they admitted me for observation at the adjacent Crouse Hospital, which had a top-notch women's center and neonatal department. If I were to deliver early, the baby would be in safe hands. In addition, I required oxygen so as not to compromise the baby's health.

Amidst the hullabaloo, I was told that Yehuda was being prepped for spinal surgery and I had to give my consent. I was desperate to see him. The crew wheeled my stretcher to where my husband lay on his, awaiting surgery. Still in intense pain, I reassured him that he would be getting the help he needed and apologized over and over for the pain I had caused him. He tried to reassure me that it was not my fault.

How bizarre. Two stretchers. Two injured spouses side by side, saying goodbye before a very delicate and vital surgery.

Meanwhile, Back in Watertown...

It was 4:30 a.m. and the scene in Samaritan Hospital was surreal. Off to the side, in an unused emergency ward, under the watchful eyes of the Burgers, the lights were dimmed and the children were trying to rest in a curtained-off cubicle. It had been a long, stressful night. The little ones were sleeping but the older children were still awake when Eliezer arrived. They immediately began to pepper him with questions.

"Is Abba alive?"

"Yes."

"I don't believe you!"

Just as I had made the decision mere hours before to be open and honest with the children, Eliezer made the same decision. We must be as transparent as possible. There needs to be trust. Trust can only come with honesty.

"I just saw Abba," Eliezer said. "He is in very serious shape. He was alive an hour ago. I will not lie to you. Now let's get a little sleep if we can because we have a long day ahead of us."

It really was only a little sleep. At 6:00 a.m. a janitor came in, pushing his cleaning cart. He flipped on the lights and declared that the space was needed and everyone had to leave. Blinking and trying to orient themselves, they gathered their belongings and shuffled into a small office that was available. Rabbi Burger and Eliezer went to the side to *daven*.

The news program on the overhead television screen was reporting on the accident. Footage was shown of the highway ablaze with lights from emergency vehicles. A blue van could be seen perpendicular to the road in a ditch. It did not seem too bad.

Dr. Sally Khandadash, a local Jewish physician, having seen the news of the accident, came to see if she could be of assistance. She graciously offered her home to the whole crew for as long as necessary. Armed with discharge papers and follow-up instructions for removing Asna's staples, everyone trooped over to Dr. Khandadash's house across the street from the hospital.[2]

Rabbi Burger and Eliezer discussed the logistics. Between them, they had two cars but not enough car seats and boosters. Someone needed to go to Walmart to purchase replacements. Someone also needed to go to the junkyard to see what could be salvaged from the van. In particular, I was concerned about Yehuda's *tallis* and *tefillin*. With the kids being cared for by the Khandadashes, Suzanne Burger went off to Walmart. Rabbi Burger and Eliezer went to find the van.

The men arrived at French's Auto Repair Shop on Pink Schoolhouse Road in the little hamlet of Theresa, New York. They pulled up next to a barn-like structure and inquired about the van. They were told to go to the grassy field behind the shop—"and be careful."

The van looked like a bomb had hit it. Its windows were shattered, with little shards jutting out where the glass used to be. The side doors were ripped off, used medical gear was strewn throughout the van, and snack crumbs and wrappers littered the seats and floor.

Eliezer's heart caught in his throat and tears sprang from his eyes as he viewed the evidence of our terrible experience. But he noticed a miracle as well. The van's roof had caved in and was being held up by the seat back of the middle bench. One additional inch forward—and

---

2.   Unbeknownst to us at the time, Dr. Khandadash had an Ottawa connection. As the mother of twins, living in a town with virtually no Jewish infrastructure, she had reached out to Ottawa's NCSY/Torah High. Yehuda and Bram Bregman, director of NCSY Ottawa, had been in touch with her about including her children in their programming.

the children in the middle bench would have been crushed. One inch backward, and it would have been the kids in the back.

Tiny slivers of glass were everywhere. Could the van be safely accessed? Gingerly, Rabbi Burger opened the hatchback and the men carefully removed the suitcases, Yehuda's hat box, suit bag, and other items. A single box of freeze-pops that had not burst or leaked was able to be salvaged. The rest of what was to be our summer supply of ices left a sticky residue all over the floor. The cracked cell phone that was being used at the time of the accident was added to the pile of rescued items.

Yehuda's *tallis* and *tefillin* were nowhere to be found. They must have been forcefully ejected from the vehicle. Despite volunteers combing the accident site on numerous occasions, they were never located.

Rabbi Burger and Eliezer were riveted to the spot. They stood there solemnly, staring. Until now they had been going through the motions, taking care of what needed to be done, not processing the horror that had transpired. A family's life had changed forever. It was too overwhelming to even take a picture. Besides, who would ever want to look at the carnage again?

Preliminary Arrangements

While Rabbi Burger and Eliezer were recovering what they could from the van, our families were mobilizing. In Syracuse, my father and brother would be responsible for Yehuda, and Ahuva would be responsible for me. This would allow Fraidel to return home to her children. My mother would be going straight to Rochester to help out there. Shmuly would be arriving by car with some New Jersey friends who had spent the weekend in Ottawa. Yehuda's sister and brother-in-law, Rachel and Michael Stein, were due to arrive shortly from Chicago. Another sister, Becky Avner, was arranging a flight from Israel. She would stay until Tuesday. Upon her departure, the third sister, Judy Newman, would arrive. My sister Elisheva Milder, her husband Dovid Shmuel, and their two children would also be coming.

Our family would be staying in Rochester for the foreseeable future and calls were made to contacts in the community for help. The first need was for transportation to take everyone back to the Lehrers. We had been gone for less than twenty-four hours. Our beds were still made. The entire extended family would need shopping, meals, rides, and laundry services. Rochester's Camp Gan Izzy was scheduled to start the next day, and its directors invited the children to attend. Camp bags, camp shirts, and bathing suits needed to be purchased. Other items of clothing had to be procured. The children literally showed up with just the shirts on their backs; our trip was meant to be a weekend getaway, not an extended summer vacation!

Three of the girls had to have their glasses replaced; they had been mangled into non-functional shapes. An ophthalmologist in Rochester agreed to check their eyes and issue new prescriptions. No cost was spared to purchase stylish glasses that would make them feel beautiful.

The children's emotional well-being also needed to be addressed. They had gone through a double trauma—a serious motor vehicle accident and their father's serious, irreparable damage. My family made arrangements for the children and me to meet with trauma specialists. They counseled us that right now it is normal to feel that our lives are in upheaval. Obstacles may seem insurmountable. However, the situation will calm down. There will be a "new normal," a "before" and "after." The adults should be patient and allow the children to process everything in their own way, on their own individual time frames. Some may want to talk now. Some may only begin to talk in three months, or six. Some may not want to talk at all. Whenever they are ready, we should just listen. We should be on the lookout for withdrawal, anxiety, and depression and be prepared to provide any necessary support. In general, as has been our philosophy over the years, we must allow the children to be…children!

On Tuesday, after the first day of camp was over, the kids asked to visit me. A ride was arranged for the one-hour-plus drive to Syracuse. This scenario was repeated many times, as the children stayed in

Rochester for the entire duration of Yehuda's hospitalization in Syracuse and a couple of weeks after he was transferred to Ottawa. The kindness and devotion of the Rochester community continued even afterward. We still feel enveloped by their warmth.

Back on the home front, our friends and community members in Ottawa were in a frenzied state, alarmed as the initial reports came in and anxious to hear updates. Rachel opened a CaringBridges account. CaringBridges is an online journal that shares health information with family and friends. A community-wide Tehillim rally was planned. Over two hundred and fifty people attended the program in the

The emergency Tehillim rally in the Soloway Jewish Community Center (SJCC). Our community and communities worldwide rallied behind us every step of the way.

Soloway Jewish Community Center. An initiative was started for people to pledge to do a mitzvah in the merit of Yehuda's recovery. Groups of Yehuda's students began organizing car washes on Sundays. They wanted to raise money to help our family.

Medical Coma

Yehuda's surgery proceeded as planned. To our great relief, the surgeon reported it had gone well. We wanted to feel confident that

Yehuda was receiving the best care possible. We managed to obtain the images of the surgery and arranged for a second opinion from a top surgeon. His confirmation was reassuring.

Yehuda had a lot of swelling due to the injuries he had sustained. In order to allow his body to begin the healing process, he was placed into a medically induced coma. The goals were for the swelling to go down, vitals to remain stable, and for him to remain intubated for up to two weeks—at which point he would have a tracheotomy. Once these goals were met, he would be ready for transfer to rehab. We would need to decide where that rehabilitation would take place.

CHAPTER SEVEN

ICU, Transfers, and Rehab

Insurance

I N CANADA, WE ARE THE BENEFICIARIES OF PROVINCIAL healthcare. We do not have to pay health insurance premiums and we can visit a doctor as often as we need without worrying about huge fees or copayments. Specialists, procedures, and surgeries are all free. Admissions to the hospital are also covered.

Having moved to Canada from the States, where we were paying thousands of dollars per year for health coverage, it sounded like healthcare utopia. But, as is the case with all things in life, there is no free ride. Wait times are common to see specialists or to have certain procedures performed. Patients are triaged, and those in more serious condition get moved to the front of the line. For less urgent situations, the wait time is longer.

Not everything is covered by OHIP (Ontario Health Insurance Plan), such as vision care, dental care, and prescriptions. One of the benefits Yehuda had when working at Hillel Academy was a reduced rate on a supplemental insurance plan, which, besides for covering vision and dental care, had an out-of-country emergency coverage plan. This meant that in the event of an emergency when away from Canada, all costs related to the actual emergency would be paid for. Once the initial emergency passed, the benefits would end.

In Yehuda's case, everything was paid for—ambulances for all of us, helicopter ride to the trauma center from the scene of the accident, and all hospital costs, including CT scans, MRIs, and surgeries.

We knew that once Yehuda was stabilized, the supplemental insurance plan administrators would find it more cost-effective to fly Yehuda back to Ottawa for treatment. At that point, the provincial healthcare plan would kick in and supplemental insurance would not be paying.

We now had a dilemma. Obviously, we wanted Yehuda to get the best care available. We wanted to be sure he had the best chance to make the greatest improvement and progress possible. We were willing to go to the end of the world to make this happen. What is money in the larger scheme of things? Would money be the factor that decided where Yehuda received care—at home in Ottawa for free, or for $3,000 a day at a prestigious rehab center in the States? And where would we get the money for that?

We decided to do the research and worry about the money later. But how would we do the research? What, exactly, were we researching?

A Difficult Decision

We contacted BINA, an organization that mainly offers assistance to stroke and brain injury patients and their families. Their mission is to work individually with each family to review options. They help formulate plans at every stage of the rehabilitation process. Fortunately, they were able to guide us regarding Yehuda's spinal cord injury.

Their suggestion was to have a family member or close friend visit each of the prospective rehab centers to tour the facility and speak to its directors. This would help us see what was being offered and judge whether it would be a good fit.

At the time, I was unable to travel. Besides, doing the research was too overwhelming for me. I was still trying to make sense of this new reality, and brain space was limited. I just wanted to know I had given

Yehuda his best chance at success from a human perspective. I never wanted to look back and say, *If only I had done X, Y, or Z…*

I spoke on the phone with Dr. Steven Kirshblum, the highly respected, internationally renowned director of the spinal cord injury program at Kessler Institute for Rehabilitation. He was kind and caring and really understood what we were going through. He knew how difficult the journey would be and described the upcoming challenges; the rigors of therapy, the loneliness, the need for endless amounts of support to get us through the difficult months ahead.

He was very frank as he explained the realities. Just because Kessler was consistently among the top-rated rehabilitation centers in the United States did not automatically mean it would be the best fit for us. There was more to picking a rehab center than researching its ranking and celebrity patient roster. The director helped us realize that our entire family would be affected by our choice. If Yehuda were to remain in the States, where would the family be? Would the children be living at home in Ottawa, or in a rented apartment in the US, attending school in the state Yehuda was in—far from home, without their friends and teachers who know them best? Did we want to add more challenges to an already challenging situation? Did we want our family to be the *nebach* cases of an unfamiliar community, relying on favors from strangers? He encouraged us to come take a look, see it for ourselves, and compare it to our option at home.

This conversation certainly gave us food for thought. We asked Dr. Moshe Lehrer and Rabbi Micah Shotkin to be our representatives. Both are very close friends of ours who, we felt, would combine their medical knowledge with a keen understanding of Yehuda's personality and help us choose the best option.

On Thursday afternoon, they met with Dr. Kirshblum and toured Kessler. In the course of their conversation, Dr. Kirshblum asked which other facilities were under consideration. When they mentioned the Ottawa Rehabilitation Centre, he revealed that Dr. Vidya Anandhi Sreenivasan, a physical medicine and rehabilitation specialist there, was his former trainee; she received her subspecialty training in Spinal Cord Injury Medicine at Kessler, with him as her program director. He gave her high accolades. He also pointed out that in Ottawa, Yehuda would be in his home environment, surrounded by people who knew and respected him. He would be a "celebrity."

With much to think about, Micah and Moshe next drove through the night to Ottawa, arriving at 4:00 a.m. After a short nap and Shacharis, they proceeded to the Ottawa Rehabilitation Centre for their scheduled early morning meeting with its director, Helen Zipes. Not by coincidence (Yehuda always said, "Coincidence? I think not!" when trying to show how everything happens for a reason even if we do not yet know what it is), Helen was our neighbor on Ardell Grove; she lived about ten houses away from us! She knew us well, had been shocked by news of our accident, and wanted to do everything in her power to help.

Although we were still blissfully unaware of how serious our situation really was, Helen knew and understood only too well what lay ahead. She gave Moshe and Micah a tour of the facility, explained the procedures to them, and introduced them to Dr. Sreenivasan. In another "coincidence," Dr. Douglas McKim, a world-renowned specialist in respiratory medicine and rehabilitation, just "happened" to be walking through the halls and spoke with them as well.

Moshe and Micah were most impressed with Helen and with the good fortune of having a world-class respiratory specialist within easy access. The rehab specialist was trained and recommended by Dr. Kirshblum. Also, the link between the Ottawa Rehabilitation Centre and Ottawa Hospital was a huge bonus. They are sister institutions and physically connected. In the event of an emergency, when seconds count, precious time would not be wasted.

The men discussed the pros and cons of the two centers on their drive down to Syracuse. They decided not to finalize their recommendation on Erev Shabbos, but to follow up after Shabbos. Moshe caught a flight back to JFK Airport and was back in Brooklyn in time for Shabbos. Micah stayed with Yehuda in Syracuse.

After Shabbos, our two friends reported their findings down to the minutest detail. They described the bells and whistles and cutting-edge technology offered by the New Jersey center as compared to the plain-Jane aesthetics and fewer specialists in Ottawa. Both men agreed that despite the absence of paintings and designer décor in the hallways of the Ottawa Centre, Ottawa was up to date with current therapies and treatments, perhaps even some that were cutting edge. As a bonus, it was close to home and our family could live at home with less disruption to our already disrupted lives. We would be within a twenty- to thirty-minute ride of Yehuda. We would be able to support him, and our community would support us.

We were bringing Yehuda "home."

Ambulance Chasers

As if the decision about Yehuda's rehabilitation and imminent transfer was not weighing us down enough, we had to deal with "ambulance chasers."

Medical insurance and auto insurance plans consider Yehuda's injuries "catastrophic." As such, it was anticipated that a large sum of money would become available to us as the result of a settlement. Our case was every lawyer's dream; a huge percentage of the funds obtained would go to the attorney who settled the claim. It would entail minimal effort on the lawyer's part, as it was an open-and-shut case.

Sure enough, we were deluged with offers "to help us navigate the system." Each attorney and advocate boasted about his credentials and ability "to save us money." We were astute enough to know that we had to do our own research before making any major decisions. This was a practice which would serve us well over the years.

I would repeat to myself and to others ad nauseam, "I might have been in a traumatic accident, my husband might be paralyzed, but I have not lost my mind." I would not sign on any dotted line until I consulted with others how to proceed. Thankfully, in the end, Micah found a compassionate lawyer who helped us reach a settlement without taking a single penny for himself.

Every Family Has Its Own Dance

I spent eight days in the hospital. In the weeks following my discharge, I was driven almost daily to visit Yehuda. On one of these trips, as we passed Junius Ponds on the way back to Rochester, Eliezer asked me how to handle the different reactions of the immediate family. Everyone was feeling the stress and anxiety of the situation and was helping—some more, some less—but some were noticeably absent.

"Every family has its own unique dance," I told him. "Whenever they get too close to a sticky situation, they dance around it. This avoids stepping on each other's toes. The relationship is more important than trying to change someone else's personality."

"But what about those who feel we should be more aggressive with Yehuda's care? They don't trust the doctors, and want us to do independent research and ask for multiple second opinions. How should we deal with them?"

"We don't. Let them be. Yehuda drilled into me when we were dealing with his Hodgkin's that we are not smarter than the doctors. They know what they are doing. We'll ask and make sure that what they are doing makes sense. But we can't knock ourselves out being distrustful of every doctor."

Imminent Transfer

It was Erev Rosh Chodesh Av. Rachel and I decided not to go to Yehuda in the morning. Instead, we would spend a quiet day with the kids.

Toward evening, I regretted my decision and felt the need to visit him. But neither of us wanted to drive back on the Thruway after nightfall. In the end, we decided to have a quick visit and be back before it got too dark. Bayla and Malka decided to come along.

As we should have expected, the drive and the visit took longer than we thought. It was already dark and we were stuck in Syracuse. What to do? Rachel remembered that she had the number of a family in the neighborhood who had offered their help. I felt awkward imposing on people whom we did not know at all. They agreed to have us, despite it not being very convenient for them.

The beautiful old home reminded me of a Victorian dollhouse. We collapsed into bed in our clothes, as we had not brought anything at all with us. It was hot and uncomfortable and I could not settle down. Nightmares ruled my fitful sleep. I had a strange feeling that tomorrow would be the day the hospital decided to transfer Yehuda to Ottawa. I had left Rochester unexpectedly and did not get a chance to say goodbye to the kids, who were on an outing when I left. Somehow, I just knew that because I had not said goodbye to them, I would not get a chance to do so before returning to Ottawa.

In the morning, we decided to visit Yehuda for a short while and then go back to Rochester. When we got to the ICU, I nervously asked the staff if there was any word about the transfer. They reassured us that it would not be taking place that day. I was quite relieved. But a few minutes later a nurse came scurrying in.

"Time to get ready!" she chirped. "Transfer time!"

"What? How can that be? They just told us that it wasn't today!"

"Well, the insurance company called and it's a go. Rabbi will be accompanied by a nurse, respiratory therapist, pilot, co-pilot, and you."

Since it was an international flight, we would need Yehuda's passport as well as mine. I needed to gather Yehuda's belongings and pack an overnight bag for myself—although there was no guarantee there would be room on the aircraft for a carry-on. When would we be leaving? Imminently. By then I knew that imminent, in hospital time, can mean several hours or very soon. I did not have time to go to Rochester and pack up and say goodbye to the kids. I burst into tears. I had only a couple of hours to make preparations to head back to Ottawa. I had not been home in three weeks.

I called our insurance company for more information. They stressed that once I was leaving, my children had to leave, too. They would make arrangements for them to get back to Ottawa.

I tried to reason with them. They cannot go with strangers on a four-hour trip. They have suffered enough from this upheaval in their lives. They are safe and protected with caring and giving family members. I do not have anyone to help take care of them back home in Ottawa. It was the middle of the summer; many people in my support system were away. If I would be spending endless hours in the hospital with Yehuda, why should they be bored and lonely at home?

The company's representative kept reiterating that if we do not send them home the same day I go, they will lose their insurance. I could not comprehend why turning down a ride would deprive them of complete emergency coverage. Were they concerned about the best interests of my children or was this merely a bureaucracy? They kept insisting and I kept pushing back.

Finally, in an exasperated voice, I asked, "If my children do not go to Ottawa today, do you mean to tell me that if they get an ear infection, or fall and need stitches, you wouldn't cover that because they don't have insurance?"

At this point, something finally clicked at the other end of the line. "Of course we will!"

"So what do you mean by not having insurance?"

"Insurance to transport them home! You will have to find your own transportation and pay for it yourself."

"Okay! That makes much more sense." I was fine with that. "My children will stay and I will go home and get Yehuda settled. When the time is right, we'll arrange to get them home."

Once we had that ironed out, we were able to focus on the technical matters of leaving. Fraidel packed a small bag for me and collected Yehuda's passport and mine. Someone else arranged for a ride for the older children to come to Syracuse, say goodbye to us, and drop off my things. At this point, Yehuda was still not looking good, to say the very least, and we did not want the younger kids to see him in that state.

The amount of stuff that can accumulate in a tiny hospital room is amazing. How many possessions can a patient amass? As we collected everything—including what must have been several hundred cards—we received a warning from the nurse. Apparently, due to some infection he either had or could have had, it was recommended to leave any non-essentials behind because of the risk of spreading germs. I really, really wanted to keep all the cards. But now I was nervous. Two things, though, were coming home with us, regardless; the pair of *tefillin* Yehuda was using daily, and two beautiful pillows that a dear friend, Orly, made for him. The pillows were blue squares with a Magen David pattern and printed pictures of our family. They are still on my bed all these years later. I have not gotten sick of—or from—them yet.

We exchanged another round of tearful goodbyes and then I followed the stretcher round and round the hospital to the garage outside the emergency department, where an ambulance was waiting to drive us to the airport. We were driven right onto the tarmac. I looked around the huge field until my gaze rested on a lone, tiny plane. When I say tiny, I do mean tiny. I was starting to realize why there might not be room for my bag. The plane was two seats wide—one seat for the pilot and one for the co-pilot. Behind them was an empty space for the stretcher. There was a seat behind the stretcher for the nurse and respiratory therapist and one more for me. That was it! Under normal conditions, never in a million years could you pay me to board such a plane. But nothing about this was normal.

After a brief, and thankfully excellent, flight, we landed in Ottawa. Yehuda was able to tolerate the change in air pressure and did well. Once again, I traipsed along behind the stretcher as we went to the next waiting ambulance. We arrived at the Ottawa Hospital General Campus, and again I walked through a medical facility to settle Yehuda in.

This was to become the story of my life for the next six and a half years.

It was hard to be back in Ottawa all by myself under abnormal circumstances. Already emotionally drained, I now had to face the reality of walking into my house alone. When I left home in June, I was planning to be back in three days. Three weeks and several lifetimes had passed in the interim.

My friend offered to come get me. She knew it would be hard for me to walk through the door, but she was not sure if I wanted my space to deal with it on my own. Honestly, I was relieved to have someone there to hold my hand.

Entering the house was surreal. I had "forgotten" what it looked like. I walked slowly, getting my bearings, patting the walls, the pictures, the furniture. Home was physically still there, but in reality, it was not. It was silent, empty, hollow. No sounds of life. I walked up the stairs slowly, as if in a trance. A few more steps and I was facing a framed picture on the wall. I looked at it and burst into fresh tears.

I had made that collage in honor of our eighteenth anniversary, and just before we left on that fateful trip, I insisted on hanging it up. Eighteen in Hebrew is *chai*, life. I had gone to Michaels and bought a frame, which had a five-by-seven window and a dozen three-by-four windows. I printed a *pasuk* from *Tehillim, V'chol hachaim yoducha*— "Let all who are alive thank You," and inserted it in the largest opening. Into the smaller boxes, I placed a picture of Yehuda and me when we were engaged, one from our wedding, and one of each child. Two boxes were left empty and waiting to be filled with a picture of our still unborn baby and an up-to-date photo of Yehuda and me.

How apropos. *Let all who are alive thank You.* Indeed, we are all eternally grateful to Hashem that every member of our family survived that crash. To this day, I thank Him for not making me a widow on the side of the road.

The Kids Need You

Once Yehuda got settled into the ICU in Ottawa, his condition slowly began to stabilize and we fell into a routine. I spent nearly all day, every weekday, with him. Being that I was in my third trimester, it would have been difficult for me to walk the distance on Shabbos.

Toward the end of our first week home, I got a call from Rochester that the kids needed me. It was hard for them to be so far from both parents during this time. Despite being surrounded by loving grandparents, aunts, uncles, and cousins, they needed a parent, so my father and I decided to switch places for Shabbos. We arranged a ride for him from Rochester halfway to Ottawa, and our friend Bram drove me about halfway in the opposite direction. My father and I then switched cars. I continued on to Rochester, and Bram drove my father up to Ottawa. We did this for two weekends before we brought the children home.

During my visits to Rochester, I tried to slip back into my role as mother. I was still recovering from broken ribs and a broken collarbone. A hug from the kids was painful; lifting them nearly impossible. As I spread my attention among the children and dealt with my two-year-old's tantrums, I thought back to the conversation with Yehuda when he told me, "Remember, we're in this together." I totally agreed. Yet, when childcare fell completely on my shoulders, with him lying immobile in an ICU in another country, I could not help but wonder: *What about this is "together"?* The "together" part would have to grow and develop as our circumstances evolved and changed. It was not an instantaneous transformation. It was a process.

As the days passed, Yehuda and I had the chance to work on the "together" part. Together, we decided that it was finally time to reunite the family. After five weeks of being nurtured by our family in Rochester and embraced by the community, it was time to face our new reality on our home turf. It was time to bring the children home.

The physical aspect of bringing the children home to Ottawa was relatively easy. We worked out transportation details with several of our friends. The logistics of getting them to Canada were simple compared to figuring out what would happen once we got them home. Who would help watch them while I was in the hospital with Yehuda? Although it was not in the original "plan" for the summer, some of the older children went to sleepaway camp. With the accident and so much on their young minds, we felt it would be good for them to get away from it all—to be carefree for a few weeks, to escape their new reality and have fun like "normal" kids.

At this point, Yehuda was stable. We were not fearful for his life. We were just waiting until he could be weaned off the respirator so he could go to rehab. Of course, I promised to keep the children in the loop and inform them of any developments or changes.

My mother's brother, Uncle Moishe Katz, and his wife, Tante Brachy, traveled to Ottawa from Chicago to spend a week with us—our first week home as a family. As the devoted parents of two special-needs boys, their days revolve around taking care of their sons in addition to fulfilling their responsibilities to home and community. I have always regarded them with awe. The boys' needs are so great that it is rare for their parents to have any sort of respite. Fortunately, the boys were accepted to summer camp for one short week—just one week out of fifty-two. How did Uncle Moishe and Tante Brachy spend their single week of vacation time? How did they recharge and reconnect? They came to Ottawa to take care of a pregnant woman with eight children and a quadriplegic husband! Vacation? Not my idea of a fun time!

The Katzes have always been my heroes and are so even more now that I have a tiny glimmer of understanding of what they must go through on a daily basis. Whenever I have a bad moment, I think of them and wonder how they get through the day. Somehow, this gives me a much-needed boost.

Ice Cream and Slurpees

The younger children had not seen their father in five weeks and we had to prepare them. Yehuda looked very different than when they had last seen him. His location, the ICU, was a place they had never been to before. The only time the children had been to a hospital was to visit me in the maternity ward after the birth of a sibling—quite a different scene than an ICU. We knew that the way we prepared them for this event would set the tone for how they would react to and interact with Yehuda in the future. We wanted to get it right the first time. We wanted them to be able to focus on their Abba and see him with as few scary associations as possible.

After many long discussions, we formulated a plan. Yehuda would be taken out of his ICU room in a wheelchair to an open area that had no equipment or machinery other than his respirator. He would be accompanied by a nurse and a respiratory therapist to monitor his oxygen and other vital signs. The area was a wide corridor, almost like an indoor balcony, behind the ICU. I would bring the children through a doorway that bypassed the ICU. We would not have to pass critically ill patients lying in their beds—a frightening scene even for adults.

In the days leading up to the meeting, I described to them what Abba looked like and let them get used to the idea. "Abba will be wearing funny pajamas—a blue pajama shirt almost like a nightgown and blue pajama pants. You will see a blue tube coming out of his throat. The tube is connected to a machine that helps Abba breathe. Abba won't be able to move; he won't be able to hold out his arms to you to hug you. I can pick you up and bring you close to Abba so that you can kiss him and he can kiss you. He'll also have something on his finger. It is attached to a monitor that helps the nurse keep track of his oxygen. Abba might also get tired very easily. He might have to go back to bed, so we won't stay for too long."

Then came the best part of the plan. It was brilliant—so brilliant that no one wants to take credit for thinking of it. It was either Michael and Rachel or Uncle Moishe and Tante Brachy; each couple says it was the other! The idea was to have an ice cream party. After all, which child—or adult, for that matter—does not like ice cream? (Well, our daughter Chan, but she is probably the only person in the world.) We would bring ice cream with us to the hospital to "break the ice" and ease the pressure of a formal meeting.

Uncle Moishe and Tante Brachy were with us for the "grand reunion." We walked through the corridor to where Yehuda was waiting for us. Everyone was very excited but slightly subdued as they sized up the situation. After giving Yehuda the once-over and hugging him, one of the kids asked, "Why is Abba wearing glasses?" I thought I had prepared them so well for what they would see. I did not want them to be alarmed by the changes. But I forgot that they were only used to seeing Yehuda wearing contact lenses. He never wore his glasses. That was the biggest difference they noticed!

Uncle Moishe is the director of the Chicago Torah Network. As part of his Torah Minutes articles, he published several about Yehuda, in which he urged his readers to pray for Yehuda's recovery and undertake mitzvos in his merit. What follows is his firsthand account of the ice cream party:

> For various reasons, after the accident, his kids did not see him for many weeks. And while my wife and I were in Ottawa visiting, *they were going to see him for the first time.* It was obviously a very emotional time and a very challenging experience for the kids.
>
> Someone had a great idea to make it easier for them; *turn it into an ice cream party!* This way, the kids will see their dad and also have some fun. So on the way, my wife and I went to the supermarket to pick up the ice cream. And it was very important that we got the right kind! So we called my niece Shaindel from

the store. She told us what to get, and then she said, *"Oh, a very important message from Yehuda."* (Remember, Yehuda was in the critical care unit. He was working so hard to talk despite a tracheotomy. And he was preparing for an emotional visit from his children.)

And what was this urgent message that he struggled to give?

"Please make sure there's enough ice cream for all the nurses!"

It was a very moving scene as each kid approached Yehuda and kissed him. Then, out with the ice cream pops! One for each kid. And one for each nurse. But there were still some left. So what did Yehuda's kids do? They learned from their father! *They walked through the corridor of the critical care unit and handed out ice cream to every doctor or nurse they saw!*

…You may have noticed that I am very proud to be Yehuda's uncle.

He has inspired me.

And I hope he has inspired you!

The ice cream party was a huge success and it helped accomplish several goals. Our children associated what could have been a traumatic experience with excitement. They made many new friends, and they felt that the ICU was a safe, warm, and fun place.

Eventually, the children and staff members got to know each other on a first-name basis. We spent so much time there that the kids became the "mascots" of the ICU. The staff truly went out of their way to be there for the children during this challenging time. One wonderful nurse, Nancy, took them to the storage room where the extra IV poles were kept. She had the children stand on the poles and gave them "rides"—like bumper cars in an amusement park!

Several weeks after the ice cream party, we had a Slurpee party.

As part of the process of weaning Yehuda off the trach, a speech therapist was called in to evaluate him. One of the necessary tests was the swallow test. Until this point, Yehuda had been tube fed. He was

NPO—nothing by mouth at all. Different liquids, different textures, and a variety of thicknesses had to be slowly reintroduced to ensure that they would not be a choking hazard. If he passed, Yehuda would be allowed to add food to his diet.

I had planned to be with him for the test. To my dismay, when I reached the hospital, I found out it had already been administered. As we were to learn over and over again, hospitals operate in a different time zone. The time you are given for a procedure, test, or discharge is merely an indicator that said procedure, test, or discharge will likely happen at some point. While I was disappointed to have missed it, I was happy to hear he had passed with flying colors.

The children and Yehuda had already had a series of discussions as to what his very first food should be. After much deliberation, they decided on a Slurpee—that sweet, sticky, brain-freezing summer treat. As I had promised the kids that they could be there when it happened, I left the hospital and returned to our side of town to pick up the kids and the drink. Back to the hospital we went with a slightly thawed Slurpee in a borrowed cooler, eager to watch.

After all that preparation, it was a total letdown! Yehuda swallowed it nicely and looked at us in surprise: *Did I actually used to like that?* I guess quadriplegia changes one's taste buds.

Reality Hits

Life in the ICU was not all fun and games and ice cream. There were times when reality hit hard. Very hard.

One day, I got a call from Rabbi Burger. "Please come. I think Yehuda needs you. He's beside himself and I don't know what is wrong."

When I got there, Yehuda was crying uncontrollably. It took a while to get the story out. A physical therapist had come to do exercises with him. During the course of conversation, the topic of walking came up. The PT, matter-of-factly and very bluntly, said to Yehuda, "You, walk? No, you will never walk again." It was a huge blow. It took him a while to recover from that.

For Yehuda, life in the ICU was hard work. Learning how to breathe again after being respirator-dependent is not easy. In fact, it is quite scary. Emotionally, a person has to reprogram his mind that his body can breathe, that if he is off the respirator for brief intervals of time, he will not die. Physically, it is challenging as well. Muscles that have not been used have to be exercised; the sensation of breathing on one's own is that of drowning. It is truly an exercise in mind over matter.

Fortunately, the process was being guided by Dr. Douglas McKim[1] of the Ottawa Rehab Centre, a world-famous respiratory specialist who has developed techniques to wean patients from ventilators and to decrease their risk of needing invasive ventilation. This was the first time these techniques were put into place in an ICU setting. In fact, Yehuda's treatments were videotaped and chronicled for various medical presentations and journals.

A very specific goal plan was devised and the steps were broken down into short and attainable goals. We hung certificates in Yehuda's room each time he achieved one. Yehuda worked hard and often met his goals sooner than expected.

One of the exercises he learned was called LVR—lung volume recruitment. For this exercise, a modified resuscitation bag was used. The mouthpiece was placed in Yehuda's mouth, and the bag was squeezed several times to fill his lungs with air. This exercise was done several times a day on a regular basis.

Our children had their own version of LVR: They would use empty two-liter Coke bottles to perform the exercises on themselves. To anyone watching, this would seem odd. But who said our "new normal" would be normal?

Bayla's Bas Mitzvah

The day of our daughter Bayla's bas mitzvah was coming up. It was

---

1. This is the doctor who so impressed Dr. Moshe Lehrer and Rabbi Micah Shotkin while they were checking out the Ottawa Rehab Centre for us.

important to us that she not miss out on celebrating this special day in her life. We chose to celebrate her birthday the same way we celebrated those of her two older sisters. Her classmates would spend Shabbos together with us as our guests and enjoy a party and craft on Motza'ei Shabbos. The key was figuring out which weekend was least likely to see me going into labor and leaving a gaggle of girls home to fend for themselves.

The other component was including Yehuda in the celebration. We turned to the ICU staff for help and ideas. They were thrilled to accommodate us and participate in the planning. They arranged to have us reserve a boardroom just outside the ICU for a special family evening.

Until the accident, eating supper as a family was non-negotiable. We ate together every single night, often with Yehuda running in to join us either before a class or between two. It was always a loud, noisy affair with everyone chatting about their day and whatever news they had to share. Yehuda would try to ensure that everyone had a fair turn. He would think of a number from one to ten. Whoever guessed the number he was thinking of got to have the next turn. He would ask questions about each child's day and share stories about his own. It was also important to him that the children thanked me for a delicious (whether or not it was!) meal.

Supper was not really as exciting without him. In truth, not much was exciting now that we were all so worried. Being with him and seeing him for ourselves was exciting. But here was our first chance to create a new supper memory. I prepared a beautiful dinner, a specially decorated bakery cake, paper goods, and drinks. I packed it all up and set up shop in the boardroom. It was beyond exciting; this was our first supper together as a family since June 19th! On that special night, we all celebrated Bayla and the milestone she had reached.

Her class Shabbos also turned out well and I was still in "one piece" to enjoy it with her.

Once Bayla's bas mitzvah celebration was behind us, we turned our attention to the next item on the *simchah* agenda; welcoming a new baby into the family. Excitement mounted as more and more details for the birth were worked out and piece after piece fell into place.

• The First Piece: Doctor and Hospital

At the beginning of my pregnancy, before the accident, I went back to the obstetrician I used for my previous three Canadian births. I really liked him and his partners. However, this time more than ever before, I was adamant that Yehuda be present at the birth of our baby—and this physician did not deliver in the hospital where Yehuda was. With reluctance on my part and compassionate understanding on his, I transferred to a different practice to be able to deliver at the Ottawa Hospital General Campus.

This transfer was really out of my comfort zone. My comfort zone had been extended time and time again, but little did I realize this was just the beginning. As the years passed, I was not sure I had any "zones" anymore. Just like a crab has to grow and grow and push out of its shell to be able to grow a new one, I kept leaving shells behind; layers and layers of me that I never knew existed.

• The Second Piece: Support

Who would be my physical support for the birth? I needed someone to drive me, someone to advocate for me if I could not do it for myself, someone to help me focus and keep me mindful of the beautiful baby that waited to be born. I hired a doula who had come highly recommended. She was compassionate and understanding of my unique situation.

It felt awkward; after all, this was my ninth birth! Was I not an expert by now? But no woman should be alone at such a time. My doula came to the ICU to meet Yehuda. She reassured him that she would take good care of me and was not replacing him. She would be there to help facilitate our birth plan.

- **The Third Piece: Including Yehuda**

This was the most complex piece of all. The ICU team and staff coordinated closely with the birthing unit. By consulting with each other, they learned exactly what Yehuda's needs were and how to accommodate him in the birthing unit.

Once I was in labor, I was to call the ICU staff at any time of the day or night to advise them. They would need as much advance notice as possible. Yehuda would be coming with an entourage of his own—a nurse, a respiratory therapist, and orderlies to push the stretcher and equipment (such as IV poles) that he would need to "stay off the floor." As hospitals are busy places, it could take time to get the necessary people to transport him to the other end of the hospital. This would be the first (and, I hope, only) time the hospital had ever done something of this sort. It was so significant, they covered it as a documentary on the hospital's 2010 annual report online!

Every mom in her ninth month prepares a "mommy bag"—a bag that contains all the essentials she and baby will need in the hospital. Of course, I had one prepared. The joke in the hospital was that Yehuda had a "daddy bag"—and his bag was bigger than mine! Every single staff member in the ICU was aware of the plans. They would pop into his room to check on me while I was visiting and see how I was doing and if "anything was happening" yet. They were all super excited and hopeful that the long-awaited birth would happen during their shift. They all wanted to be there!

As I mentally prepared myself for the birth of our baby, I kept praying that Yehuda would make it.

- **The Fourth Piece: The Children**

Who would stay with our children when it came time for me to give birth?

This time around, these arrangements were easier than they had been by previous births. Our eldest two were seventeen and fifteen and a half. They were very capable and responsible teenagers and we counted on them to keep everything running smoothly.

• The Fifth Piece: Rosh Hashanah Plan

In 2010, Rosh Hashanah fell on Wednesday night, September 8th. As I was due around then, it was very likely I would give birth on or around Rosh Hashanah.

Running the family on a weekday is one thing; adding in a Yom Tov with its *minhagim* and meals, as well as restrictions, is in a completely different ball park. To add to that, the day after Rosh Hashanah was Shabbos!

We yearned to be together for Yom Tov. After pulling off a successful bas mitzvah dinner in the ICU, we were eager to do it again. But the logistics would be more challenging this time. For one thing, we lived in the Craig Henry neighborhood in Ottawa's West End. The hospital is in the Alta Vista neighborhood in Ottawa's East End, a distance that takes three hours to walk. Not feasible. Our close friends, the Burgers, lived in that neighborhood and graciously let us use their home, as they would be away for Yom Tov.

Bit by bit, the plan slowly developed. My brother-in-law Michael would fly in from Chicago. He would be "in charge" of Yehuda and would eat the two Yom Tov night meals with him. My brother Avrohom Dov, together with his wife Gila (and their little Yitzy), would come in from New York and be "in charge" of me and the kids. We would all stay together in Alta Vista.

Going out at night with the children to walk to and from the hospital would be too hard. For me to walk back and forth several times a day would be too tiring at this advanced stage of pregnancy. We made the decision that we would eat the night meals without Yehuda and Michael and walk to the hospital only for the day meals.

Food would be needed in three locations; the home we were staying in, Yehuda's hospital room, and the location in the hospital where we would all be eating.

With the help of numerous friends from both Ottawa and Montreal, food became a non-issue. Every delicacy imaginable was provided. I had not prepared myself for what I would do when the boxes and boxes of food would arrive. When the delivery showed up, I could not help bursting into tears. The task of organizing the food completely overwhelmed me. How should I divide it up? Where will it all go? Did I even have enough room in the freezer?

I called my mother for help; she lived in New York, an eight-hour ride away. With grace and understanding, she assured me she would take care of everything. Within moments, my doorbell rang. A friend had come to help. She had dropped everything she was in the middle of because my mother called her. As I sat on the floor feeling completely useless, she unpacked, rearranged, and repacked several days' worth of food. Soon everything was neatly organized and labeled. In addition, arrangements were made for the purchase of paper goods, drinks, and non-perishables for each of the three locations. As Rosh Hashanah drew closer, my friend helped me pick out a menu based on the available food and determined what would go where. Finally, there were three labeled boxes, ready to go.

To add to the general chaos, the school year was due to start on Tuesday, September 7th, the day after Labor Day. The children needed to get prepared. Once again, friends stepped in, purchasing and labeling all the supplies that were requested in advance of the school year.

Nochi's Arrival

Late Tuesday night, I began to suspect I was in labor. As my previous labors had been fairly quick, and I wanted to give the ICU staff plenty of time to get Yehuda ready, I called my doula. She said that based on my description it surely made sense to head to the hospital right away. She was coming to get me. My "mommy bag" was ready. Hiding at the bottom was an unopened package containing "It's a boy!" and "It's a girl!" oversized banners, one of which would be hung on the outside of Yehuda's hospital room door for all to see!

I gently woke Shmuly to tell him I was okay and was headed out to have the baby. I assured him I would call just as soon as there was good news to report.

Upon arrival at the birthing unit, fearing that our plans would not be realized, I used my most confident voice and stated, "Hi. I'm Shaindel Simes. I'm the lady you're waiting for. My husband will be meeting us here; he's coming from the ICU. I was told I would be getting the largest room you have to accommodate us."

They seemed a little taken aback by my assertive manner but assured me they were well prepared. I urged them to keep calling the ICU to speed them up. I was so afraid Yehuda would miss it. All I could do was keep repeating: *He better make it. They better bring him. They said they would bring him.*

In the birthing room, I was feeling more and more certain the baby would be born at any moment. Just then I heard a yell: "He's here! He's here! *He's here!*"

The baby and my husband arrived at the same moment. "It's a boy!" we heard them shout. With tears of joy, relief, and immense gratitude, I looked up to see the nurses gently placing our newborn son into my husband's arms as tears rolled down his face. I looked at the two of them and sobbed. Words can do little to describe the emotions of seeing our miracle baby and his equally miraculous daddy, as he was to be dubbed in one of the many articles recounting our story.

The miracle and beauty of birth is always special, but a baby born to a father who defies odds is spectacular. The injuries Yehuda sustained should not have allowed him to be alive and present at that moment. Watching our baby breathe easily on his own after watching Yehuda painfully relearn how to breathe reminded us yet again of the miracle of each breath. Breathing is something we do not take for granted anymore.

We got to spend time together as a threesome, looking at our beautiful infant son and holding him. After a while, Yehuda reluctantly asked to go back to his room while I was readied to be taken to mine. The nurse filled in all the details on the "baby boy" banner to be displayed on Yehuda's door. This time, I was the "patient" and he was the "visitor."

In the early hours of the morning, I made calls to our family to share the wonderful news. Everyone was thrilled. Our joy was shared with many around the world.

The timing could not have been more perfect. Wednesday was Erev Rosh Hashanah. Plans were in place for Yom Tov and now we just had to await the arrival of the relatives to assume their positions. Michael was in flight and found out about the baby's birth upon landing. Avrohom Dov and Gila were told to go straight to our house, pick up the kids and whatever they needed for Yom Tov, and bring them to see the new baby. Then they were to set up the house for Rosh Hashanah and return to pick up the kids.

While I was resting a bit between phone calls, I had an exciting visitor: Yehuda had come to see me! I did not know how I would get to see him that day—we had not planned that part. He was grinning from ear to ear, so happy to have accomplished coming to the birth and now to see me. His nurses were only all too eager to bring him, as they wanted to see the baby too!

I did a double take as I noticed a white gauze bandage on his throat, covering the area that had, until now, been the location of his trach. Yes, two unbelievable events happened on September 8, 2010. As Yehuda later said, both he and his youngest son took their first breaths on the same day.

Yehuda had been working all summer on being weaned from the respirator. As he progressed, he was able to go for longer and longer stretches without it. The trach had not been removed; rather, it was capped and left in his throat for whenever he might need help from the respirator. This was the day the doctor deemed it safe to remove it entirely. Yehuda no longer needed the respirator to breathe at all. Free at last!

During the course of the day after our son was born, my mind wandered a bit down memory lane. When we first found out I was due Rosh Hashanah/Yom Kippur time, I remember thinking, *Yom Kippur in the hospital? How depressing!* When I was fourteen, my youngest sister, Ahuva, was born Erev Yom Kippur. I remember my mother describing how she was in the hospital on that solemn day while I held down the fort at home. Right after the accident, I remember saying to myself, *Depressing? What made me use that word? Having a paralyzed husband in the ICU when I'm having a baby—now, that is depressing.*

Well, here I was in the hospital, with my healthy baby boy, my husband no longer respirator-dependent and on the cusp of recovering and rehabilitating. It was far from depressing! It was probably the most meaningful Rosh Hashanah I ever had. Perhaps it was even the most well-spent one, spent appreciating life and looking toward the future with an eye on the past.

That night and the next, Yehuda and Michael came to my room for the Rosh Hashanah meals. During the day, we ate the meals with the rest of the family in the boardroom that was reserved for us.

Rosh Hashanah 5771; a new year, a time for new beginnings, a new baby, a new lease on life.

Once again, a curveball was thrown our way. Now that Yehuda had been weaned off the respirator, he could be transferred to the rehab center. With barely any time to get used to the idea, I was told that Yehuda and I would be taken that very day to tour the center, which would become the next step in our journey.

A nurse pushed Yehuda in his wheelchair, Michael pushed me in mine. It was a long distance to the rehab wing. Sometimes you have to try to find humor in a situation. There we were, two parents of an hours-old newborn, being wheeled around a hospital. Actually, it was not funny at all.

Nochi's *Bris*

Yehuda was set to be admitted to the rehab center on Tuesday, September 14th. Our baby's *bris milah* was to be held on the eighth day of his life—Wednesday, September 15th. There was a lot to do and plan for both milestones. Once again, our family and friends came to the rescue. We needed two teams; one to get Yehuda organized, and one for me, eight kids, and a newborn.

Rachel came to pack up Yehuda's belongings from the ICU and purchase the items he needed for rehab.

The *bris* would obviously have to take place where Yehuda could attend. We are so grateful to Helen Zipes, then-director of the rehab center, for enabling that to happen. The patient lounge was reserved for us to use that Wednesday morning, barely twenty hours after Yehuda became a resident there.

Yehuda holding Nochi at the *bris*.

A friend came the night before to cut Yehuda's hair and trim his beard in honor of the festive occasion. We prepared a dress shirt, tie, and suit pants. This was his first time in real clothes since the accident.

A group of our closest friends and family were in attendance, some having come from as far away as New York, Chicago, and even Israel. As the baby let out a wail, there was not a dry eye in the room.

Our son was named Alter Chanoch Henoch after the Rosh Yeshivah of Yeshiva Chofetz Chaim, where both Yehuda and my father had received *semichah*. Rav Leibowitz's teachings helped us navigate our lives up until this point, and we hoped they would further guide us on our journey through uncharted territory. The choice of name also reflected our aspirations for our son, that he grow up to be an outstanding individual like his namesake.

All our children have Hebrew names. These are the names they go by. Some of the children have an English variation on their birth certificate and legal documents. Even for us, both fluent in Hebrew, three names are a mouthful. And combined with the guttural "ch" sound three times in succession, they truly made for a tongue twister. We decided to call him Nochi for short. For the rest of the world, we came up with a nickname; in public, we would call him Charlie.

At the *bris*, Yehuda was able to personally thank everyone for the support and encouragement which enabled us to reach this point. As well, our children had prepared a scrapbook, one page per child,

Our first family photo "after" the accident. We had this picture enlarged to 11" x 14" to hang in Yehuda's room in the rehab center. Our dear friends snuck it out one day and surprised us by having it professionally mounted. This picture accompanied Yehuda on every hospital stay.

expressing gratitude for the devotion and care the ICU staff showered on Yehuda. This was presented to the staff members who were present at the *bris*.

In addition to the gifts received at the *bris*, numerous gifts were dropped off at our house in the following days. It seemed as if the whole city wanted to reach out and be a part of our celebration!

One gift in particular stands out in our minds. A parcel arrived in the mail. A family member was asked to open the package. Not really sure what it was, she held it up for all to see. As realization dawned upon us, we screamed. My sister threw it out of the room as we all burst into nervous laughter. It was a brown hooded baby bunting. But not just any brown hooded baby bunting—it was a deer costume! Of all things! Needless to say, our baby never wore that!

Life in Rehab

Once Yehuda was transferred to rehab, we faced new transitions. Yehuda was assigned a private room and set up with a team which included a physical therapist, occupational therapist, speech therapist, and nurses. A care plan was designed to meet his needs and goals.

CaringBridges: Journal Entry by Rachel Stein (Yehuda's sister) — Sept. 16, 2010

We were warned that the first day in rehab would be overwhelming—and it was. So many new names and faces, and Yehuda tries hard to learn them all. From the beginning, it was obvious that the rehab staff is truly exceptional. Unlike being in an ICU, in rehab the patient is very involved in the process. Yehuda will be setting his own goals and working toward achieving them. Everyone in rehab is very focused on improving your quality of life—not just keeping you alive, as they were in the ICU. Moreover, they really understand how much little things can make a difference in making people feel like they still have their identities. For example, although they probably have never seen *tefillin* before, it is not a nuisance for them when Yehuda takes time to put them on, because they really get that for him this is an important piece of his identity. They are even going to set up a sukkah on the balcony next week! Even a small thing like the sign on his door which says "Rabbi Simes" is a gift, because it preserves Yehuda's identity—he is more than just an SCI patient. In thousands of subtle and not so subtle ways, the rehab staff shows that they understand the importance of getting your life back—as much as possible.

Right away, we could see a difference between the ICU and the rehab center. Prior to the transfer, we were given a clothing and supply list that reminded us of the lists our children get when packing for summer camp. In rehab, one gets dressed every single day—no hospital gowns. One is no longer a "patient"; one is being prepared to re-enter the community. "The community" is a big concept in rehab. It refers to real life outside an institutional setting, and those words are uttered with near reverence.

When we entered the rehab stage, I thought rehab was a magical place, a place where people who are very broken go to be fixed, where people are put back together and relearn all they lost. But soon I learned that just like Humpty Dumpty, not all broken people can be fixed, and even if a person can be fixed, it certainly is not magical or instant. Improvements cannot be measured by leaps and bounds. One does not suddenly wake up in the morning able to do something one could not do before. It was so frustrating to be asked by well-meaning people, "What can Yehuda do now?" How can you explain to them that progress is often something they cannot see, that it cannot always be measured, and that to an outsider it might not appear significant at all? We did not exactly have the town crier announce that Yehuda could now tolerate sitting up in a wheelchair for four hours at a time, that he could handle range-of-motion exercises without getting dysreflexic,[2] that he would now be allowed to sleep without a BiPAP machine, that he could say a few words without becoming short of breath. I had to reprogram myself to the harsh realities of the hard work therapy entails, to the fact that as much as we were in a rush to get moving, the body does not work as fast as we would like.

Yehuda was optimistic and gung-ho to improve; he wanted to push harder and do more. It was frustrating to be slowed down to the pace his body could handle. There were days when his body could not handle much at all. The physical pain was intense. For a long time, one of the goals of rehab was to get the pain under control. It was hard to believe the pain could reach such intolerable thresholds in a body so paralyzed.

Rabbi in rehab.

Yehuda was on all kinds of cocktails of pain medications. Methamphetamine was a drug of choice, though it had some interesting side-effects; we laughed so hard when Yehuda sent my brother Avrohom Dov to locate the source of the music he heard playing—music only he could hear!

Shabbos in the Blue Room

The first few weeks Yehuda spent in the rehab center were mostly

---

2. Autonomic dysreflexia is a syndrome in which there is a sudden onset of excessively high blood pressure. It is more common in people with spinal cord injuries that involve the thoracic nerves of the spine or above (T6 or above).

yamim tovim. Meanwhile, I was recuperating from Nochi's recent birth.

Becky called to let us know she would be flying in from Israel for a visit. She planned to stay with us for about eight days and wanted to spend Shabbos with Yehuda in rehab. I knew how good it would be for Yehuda to be with Becky, but I was feeling selfish and wanted her to spend Shabbos with me and the kids at home.

There had to be a way for all of us to enjoy the visit. Every visit from family or friends provided an incredible boost, a much-needed injection of support and optimism that had to last us until the next visit.

I had a crazy idea. What if we all went to Alta Vista for Shabbos! Could we stay with our friends, the Burgers? What about the baby, Devorah, and Yitzchak? It would be too hard to walk with them a half hour each way, both Friday night and Shabbos day.

I need not have worried. Once again, the Burgers went above and beyond, doing anything they could for us. They assured us that it was not a crazy idea at all. They would be happy to host us all and we could leave the littlest children home with their family when we walked to the rehab center.

This exciting new development was another "first" for us—the first time our family would be together for Shabbos in three months. Yehuda always had a family member or close friend with him for Shabbos—he was never alone—but I had never spent Shabbos with him in all that time. (I would not count the first Shabbos after the accident, when he was in the ICU in Syracuse and I was still a patient in Crouse, as "spending time on Shabbos.")

We turned to the rehab center for help in facilitating the special experience, and once again they came up with a plan. Right across from Yehuda's room was a conference room that was used Monday through Friday for various meetings and workshops. It was not used on weekends, and before we knew it, a "Reserved for Rabbi Simes and Family" sign went up. The staff referred to the room as "the blue room" for the color of its walls, but from that week on we called it "the Shabbos room." On Friday, we brought over everything we would need for the twenty-five-hour duration of Shabbos, and hoped for the best.

We spent a lovely evening chatting, sharing, and catching up. It was so wonderful to be together! Even the walk home was exhilarating as we rehashed and relived the experience.

This became our new ritual. We went back for nearly every Shabbos until December, except when the Burgers celebrated their son's bar mitzvah. For some of those weeks, either my mother came from New York, or my sister and brother-in-law came from Rochester to join us. When Fraidel and Eliezer came, it meant leaving their babies with the Burgers as well!

Not every Shabbos was as smooth as the first. Several times, Yehuda felt unwell and was unable to join us in the blue room. He was just across the hall, but it was not the same without him. On those Shabbosos, watching him suffer drained all the joy out of the evening. Irrational as it may have been, I found myself becoming frustrated that he was "ruining" the special time I had planned and hoped for.

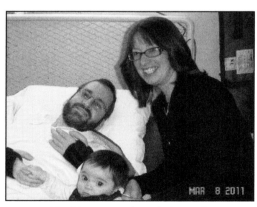

Nochi came to the rehab nearly every day to cheer his Abba on.

When he was with us, we considered it normal—even when there was nothing normal about it. Our definition of normal just kept morphing to accommodate whatever situation was at hand. Good to bad, bad to worse, worse to good—each in its time seemed normal. It is mind-boggling what a person can get used to.

My maternity leave dreams soon became an illusion of the past. I bundled up my baby to spend day after day at the rehab center. I would get there in time to feed Yehuda his homemade lunch and accompany him to his afternoon therapies. "Charlie" became the mascot of the center; his milestones were celebrated as much as Yehuda's.

In between dealing with pain management and keeping bouts of autonomic dysreflexia at bay, therapies continued as much as possible.

It was important for Yehuda to be fitted for a power wheelchair that would accommodate his needs. As he had no use of his hands, alternative means of driving had to be explored. Head-controlled seemed like an obvious choice; however, it caused too much pain. After much trial and error, a modified joystick was created. Typical joysticks can be operated by using palms or fingers, neither of which was feasible for Yehuda. Instead, an OT devised a two-pronged stick that had success. If we placed Yehuda's hand in between the two bars, he could use the muscles in his arms to direct his hand. It took a lot of exertion to be able to maneuver the chair.

As is the case with muscles, the more they are used, the better they become. Yehuda's strength grew and he became an expert at maneuvering his chair through the tightest curves and corners. He also gained the strength to raise his arm independently to place it into position to drive. While this may sound easy, it took a lot of effort and time to develop this skill.

On one occasion, I arrived at the rehab center to feed Yehuda his lunch. As I had reached the cafeteria before him, I used the time to catch up on my emails. I was pleasantly surprised to hear my name being called; it was Yehuda, who had come to find me all on his own.

Regaining a measure of independence had a positive impact on Yehuda. He had come a long way from relying on others for every step he needed to take. No longer would the nurses have to call a porter to take him from one therapy to another. No longer would he be left in a room by himself, hoping that someone would remember he was there and needed to go someplace else.

Yehuda *davening.*

Some time later Yehuda was able to raise his hand to his chin, then his mouth, to feed himself, an accomplishment we hailed as a major milestone. But the single moment that remains indelibly etched in my memory is when he was first able to lift his hand to his eyes as he recited Shema. Holiness permeated the atmosphere. Something deeply spiritual was unfolding before my eyes and I had to turn away. I felt as if I were invading something personal between a man and his Creator. Despite having been tested to the nth degree, Yehuda was expressing his unwavering faith and devotion. I imagined that the spirituality in the Beis Hamikdash was parallel to that experience.

"You Are Still You!"

Spending endless hours in rehab gave us lots of time to talk. Yehuda was concerned that he was no longer himself, that he had lost so many parts of the real him. Who was he now? What would become of him? What would he do with his life? Until the accident, he knew exactly what his goals were. Did that all change? Would it have to change? What did I think of him?

I reassured him, on countless occasions, that as far as I was concerned, he was still Yehuda. Humans are made up of many different components—mind, body, and soul. True, his body was broken, but his mind and soul were intact. I could look past the wheelchair. It was just that—a chair. His mind, his intelligence, his personality, his mannerisms were still there. That was the part of him that I knew and loved. We could still relate to each other; we could converse, make plans, make decisions together. We could still be a team. We could have fun together, respect and appreciate each other. None of that had been taken away. Things may look different, but much could still be the same.

"You are still you" became my refrain. I meant it. I had heard a story about a young girl who suffered a traumatic brain injury. She lost her memory, her personality, and her previous level of intelligence. How devastating it must be to see the person you know and love right before your eyes, so real and tangible, yet it is not her. She cannot remember you or your past relationship history with her, and reacts uncharacteristically and unpredictably. To me, that seemed like a terrible tease—to have, yet not to have.

I was so grateful I had Yehuda—that he was there in front of my eyes in the true sense of the word. My best friend may have lost some of his abilities, but I did not lose my best friend. I could handle the physical losses. I admit, though, that it took time to really mean this on a deeper and non-superficial level.

Weekend Pass

Toward December, the rehab center began to discuss Yehuda being able to get a "weekend pass." This would mean that from Friday afternoon to Sunday evening, Yehuda could come home!

It was very exciting, but frankly, it was nerve-wracking as well. Would we be able to manage his care at home? We would have to get caregivers for a good portion of the time he would be home. We would also have to get equipment and supplies. It would take time to coordinate all that.

Our home, which my children had dubbed "the upside-down house" or "the house with two basements," was in no way designed with the needs of a wheelchair-dependent person in mind. In fact, when we had an accessibility expert come to our home, he took one look around and shook his head. "I have seen everything and done all kinds of crazy things, but with this house, I'm coming up blank."

To get into our home from the front door, you had to go up two short flights of steps. Once inside, there was another set of stairs. These short flights added up and brought you to the second floor of our home, which was laid out like the first floor of a typical home with a living room, dining room, kitchen, bathroom, and two bedrooms.

From the kitchen, there was one long flight of stairs to get down to the first floor, which was on street level and could also be accessed from the side door. That floor had a family room, a bathroom, and two bedrooms.

A basement was one level below that.

Yehuda would only be able to enter our home from the side door and stay on that level. Luckily, our bedroom was on that level. We would need to have a ramp built on the side of the house to get into the side door. We would have to rent a portable manual lift for getting Yehuda into and out of his chair and bed, a hospital bed with a special mattress (to prevent bedsores), and other equipment.

A tentative date—December 3, 2010—was set for Yehuda's first visit home. As his weekend visit coincided with Shabbos Chanukah, it would be the perfect Chanukah gift. However, I was too scared to say anything to the younger children in case it did not work out.

It turned out that I had valid reason to be nervous. Yehuda had been having episodes of autonomic dysreflexia during the week before he was scheduled to come home. He was afraid to leave the comfort and security of the rehab center, where a nurse was present at all times and a doctor was just a few steps away. What would happen to him at home if he had an episode?

As much as I feared the same thing, my attitude was different. I was not the patient who had been living in a hospital environment for six months. I was the wife at home without her husband for six months. I wanted my family under one roof. I was very afraid of AD; it was terrifying. However, I had received extensive training on what to do in such an event. I knew that I could always call 911 for backup and transfer to a hospital setting. It was to be something we would have to live with forever. Waiting to go home was not going to change that; it would still be a fear and a reality.

Buoyed by the support of his family, Yehuda worked hard to be able to be discharged from rehab as quickly as possible.

All week long, Yehuda wavered between wanting to go home and being afraid to. In the end, he agreed to come home! When the children returned from school on Friday, guess who was waiting for them? Of course, they were surprised and happy—but they wanted to know if they would also be getting "real" Chanukah presents.

CaringBridges: Journal Entry by Rachel Stein — Dec. 17, 2010

...I am happy to report that Yehuda is now able to go home for Shabbos and Sundays! He spent the last two weekends at home, and as you can only imagine, it was wonderful to be at home again with his family! Shaindel says it is such a big difference for all of them—it really changes the tenor of the whole week because they are looking forward to spending Shabbos together.

...Next week Yehuda will be home for a very extended weekend—from Friday afternoon to Tuesday night or Wednesday morning. Then, with New Year's, the following weekend is also extended from Friday to Tuesday morning. So far they have hired full-time nursing help for these visits, but beginning this week, Shaindel says they are feeling more comfortable and don't really need the nurses full time. They have built ramps to the side and back doors of the house, which are really the only entrances they use. Then they set up their family room as the dining room and camp out on the first floor for the weekend. It works for now. Since we are all hopeful Yehuda will continue, with G-d's help, to make progress, it is still unclear what modifications will need to be done in the long term. We will have to wait and see.

Another development is that Michael and Yehuda are going to start learning together via telephone. Although we have been looking at different voice-activated software, in the meantime the phone is a workable option. Skype works when Yehuda is at home, but it is blocked at the hospital, as are other social network sites. I don't think they've decided what text they will study, but I know they are both looking forward to it!

I wanted to share a story about a special student of Yehuda's. The young man very much wanted Yehuda to be able to attend his bar mitzvah, if at all possible. His family is secular, and they did not belong to a synagogue. He had a connection with Yehuda, and felt he was his "*rebbi*" and enjoyed studying Torah with him. The family had no idea if Yehuda would even be able to leave the hospital, but decided to make the bar mitzvah at Yehuda's shul so that if there was even a small chance for Yehuda to attend, it would be most comfortable for him.

In the meantime, the family asked if there was any

possible way for the boy to put on his *tefillin* with Yehuda. They would meet him anywhere, anytime—just name the place and they'll be there!

The first weekend Yehuda was home, Yehuda called the bar mitzvah boy. He came over with his parents on Sunday and put on his *tefillin* with Yehuda for the first time, and they said Shema together. It was quite an inspiring moment.

As it turned out, Yehuda was even able to attend the bar mitzvah! It was his second Shabbos at home and Yehuda felt up to it, so he was able to go to shul. (Shaindel had called the rabbi on Friday to give him a heads-up—but he was the only one who wasn't surprised!) The entire shul was so happy to see Yehuda after over five months—especially the bar mitzvah boy and his family. ... The Ottawa community is really so very special and very close-knit and were so happy to celebrate Yehuda's return to the shul. Shaindel said many people said that shul finally felt "whole" again—something had been missing. The rabbi warmly welcomed Yehuda, with thanks to Hashem. After *davening*, there was a long line of people who just wanted to greet Yehuda and say good Shabbos. I know Yehuda and Shaindel are both very moved by the warmth and strength of their remarkable community, and feel thankful to be a part of it.

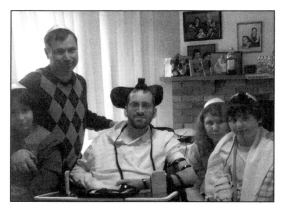

Yehuda forged close connections with his
students, sharing in their milestones.

CaringBridges: Journal Entry by Rachel Stein — Mar. 13, 2011

So much to report! I was in Ottawa last week for
another transition: Yehuda is moving back home! After
almost six months in rehab, Yehuda is now home for
good. He will be continuing therapy at home—with
his own cheerleading squad to encourage him. After
living apart for so long, it will be a nice change to have
everyone under one roof again.

I was fortunate to be there for Yehuda's goodbye
speech. Many of the therapists and nurses from the
ICU and the rehab center attended his presentation—
it was really nice to see them again! The speech, titled
"A Rabbi in Rehab," was basically about Yehuda's
perspective on his new reality, and how he is able to
remain positive by drawing strength from Jewish texts
and traditions. Yehuda says we all are challenged
in life, but the challenges that Hashem gives us are
the ones we need on our life's journey of personal
growth. He knows his injury was a challenge he was
given specifically, and he feels he must use his special

circumstances "for the best"—to become a better person and to share with others as a teacher. ...

Yehuda really spoke so beautifully, from his heart. A few months ago he could hardly speak a few words without becoming exhausted—and this was almost half an hour of uninterrupted speaking!

What Is It Like for a Rabbi to Be Going through Rehab?

I would like to thank everybody here. ... Every person sitting here now has had a great impact on my life and the life of my family. Many people sitting here have seen me through some pretty difficult and—I dare use the word—torturous times...

I assume I am probably the first rabbi to be going through this particular rehab. I don't think there are too many rabbis going through rehab in Canada. So I might have a particular viewpoint I would like to share, give you a little bit of a window into what it is like for this rabbi to go through this experience.

In terms of who I am, I am a believer in G-d. It is a strong identification of my personality. Even when I think about how I serve G-d in my religious life 24/7...the fact is that even those religious things are linked to my body. Most of the things I do, the commandments I fulfill, are tied to performing those commandments with my body. There are very few things that are only done with my mind, so, consciously or subconsciously, I have always thought of myself...as a body which has a spiritual side, the soul. Once I lost most control of my body, I had to grapple with the difficult question at the very core of who I am... Now I have to view myself [as] more of a soul that has a body, not as a body that has a soul. It is sort of like when in the winter you wear a coat, and at the end of the day you take off your coat, you are still around, you still have your body. My body is really like the coat. It is not really me… In a certain way, I shed my body, but I am still around, I am still me. My children and my family do not look at me like a coat, like a body, they view me as a Dad. I am still me; I have had to internalize that in a very personal way.

It's pretty tough. So how did I do that? That's what I would like to give you a little insight into… What are the resources I have drawn upon…to face the challenge of changing my personal identity?

There is a story in the Bible about Job, who went through a very interesting challenge. Satan went to G-d and said, "Of course, You see that Job is such a righteous man—You know why? Only because he is so rich, only because he has a large and beautiful family, only because his body is strong. I bet if You gave me permission to take away some of those things, he probably would not be so righteous anymore. He probably would not believe in You as much as he does now. Do I have permission to take something away to test him?"

And G-d said, "Yes. You will see that he will still believe in Me."

So Satan started. He took away Job's money, he burned down all of his warehouses—and Job still believed in G-d. Satan went back to G-d and said, "Okay, he still believes in G-d, big deal. What if I took away his family? There is no way he would still believe in You."

G-d said, "You have permission to test him."

Satan took away his family, and…Job still kept his religious belief in G-d.

G-d said, "You see? He still believes in Me."

Satan said, "He has one more thing. Do I have permission to take away the health of his body? To torture his body so that he should not have good health and control of his body?"

G-d said, "You have permission."

So Satan took away his last thing, the health of his body. And it says after that, Job no longer believed in G-d; he lost his faith for that time.

Of course, the end of the story is that he gets it all back. What I want to share with you is the enormity of that challenge. That even Job, the great righteous man, the Biblical figure, lost his faith for that time. The loss of his money could not cause him to lose his faith, even the loss of his family did not cause him to lose it, but the loss of the good health of his body is what caused him to lose his faith. So that challenge, we learn from this, must be tremendously enormous. I have had to stay positive; most of the time I think I have.

I just wanted to share some of the resources I have…drawn upon to keep a positive outlook.

The first thing is that I firmly believe, based on many Judaic sources, that G-d never gives challenges in our lives that are beyond our personal potential to pass.

There is an old Jewish story that talks about the challenges we all have. All the billions of people in the world have problems and troubles and challenges; that is just part of life. Meeting those challenges is a way we can advance to become better people. Every person has his or her own tailor-made set of problems. Nobody escapes it. The only thing is, everyone thinks they wish they had other people's challenges. We do not want our own, we look at other people and say, "If I only had their troubles and I did not have mine, my life would be so much better."

One day G-d looked down at all the billions of people in the world and said, "We are going to have a day of amnesty. Everybody gets to shed their backpack of troubles. And you can line them up against a huge wall, and every person can choose somebody else's, because that is what everyone wants, somebody else's… You can inspect each backpack and if anything suits you, you can just put it on yourself."

Everyone was so excited! All the people lined up, and everybody shed their backpacks and got to pick somebody else's! They looked around, took their time…and assessed all the backpacks—billions of backpacks that were available—and were so happy that they were [each] able to take a new, fresh one. But then they looked inside, [where] there was a little nametag. They were shocked, because the nametags had their own names!

Every person has the backpack that is completely and totally suited for the tools that they have. Everybody has their own laboratory, and the problems they get are the ones that are totally fitted for them.

So I never changed, just like everybody in the

world. I am still the same person. Just the set of problems has changed. Everybody's sets of problems change as they go through life. So that is the first thing that has kept me strong, that this is not just some random thing. We had an accident—of course it was an accident—but it was not random. It was exactly what I was ready for; if G-d gives, I am ready for it. It means I have to step up to the plate and get ready for where this journey will lead me.

The second thing is very similar. I have had to tell myself [that] this is very individual; this paralysis is extremely fit and individualized for who I am. If that is the case, then I have a unique role to play. I have to use these sets of circumstances to keep on doing what I am able to do. I feel that my…job in life is to share with others, to teach children and to help them grow. I just have to keep on doing that, the way that I am now, for the very way that I am now could only help me…the paralysis is so unique to who I am, so my role as a teacher is going to become very unique as well.

There is a third thing that keeps me going, and that is the story of Jonah and the whale. Jonah lived through the loss of control of his body because he lived inside the belly of a whale for three days and three nights, so he could not go where he pleased and walk around where he felt like going. The Bible tells about the prayer he prayed during those three days. One of the themes of his prayer was that he lived through miracles and G-d does not do miracles for nothing… There must be a reason for it.

…I have lived through miracles. I have gotten off the trach; that did not have to happen. I am able to swallow; that did not have to happen. I am able to move around—I have a chair that can move; that did not have to happen. Many of the things in my life—I did not have to get out of the car that night when I was trapped—all those little miracles and many, many more. If G-d allowed those miracles to happen, I have to say the same thing Jonah said, and that is that G-d does not do miracles for nothing. There is a reason. If these miracles happened, that means that G-d wants something from me and that my family wants something from me as well.

The last two things I wanted to do with you is a visual display. The first [item] is a T-shirt; I will ask Shaindel to hold it up. I will tell you the story behind the T-shirt. A couple of weeks ago, one of my friends came by to visit me in my room. It was a Friday, before the Sabbath, and he asked me to give him an inspirational idea before the Sabbath. So I told him the idea and he liked it a lot. He actually has patients who are paralyzed, and he said he would use it often for his patients. Not only that, but he also made a T-shirt and I'd like to show you that T-shirt:

"Simesism #1: Walking is overrated."

I noticed that he put #1. I was waiting for #2, but he went away to Israel for a couple of weeks so I did not have the chance to tell him the #2. But I will tell you if you are interested what #2 would be: "True happiness is underrated." I think all of us want happiness. In another speech maybe I will fill you in on what I think true happiness is—not being connected to the body. But true happiness is underrated.

And the second thing I wanted to show you; we

found a quilt in our house. You will notice that the ends of the quilt are confused or unplanned strings. The strings are just random, just hanging there. But the middle of the quilt is crocheted very deliberately and it is planned out.

We find ourselves...often being confused and asking, "Why is our life this way?" "Why did I have to have this challenge?" We are all equal in our challenges. We all have those backpacks. It is true that some backpacks may seem a little heavier, so those of us who think our backpacks are heavier ask ourselves, "Why does it need to be so heavy? Why did G-d have to do this to me?"

But that is because our lives are the fringes, the strings that are so confused and disheveled. But G-d's ultimate plan is the middle of that quilt. It is all very planned out, it is all very deliberate. And at some time, either in This World or the Next, we will know the answer, why our life was this way. Then we will be in the middle of the quilt and not stuck outside.

I myself have already seen so much good that has come directly from the situation I am in. So much good in my family, my community, the people sitting here, there is so much good in my life, my family's life; I see that already. I never would have seen those things if not for this situation. I am thankful for that. And I know there is so much more good that is going to come from it.

On that note, I want to wrap up with one final short story about probably the greatest Jewish sage of all time. His name was Rabbi Akiva. He had a saying, "This too is for the good." Any bad thing that happened in his life, he would always say, "Even this that looks so bad—it looks like such trouble—is only for the good."

One day he was put to the test. He was traveling on a donkey and he had with him a rooster to wake him up in the morning, and a lantern so that he could see in the nighttime, so he could study. It was getting close to nighttime, so he had to find a place to stay. He found a village and knocked on a door and asked for lodging. The person just closed the door in his face. What did Rabbi Akiva say? "This too is for the best." There has got to be a good reason. I will just look for another place.

He walked a little more, found another house, knocked on the door, the person came to the door. Rabbi Akiva said, "Can I spend the night?" The person said, "Don't bother me! I'm not interested in having guests!" and closed the door. What did Rabbi Akiva say? "Even this has got to be for the best."

He went from door to door asking people, and that village was not very hospitable. No one was interested in having Rabbi Akiva spend the night. But he was not upset or troubled at all, because he knew that there is a G-d in the world; there are reasons why things happen and this is for the best.

He looked around and realized he would not be spending the night inside a house. There was a forest nearby. "I'll have to lie down and sleep in the forest, but even this is for the best." He did not know why, he did not know the reason behind it, but he knew it was for the best.

He went into the forest, riding his donkey,

carrying a lantern, with his rooster, and he lay down and started to study. He was happy...until a wild animal came and mauled his donkey. So he lost his transportation. But what did Rabbi Akiva say? "Even this is for the best. I do not know why, but it is for the best."

He continued studying, so he was happy. But then a fox came and ate the rooster. There goes the alarm clock! However, he comforted himself by saying, "Even this is for the best. I do not know why, but it is for the best." He continued studying and he was happy. At least he still had a lantern.

After a short time, a big wind came and blew out the candle. Now it was pitch dark. (By the way, this story happened about 2,000 years ago, so there were no electric overhead lights.) He could not even study, except by heart. But he said, "This too is for the best." He fell asleep, and everything was great, because he knew that this whole string of misfortunes were not real misfortunes; if you are looking from the center of the quilt it is all for the best.

He woke up in the morning and had to walk instead of [riding] his donkey. No light, no alarm clock. He walked out toward the village and saw something shocking and devastating. The village was burned down to the ground! A mob, I guess Romans, must have gone through the village and destroyed and killed. And in this instance, he was able to see the why, the answer. If he had been taken into one of the houses, he also might have been killed. If he had still had the rooster making noise, the mob would have heard the rooster. If he had had the lantern, the mob would have seen the light and they would have gotten him. The same thing with the donkey. So in that instance, Rabbi Akiva was able to see how all that string of misfortunes were all for the best.

I want to end with a blessing for all of us, that we should use our backpacks to our advantage, and realize that everything in there—all of life's troubles and misfortunes—are all for the best and are all to help us grow in life, to beat the challenges, to overcome and become better people.

Thank you for listening.

CHAPTER EIGHT

Moving Beyond Our Comfort Zone

RACHELI WAS A MEMBER OF YEHUDA'S FIRST CLASS AT HILLEL. We had invited her and her family to eat with us on Shavuos night of our first year in Ottawa. Being new to the Great North, we did not realize just how late that was going to be! Sunset that night was at 8:47 p.m., meaning we could not start our meal until after 9:47 p.m.! We had a very pleasant time but the children were getting tired. Racheli and our daughter Malka each lay down on one of the couches and promptly fell fast asleep. They were only six years old. When we concluded our meal, we suggested that Racheli sleep over. Her parents, Barry and Barb, toyed with the idea, concerned that if Racheli woke up she would be unfamiliar with her surroundings and be scared.

At that, Malka's eyes popped open. "I'll stay on my couch so if Racheli wakes up, she'll remember where she is."

Sure enough, a few hours later, Racheli awoke with a start. "Malka! Malka! We were kidnapped! Where are we?"

That was the start of our friendship. Years later, Racheli pursued a degree in education because of the impact Yehuda had on her.

Barb has a friend Howard Goldenthal, a producer for "The Current" for the CBC (Canadian Broadcasting Company). This nationally syndicated radio program, listened to by millions, airs weekday mornings and features interview sessions and radio documentaries that typically take a half hour each.

Barb shared our story with Howard. It was now nine months after the accident. Yehuda had been in the ICU for three months, rehab for six. We would be celebrating Pesach, the holiday of our freedom, at home at last! Howard's idea was to document Yehuda's story and connect it to the theme of freedom from bondage and what that meant to Yehuda. Knowing how beloved Yehuda was to his colleagues and students at Hillel Academy,[1] he suggested making a surprise return visit to be recorded.

It was a fabulously exciting idea. Hillel's administration was fully on board and eager to make it happen. For days, the students were prepped and told only that a special surprise guest would be arriving

Yehuda surprising his students as
part of the documentary.

in just a few days' time. All students would gather in the gym; they were coached to be on their best behavior.

Yehuda and I were to arrive after all were assembled to keep the secret safe.

Once the students were seated, the assembly began.

"Today, we would like to share with you a very, very special

---

1. In 2009, Hillel Academy was renamed Ottawa Jewish Community School (OJCS).

guest"—the doors opened—"our very own and beloved...RABBI SIMES!"

The room erupted into thunderous applause, shrieking, and cheering that continued nonstop for what felt like half an hour. There was no containing the joy everyone felt at seeing their beloved teacher. It was electrifying.

When the tumult subsided, Yehuda began to speak:

> I have always loved and respected each of my students. You are all very, very special to me and to my wife and family. I don't know why things like this happened. But I will share with you a secret: I don't need to know why. Because I believe in a higher purpose and something good. G-d only does good. The only question I ask is, "What does G-d want of me?" I don't know if I will ever walk again, but that's okay. I'm still me. I am still a person, still a teacher, still a father, still a husband. I can do all those things. I'm still me—Rabbi Simes. But I pray to G-d to know what I need to do to get closer to Him, to serve Him and to serve you, my students.

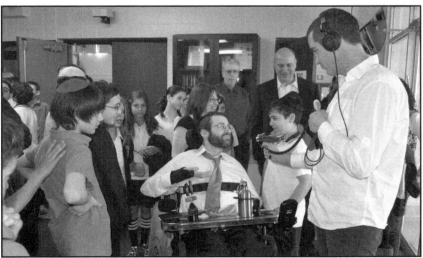

Students surround Yehuda.

Afterward, the students were given an opportunity to ask questions, which Yehuda answered openly and honestly.

The documentary, named "The Unfinished Journey of Rabbi Simes," was so well received that the CBC replayed the broadcast annually at Pesach time. As a final tribute to Yehuda, they announced his passing and replayed excerpts on the day of his funeral.

Jewish Unity Live

JET (Jewish Education through Torah of Ottawa) provides a wide variety of classes, programs, small-group study opportunities and more to Jews of all backgrounds and levels of knowledge and practice. Our friends, the Shapses, are the directors. One of their main events and fundraisers is the yearly Jewish Unity Live program. The event highlights members of the community who have made an impact. Knowing how beloved Yehuda was to the entire community, Yehuda and I were asked to accept this honor. The sold-out event was attended by hundreds on May 31, 2011.

Montreal Seminary Visit

The proximity of Ottawa to Montreal provides benefits to both communities. Every spring, the staff and students of the Montreal seminary take a trip to Ottawa during which they combine the pleasures of exploring the nation's capital with hands-on learning experiences. Aspiring teachers plan engaging model lessons and age-appropriate activities for the various classes at Torah Academy. The elementary students look forward to a change in their routine. I benefited from the energy and excitement they brought to my class. Having heard about our accident the previous year, the principal asked if she could bring the girls to our home in June 2011. At this visit, Yehuda and I shared our perspectives of the accident that changed our lives.

After giving the girls some background about the terrible events of June 20, 2010, I turned the mic over to Yehuda.

Let's talk a little bit about life. The story you are hearing is the story of all our lives. I don't know if when you look at me you feel awkward, if you think I am different than you. I am just a regular guy, it just happens to be that I am a quadriplegic, which means that I have no control from the top of my body to the bottom. When we say *nissim*, we really mean *nissim*, because I started to move and have feeling, sensations in my body, more than I was supposed to according to the textbooks. In fact, I am breathing on my own, which is a *nes*, and I am able to swallow. But our goal, my goal, is to get back into the classroom, back to teaching, and the *tovos* of Hashem are very difficult to put into words.

Everybody here knows that we have identities... The most important thing is to be comfortable with who you are. So here's the thing—I was really comfortable with who I was... I was at the top of the world—in my mind, at least. It was all taken away from me. Imagine, in one moment, not being able to move or feel anything.

I had to become comfortable with the new me, and that was really, really tough. Things happen to other people...but for the first time in my life, it happened, not to others, but to me, which I never thought would ever happen.

What does this have to do with you? Because the things you learn have to become more than just words. I have quite a background in *Limudei Kodesh*. I learned post-high school for fifteen years, in *kollel* for ten years, I went to what is called a *mussar* yeshivah, Yeshivas Chofetz Chaim... You all know what *mussar* means. I thought I knew what *mussar* meant also. But I am going to share a secret with you, a personal secret: All those *mussar shmuessen*, all those *sifrei mussar*, all the internalization of the words…it was not enough. There is something called *chinuch* of *mussar,* which is putting the words into practice. All the *ma'amarei Chazal* that you learned, they have to penetrate, but to make it really real, they have to be put into action. So let's say you learn about *chessed.* Until you put it into action, put the *chessed* into action, it does not really become part of who you are. …

So everything that I was—rabbi, teacher, father, husband—it all became a question mark, because who am I now? I cannot move, I am not a teacher, not an adequate husband, not an adequate father, so to accept the *gezeiras Hashem* is very, very difficult. But I can honestly say—and I hope Shaindel will agree—that we never asked why Hashem did this to us… Not once did we kick at the *yissurim* to say, why did G-d do this to us? But the devastating question that we did ask was, "What does Hashem want from us now that we are in this state?"

We thought we knew before what Hashem wanted. We should be teachers and *mekarvim,* touch lives, bring people to our home—but now what? What can we do now? That took a little while, a lot of tears, and a lot of *davening.* At one point the question arose… "Why should I be *davening* and pleading with Hashem to get my *kochos* back if I'm working so hard to be *mekabel* what Hashem has done to me? If I'm *mekabel,* I'm accepting this harsh *gezeirah*… I'm going to accept it and savor it with *simchah.* I don't know if I could do that, but at least embrace it to a certain extent. So if I am embracing it, then how can I at the same time ask that it should leave, and if I am asking that it should leave, then how am I able to embrace it?" You see the contradiction?

If the *sefarim* say that you have to accept *yissurim* with *simchah*, what right do I have to ask that I should actually walk again? Yet I do ask to walk again, and that is where I focus my dream, my yearning—please, Hashem, let me walk, let me move—so am I really accepting where I am today? Got the question? I am going to try to answer.

...The human being is able to live with contradictions. We have the capacity to live in a state of questions and contradictions. And we can operate simultaneously on asking for more and at the very same time accepting where we are. We are so deep and delicate that we are able to have these two opposite contradictory forces coexist within us. We are happy, we want more. It does not make sense intellectually, but on an emotional level, that's how it is....

I will tell you one thing; I am a little happier, I get a little more pleasure, and sometimes a lot more pleasure from things I missed before. Last week we went on a walk for the first time. "Walk" means that we had two carriages. My son Chanoch was in one, and I was in the other. His was being pushed by Shaindel, mine was being moved by this handle—I can move this basic wheelchair around. So we went to a bike path for the first time. [Actually] I went on that bike path many times before... But now I felt something. Hashem's *briyah*. Hashem put us here, He connects us...so I think about that, how I felt the sun, the simple things, trees, the weather...and isn't that a *tovah*? I missed it and I think that is something special, a way of accessing pleasures I did not have before.

Q: How is it possible to never ask why?

Rabbi Simes: I think it depends what you mean by why. When I say why, what I mean is, why do I deserve this? What did I do wrong that this should happen to me? That is what I never asked. I firmly believe that Hashem is good and He knows what He is doing. I don't know what Hashem has planned for me, maybe it was all training up until this point, Hashem wanted me to get here to do other things. My life was in one direction until now. Life is too short to be worried about whys. It's not worth it. Think about *what* instead of *why*.

Q: Would you want to know what is going to happen?

Rabbi Simes: Oh, yes. We all want to know. I am no different than you. You guys want to know about your future. You want to know about what you are going to be doing. What your life is in the future. Don't you? So do I. Just because I am a little older, and I seem to have been set, Hashem is teaching me no one is ever set. Things change in life, and you just keep on going, so of course I want to know what is the future, but I know that whatever happens to me is *gam zu l'tovah*. …

Everything Hashem does is because you need it and you deserve it and it is all gifts. I know you are not going to believe this one. This is actually a gift. So many good things happened. My relationships with my whole family are different. My access to the world is different. I can't walk? There are a lot worse things. I could be dead. I was very close to being dead. So this is a million times better. I am not going to waste my time being depressed, it's not worth it.

There's not a person sitting here without problems. Some of them are secret. Some of them are not secret. But Hashem tailor makes a person's problems for each individual. Nobody can tell me their problems are too big to handle, because they are for you. Hashem gave them to you because you have the *kochos* to meet your personal challenges, no matter what they are. So these are my challenges. I do not think mine are any harder than anybody else's because they are tailor-made for me; they are what I need. And each person has what he or she needs to become a better person.

Q: Is teaching something you are thinking about?

Rabbi Simes: It is. It's scary, though, because…last I knew my lung capacity was 35 percent of what it was before, which makes me very tired and…causes pain. So I do not know how exactly it is going to happen. I will probably go slow in the beginning. Of course, *parnassah* is something I think about, I have nine children I have to support. But if Hashem didn't believe in me, Hashem wouldn't have given this to me. So if He believes in me, then I have to believe in myself. That's the same for all people. If Hashem gave you your life and your situation, it means He believes in you, that you can do it. So you have to have the courage to believe in yourself. To believe in Hashem.

Q: How did your children handle the whole situation?

Rabbi Simes: We talk a lot about it. We're very, very open. It's something the kids need to speak about.

Q: This is really a question for you and your wife. Was there anything in your life before that you think gave you the strength to not fall to pieces and to be able to make some of the decisions and acceptance that you have?

Shaindel: …There are a lot of clichés you hear again and again. I remember at one point in school hearing stories about people's *mesiras nefesh* and *kiddush Hashem*. You say, wow, how did they have the strength, and how were they able to do that? You say, I wonder if I'd be able to do that. And you learn that it's part of our DNA that a Yid knows *kiddush Hashem,* and if someone is put to the test they have that power in them.

There are times in history of people dying *al kiddush Hashem,* and there are times in life when it might even be hard to live *al kiddush Hashem.* To go outside and still have a smile on your face, to smile at the world and smile at people when things are very challenging is a *kiddush Hashem* as well. ...

Hashem felt I am up to this test...we need to stand strong and Hashem gives the *kochos* to handle things. Sometimes you might feel like you are in a canoe and the waters are very treacherous, but Hashem throws you paddles so that you can guide yourself through the rough waters. ...

Nobody wants to be a taker; we all want to be givers. But there are times in life when it is our turn to be takers, and we'll have the turn again to give back. I think those are things that keep us going.

One of our *rebbeim* said, "Just remember Hashem is with you...talk to Him, He's beside you, just keep talking to Him." It took a little while until I knew what he meant, but soon I found myself talking to Hashem a lot more than I ever used to. ...I just *daven* that this one should be *matzliach,* that one should be *matzliach,* let the doctor say good things, let the procedure go smoothly, let this therapy work. [My husband] takes his medicine before the therapy and he says, "*Yehi ratzon* that *esek zu* should be for a *refuah, ki rofeh chinam Attah.*"

So just talk to Hashem and you'll see that the more you do it the more comfortable you feel with it. ...

Rabbi Simes: Lots of mitzvos [are being done in our *zechus*]. There are a lot of people who are lighting Shabbos candles, having something of a Shabbos *seudah* for us— those things could not have happened before. I'm much more direct with people. The director of a radio program from Toronto was here; I didn't know he was Jewish. He said something about going to a Jewish school so I asked him if…his wife would consider lighting Shabbos candles. I'm very comfortable asking now. I would have never asked that before… But he said he would seriously consider it.

Torah High Five-Year Celebration

June 2011 was a milestone for our community. Torah High, founded by Bram Bregman and Yehuda, celebrated its five-year anniversary. Even though the program started out with only a small class of pioneering students, it quickly expanded to over one hundred students. The program was a popular option among students. Yehuda, as principal, was chosen to address the community as keynote speaker on June 14th. The capacity-filled room was the same location as the Tehillim rally one year prior. His speech, "My Life on Wheels: Navigating through the Detours of Life," met with great acclaim.

Yehuda addressing the Ottawa community at the
Five-Year Celebration of Torah High.

CHAPTER NINE

Life on a Roller Coaster

WHAT WAS HARDEST TO GET USED TO WAS THE UNCERTAINTY of life. For six and a half years we were living on the edge, never knowing when the next episode, the next medical scare, would occur. We learned to live waiting for the other shoe to drop. We became very familiar with symptoms, causes and treatments, 911 calls, and ER visits. Sometimes the emergencies were further apart, other times they were so frequent we could barely catch our breath.

The "Perks" of Quadriplegia

Living with quadriplegia is neither easy nor fun. It is downright hard and unpredictable, and often painful and gut wrenching. Yet there is meaning in such a life. Good times can be had—it is important to be mindful and live in the moment.

We would try as hard as we could to find the "perks of quadriplegia." It actually became a running joke. If something good came our way specifically because of the paralysis, we would say, "Oh! Perks of quadriplegia!"—and burst out laughing. One item on the very short list of perks was using our handicapped-parking pass to park in spots close to stores and events. Another: Three of our children were chosen to go to Disney on an all-expenses-paid, no-expenses-barred trip with Chai Lifeline.

For the family as a whole, the best perk was the visitation benefit for which we qualified. Due to the severity of Yehuda's injuries, the insurance company paid for unlimited visits by immediate family, including parents, siblings, children, and grandchildren.

Becky, Rachel, and Judy were able to visit several times a year. Those visits were a huge boost for everyone. For Yehuda, it enabled him to be supported in a way that only siblings can do. They would reminisce and roar with laughter as they remembered their childhood shenanigans and dramas. For the kids, it was a chance to be doted on and to connect to their roots, to see Yehuda from another angle. For me, it was a relief, a chance to lay down my burden and allow someone I trusted to take care of Yehuda. It was also a chance to have some fun and get spoiled a little.

In the summer of 2011, just one year after the accident, Becky had a fabulous idea: She would come for a visit, and while she was there, Yehuda and I should go away for two nights together, without the children. Now that was exciting! But how on earth would it happen? Where would we go? What accommodations would the hotel need to provide? It seemed a little outlandish but worth pursuing. We got our PT and OT on board to help facilitate the endeavor.

Yehuda liked to dream big. He decided we were going to stay at the Ottawa Fairmont Chateau Laurier. Rumor has it that the Queen of England stayed there when she visited Ottawa. If it was good enough for the Queen, it would be good enough for us! Yehuda was also of the opinion that a vacation means a minimum of two nights away from home. Two nights were booked, equipment was rented and delivery arranged, and the caregiver was notified of our temporary change of address.

Off we went! Could this, would this, work? Yes! We left the worrying to those we left behind.

Our mini-vacation may have looked different, but it was still very much the same. Yehuda was still Yehuda. We strolled around the scenic ByWard Market, walked around the Rideau Canal, and explored a museum. (Another perk of quadriplegia: As companion to a wheelchair-bound guest, I got to go in for free!) We were a perfect couple on a summer holiday. It was certainly less spontaneous than in the past but definitely enjoyable, pleasant, and meaningful.

We would beat this quadriplegia thing, by hook or by crook.

Something Is Off

A few weeks later, Yehuda complained of feeling unwell. Something was off, but he could not describe what it was. He felt tired and was too fatigued to do his therapies. Soon he was able to pinpoint the feeling as coming from his chest—he felt like he was being crushed by a truck, like a huge weight was on him. Fearful he might be having a heart attack, we called 911.

Yehuda was rushed in for testing. There were no signs of a heart attack, but something was definitely wrong. He was admitted to the hospital. I panicked and called Fraidel and Eliezer. Although they lived in Rochester, four hours away, I could always count on them to drop everything and come help me at a moment's notice.

During this hospitalization, we first met Dr. Omer Choudhri, who became one of our dear friends.[1] Right away, I was struck by his humility. He had originally suspected a specific ailment as being the cause of Yehuda's symptoms. On further persistent review, he revised his diagnosis to myocarditis/pericarditis—an inflammation of the muscles surrounding the heart. No wonder Yehuda felt the way he did! He was connected to a telemetry device to track his heart rhythm.

Those several days in the hospital were tense, as we were afraid that in addition to paralysis, Yehuda would suffer heart issues. What more could possibly go wrong?

Never, ever ask that! More could go wrong, and it would. We just did not know it yet.

---

1.   He even spoke at a memorial service for Yehuda, leaving the ICU briefly to pay his last respects to a patient whom he so admired.

Wheelchair Issues

I had to get Yehuda out of the hospital. We had a very important appointment on the other side of town with the medical equipment and supplies company. Several major issues with Yehuda's power chair were hampering his mobility and comfort and causing him pain. This meeting had been booked a while before, and I did not want to reschedule it.

Fortunately, Yehuda was discharged from the hospital on the morning of the scheduled appointment. I hastily collected his belongings and called a cab. On the way, I called to confirm the company's address.

"Thanks," I said. "We'll be there soon."

That was when the trouble began.

"I'm sorry, but we don't have you on our appointment list for today...[pause]...or any other day, for that matter."

I firmly stated that this appointment had been made several weeks prior. "Our therapist booked the appointment and will be meeting us there. For your information, Rabbi Simes was literally just discharged from the hospital after several days due to a suspected heart attack. We are on our way and will be there shortly. Please ensure the technician is available."

Needless to say, the technician we had been supposed to meet was not there, as "there was no appointment." Instead, we were assigned to someone else. This turned out to be one of the best mistakes! This technician was amazing, capable, creative, and ambitious, and devoted the entire afternoon to us. He went through the issues one by one and did not stop until he had a plan. It was a productive—albeit exhausting—day.

New Van

We relied on accessible taxis to take us wherever we needed or wanted to go. On one such occasion, when the taxi arrived, we noticed it was a different model van than usual. No matter how hard we tried, we could not fit Yehuda into it. We dismissed it and called the doctor's office to reschedule the appointment. Expecting compassion, I burst out crying when the operator berated me for the last-minute cancellation. Tearfully, I explained what happened. To her credit, she softened and expressed regret.

Scheduling our trips was also an issue. Sometimes, due to a driver's availability or lack thereof, we had to leave events earlier than we would have liked. As we felt our independence eroding, we eventually reached the point where we could no longer handle any further infringement on it.

The rehab center hosts a department that deals with transportation needs—helping people with disabilities learn how to drive, where feasible, or purchase a van to accommodate a wheelchair. Yehuda was not a candidate to learn how to drive using hand controls (for which, truth be told, I was grateful). We spent time researching vans with accessibility options which, we learned, included a rear-entry or side-entry ramp. The rear-entry ramp meant that, in essence, Yehuda would be sitting in the trunk. I did not think it was appropriate for the head of our family to be relegated to the back like a piece of luggage. The side entry meant that Yehuda could swivel his chair once inside the vehicle and sit up front in the passenger seat. The actual passenger seat would be removed to make way for the power chair. This was a much better and more respectable option for us.

Yehuda got to choose his color. Boys will be boys, and yes, he chose red. Not quite a convertible, but it would have to do.

Delivery was expected in the early fall of 2011.

Unusual but Meaningful

Once again, Rosh Hashanah was approaching. Our baby would be one year old—what a milestone for all of us!

In the days leading up to the Yamim Nora'im, I sensed that

something was slightly off with Yehuda medically. It was nothing specific, just something to keep an eye on. My brother and his family were once again coming to be with us for Yom Tov. This time we would be home.

On Rosh Hashanah morning, we got dressed and ready for the special services. The intense *tefillos* usually evoke powerful emotions in me, but this year, as I sat in the shul, I felt strangely unmoved. I looked around the room at all the members. It was a packed room, yet I felt alone. I had undergone so much in the last year. My life had been turned upside down. As I skimmed through the *tefillos*, I felt like I had already said them dozens of times throughout the year. My whole year had been Rosh Hashanah. *Who will live? Who will die? Who at their right time? Who at an earlier time?* I did not belong here now; I said those prayers already.

My eyes brimmed with tears. I leaned over to my sister-in-law Gila and whispered, "I need to go out; I can't be here anymore." Gila offered to accompany me, but I said I would be fine alone. I went down to the social hall where the babysitting service was. I took Nochi, put him in his stroller, and exited the shul.

I started walking aimlessly. I did not want to go home, yet I could not remain in shul. I kept walking. We lived in a beautiful residential neighborhood which is home to numerous parks, playgrounds, and bike paths. As I walked toward a path, I poured out my heart to Hashem. I told Him that Rosh Hashanah was the day we coronate Him as King. I too would coronate Him and place my trust in Him, trust that He knew what was good for me, that He would guide me through this uncharted territory, that I could not do it alone without His help. As I walked, I talked. It was the second-most-meaningful Rosh Hashanah of my life. Why does it take something so drastic to appreciate life and its meaning?

I found myself at my dear friend Kathi Kovacs's door. She was surprised to see me and immediately worried that there was an emergency of some sort. I assured her that technically all was "fine" for the moment but shared my concerns about Yehuda. We agreed that I should keep a close eye on him to see what transpired.

It Could Have Been Avoided!

Within a week, Yehuda had an episode of autonomic dysreflexia. I had feared it would happen, so I was not surprised. Yehuda's blood pressure was well over 140, the level at which treatment becomes necessary. Post-accident, his blood pressure was in the eighties. I did what I was trained to do, loosening tight-fitting clothing, sitting him completely upright, and monitoring his blood pressure at the prescribed intervals. There was no major change, so I applied Nitropaste as directed.

AD is a true medical emergency which, left untreated, can lead to stroke or death. I could not let that happen on my watch! After several hours with no end in sight, I called 911 for backup. Armed with all our supplies and an AD information packet, we headed to the emergency department for help. Due to her medical background and connections, I also put in a call to Kathi to meet us there.

When we arrived, I felt confident that Yehuda would be treated immediately. The rehab center had prepared us very well for this eventuality, reassuring us that when treated right away, AD had no lasting consequences. If not, the results could be deadly.

We were questioned by the triage nurse as to why we were there—Yehuda looked fine. I pulled out my pamphlet and stated that Yehuda was a quadriplegic in the process of an AD episode; if left untreated, he could stroke out. At the time, he had Nitropaste applied and his blood pressure was still too high. I explained our fears and handed her our treatment information card. She looked at it and handed it back disdainfully.

"This isn't protocol from our hospital," she sniffed. "We cannot follow other protocols. We can only follow *our* protocol."

I said that I was okay with that, as long as she followed any protocol that prevented him from having a stroke.

Somehow, she did not quite comprehend the seriousness of the situation. "You'll have to wait," she informed us.

I told her that we had to keep checking his blood pressure at prescribed intervals.

"In this part of the hospital, we do not check BP that frequently," she said, as if speaking to a small child.

"Then please take us to a different part of the hospital!" I requested firmly.

She shot me a look that spoke a thousand words, and walked away.

I looked around the room to further assess our surroundings. The room was packed with people; stretchers lined the walls and the corridors. Did people come here to hang out because they were bored? It was the most crowded waiting room I had ever seen. I feared they would forget about us. We would get lost in the shuffle.

Indeed, we did.

As the hours ticked by, we did not seem to be getting any closer to testing or examination. I kept going to the nurses for help, again and again, to no avail. I was in a state of panic—for this, we could have stayed home. There was no reason to be here. We came here to get help and were not getting any. The fear of stroke hung over my head.

Finally, it was our turn. Once again, I explained to the intern what was wrong, what I suspected the causes could be, and what needed to be done. The symptoms must be treated as well as the cause.

Upon examination, they discovered two possible causes for the episode. Based on my experience and training, both were possible and both needed to be treated. The doctor on call felt that neither of these two was serious enough to cause such an extreme reaction by Yehuda's body.

But that is exactly the point! A paralyzed person's body cannot feel pain the way we can. The message pathways from the brain to the spinal cord to the affected area have been severed. The brain goes into overdrive to alert the body that there is something that needs to be taken care of. The problem can be as simple as sitting in one spot for too long. An able-bodied person shifts and squirms constantly; a quadriplegic does not.

I pressured them to take further measures to treat him. They insisted there was no need, as he was fine now. Fine now, well, maybe; depends on what you call fine. Besides, if the cause is not treated, soon he will not be fine. Once again, they insisted there was nothing to do and we could go home.

How on earth am I supposed to take him home at 4:00 a.m. without a wheelchair?

"Do you have someone to call who can bring it to you?"

Are you for real? At 4:00 a.m.? In a taxi? "No, sorry, there's no one I will ask to do that."

They offered to call us a medical transport—basically, a nonemergency ambulance service. I told them that if I was not comfortable with how Yehuda was feeling or his symptoms, I would not be taking him home. He was in a hospital and I expected him to get treated. They just humored me and went about their business.

An hour later, the transport arrived. The personnel came over to prepare Yehuda for discharge and to transfer him from one stretcher to the other. I reminded them of what I had said. They assured me that once he was transferred to the other stretcher, they would check his BP.

"Are you kidding me? Is there something here that *I'm* not getting? Why on earth would you transfer him to a stretcher to take him away if he isn't going anywhere? And you people should know that when a person is handled, especially during a transfer, his blood pressure will go up. It will not be an accurate at-rest reading!"

Why do I have to tell these people these things? I do not have a medical degree! Do they? By this point, I had serious doubts. I thought I was going to be in need of medical attention myself if this farce went on any longer.

To make me happy, a nurse came over to take Yehuda's blood pressure prior to transferring him. What a shock! It was over 150! Sheepishly, she canceled the transfer. No way was he leaving that facility.

His condition deteriorated rapidly after that. The staff began to realize that maybe I knew a thing or two, but were not quite convinced until they took his BP again—250! That did it! There was a flurry of activity as they went into emergency—I would even venture to say panic—mode: "Quick, quick, hurry, we need to get the antidote, he could stroke out!"

I was absolutely livid! I had been saying that for nearly TEN hours!

Yehuda was rushed to the ER's critical care unit (I guess it was where they do check BP frequently) and was hooked up to numerous IVs. I was beside myself. This was exactly what I had been hoping to avoid. The staff finally made plans to treat the two issues that were initially diagnosed. He was in critical condition. Would I lose him this time?

Finally, Yehuda was stabilized and moved to the ICU. This time, his hospital stay lasted ten days, including Yom Kippur, the holiest, most serious day on the Jewish calendar. Afterward, he was not medically able to go straight home. His body needed more time to recuperate, so he was readmitted to the rehab center for ten days. It was a horrific situation, made even more horrible by the fact that nearly three weeks of hospitalization could have been avoided.

Once again, our family rallied behind us. Yehuda remained in rehab over the joyous Yom Tov of Sukkos. Some relatives went to the other side of town to be with Yehuda. Some stayed with me and the children.

The previous Simchas Torah, he had been just two weeks into his stay at the rehab center. Rabbi Burger had borrowed a small *sefer Torah* from Congregation Machzikei Hadas and brought a *minyan* of men to celebrate with him. I wish I could have seen it in person. I heard it was very emotional. Yehuda was given an *aliyah*—it was his first one post-accident. How he treasured that moment! Would he be having a repeat of that experience this year?

We asked the physiatrist if there was any way Yehuda could celebrate with us. To our tempered joy, he was granted a pass to leave the rehab center for several hours on Simchas Torah night and Simchas Torah day. We had to work hard to focus on the moment and not think about the fact that he would have to return to rehab once the *hakafos* were over.

Physically, it took Yehuda a while to recover from this setback. For me, the aftereffects were not physical but rather emotional, as I questioned the system that had let us down. It left a lasting distrust that I constantly tried to push aside.

Later on, after the dust had settled, I had our PT help us draft a letter to the CEO of the hospital to apprise him of our awful experience. In a return letter, he validated our concerns and expressed his regrets along with the assurance that the hospital would be reviewing its protocol for AD in order to revise and amend it. As they treat very few quadriplegics, the staff was not trained well enough on how it should be treated. They should have followed the exact protocol I gave them. I kept that letter in Yehuda's chair bag in case of future need. I made the decision not to bring Yehuda to that hospital ever again if I could help it.

"EZ" Lock

In the midst of all the chaos surrounding Yehuda's hospitalization, we got a call from the car company. Our new van was ready to be delivered. When I got the message, I announced to the family that I was not interested in the van—I did not want the van—I will not drive the van—I will not go in the van! Yehuda is in critical care. I do not know if and when he will recover. Of what use is a van? I could not cope with the dealer and had someone else tell him to hold off on the delivery until I knew Yehuda would recover. The dealer was adamant that I wanted the van ASAP, so he was going to follow my orders to a T.

We tried to reason with him and explain that that was before Yehuda got sick. The situation had changed.

Our explanations fell on deaf ears. The car was getting dropped off, like it or not.

If he was so intent on following my orders "to a T," the dealer should have inspected the car before having it delivered. We had a special mechanism installed called an EZ Lock. The name should have given away its purpose. It was a lock installed under the wheelchair with a corresponding latch installed in the floor of the van. Once wheeled into the van, the wheelchair would click and lock into place so it would not move around.

The mechanism, however, was very unreliable. It would take try after try until we finally heard the "click" of success. Sometimes I literally had to lie down with my face on the ground to look up at the van through the open door to guide Yehuda's chair to line up properly. Other times, it would glide in easily. Every outing was an exercise in frustration. We avoided going out any more than was absolutely necessary.

Finally, one snowy freezing day of face in the ice, I had had it! I wanted the dealer to just take back his defective vehicle!

When the dealer took a quick glance at the mechanism, he confirmed that it had been installed incorrectly—get this!—on purpose. *On purpose? You mean there were people who were purposely messing with my life?* Yes! The technician knew the car came with a standard passenger seat. He wanted to give us the option of being able to reinstall it and use it if/when necessary. If he were to install the EZ Lock correctly (so we could actually use it as indicated), the standard seat would not fit.

I could not make this stuff up if I tried. *Hello!* We do not need a standard seat! We need a power chair. That is what the EZ Lock is for!

Connecting with Other Quad Families

Life as a quad family meant getting used to a constant state of flux—ups and downs, gains and losses. We always anticipated and awaited the gains. The losses and setbacks were real blows.

The rehab center recognized this fact. They encouraged us to get a lot of peer support, to find people living under similar conditions whom we could befriend, from whom we could learn and get support. As much as they meant well, we did not find their advice practical. We could not find anyone like us at all. We were an anomaly: a religious, large family, a patient with a high-level injury living at home. Where would we find that? At times we preferred to go it alone. It was hard, very hard, but we were already in uncharted territory. We did not want to get influenced by the naysayers. Practical advice we were ready for, but there did not seem to be much available.

My friend Lauren had heard a speech given by Aliza Bulow and forwarded it to me. Aliza has a daughter named Elisheva, who married Yehoshua, a young man who was a quad as the result of a car accident. The speech was a very inspirational and moving account of how the couple met, their decision to marry, and their journey together.

I listened in disbelief to their story. Yehuda often asked me if I would have married him after the accident. I managed to avoid answering him by insisting that it was not a fair question. After all, we had been married for eighteen years already; we had a history and a commitment to each other. We had nine children. I was not going to give up on him.

I sent an email to Aliza and thanked her for publicizing the story. I explained to her what our story was and that I was looking for peer support. Aliza and Elisheva graciously agreed to talk to me. I gained so much from their encouragement and advice. Yehuda and Yehoshua connected in a very deep way. For a while, they had a weekly learning session. We were able to complain and vent to them. They "got it." They were not judgmental and we did not have to put up a front for them.

An article was written about us in the December 12, 2011, issue of *Mishpacha* magazine. Shortly afterward, our friend Rabbi Micah

Shotkin told us that if and when we felt ready to speak to others in our situation, we should let him know.

Tracey Ribeiro in South Africa had read our story. She and her husband were the same ages as Yehuda and I. Several years earlier, when their children were a few months old, two, four, and six, her husband, José, had been in a car accident. He, too, became a quadriplegic. They had been on this journey for longer than we had and could fully relate to what we were going through. Tracey recognized that we might not yet be ready to share our story, yet she wanted us to know that she cared. It was the perfect combination of sensitivity and warmth. I did reach out to her. She was also a huge support for me. We got into the habit of communicating weekly.

Both Yehoshua and José have C5/C6 spinal cord injuries, which do not affect the diaphragm. They did not incur the breathing issues that ultimately took Yehuda's life.

Confusion

"You are still you" continued to be my mantra, along with gratitude that his essential "Yehuda-ness" remained intact. This would explain my fear and anguish when, several months later, in the late winter of 2012, things seemed to change. Yehuda was becoming unpredictable. Conversations confused him, doing homework with the kids had him going in circles.

I could not understand what was happening. I sensed I was losing him, and I was terrified.

We had an appointment one afternoon on the other end of town. It was a snowy day, and between the snow and getting the wheelchair in and out of the car, we needed to allow a lot of extra time. I had arranged with Yehuda and his physio (Canadian term for physical therapist) that after his session was over, he would not be put into his bed for a nap. It would take me too long to transfer him from the bed to the chair, and I was already feeling rushed and pressured. Instead, he would tilt back in his power chair and we would quickly (if you could call it that; it was anything but) put Yehuda's coat and winter gear on.

At the prearranged time, I went in to get my husband, only to find him sound asleep in bed. I was beyond confused. Yehuda was even more confused than I was. Why should he not be in his bed?

We had several similar scenarios over the coming months when I would sense that something was not quite right. It left us both frustrated and upset. I discussed it with every doctor and therapist on our care team. I questioned medical personnel: If something seems off, why, oh why, can we not get to the root of it before it explodes? No one had a good answer. They all explained that traumatic injuries can bring on drastic changes. I kept fighting them and disagreeing. He had no drastic changes while in the rehab center or during his initial months at home. Why would it manifest itself months later? Another explanation they offered was that being part of "the community" is hard work and requires a lot of head space. That answer did not sit right with me either. Why would it be harder to adapt to being home, surrounded by a loving and caring family, than to living in a rehab center?

Unfortunately, even with excellent care, unless medical science can prove something is indeed wrong, nothing can be done. It would take a crisis to finally get a diagnosis.

One night, as I was discussing the situation with Yehuda, he did not respond to my question. I yelled at him to answer me—again, no response. With a shock, I realized he was not breathing. I immediately called 911. My next call was to my brother, Avrohom Dov, who was staying in the neighborhood with his family to be with us for Pesach.

When the paramedics arrived, they determined that Yehuda was in respiratory arrest. They immediately transferred him from his bed to the floor of the family room to perform CPR. My kids were sleeping in their rooms. I was terrified I would lose Yehuda and terrified the children would wake up and witness the resuscitation efforts. One child actually did wake up. Avrohom Dov pushed her back into her room and shut the door.

Thankfully, the paramedics were able to bring him back. As we were transporting him to the hospital, they gently made sure I understood the severity of the situation.

Was I aware CPR was performed? Yes.

Was I aware he had stopped breathing? Yes.

Was I aware that means he was dead? Yes.

Was I aware that means his situation is serious? Yes.

Numerous tests were performed to determine what had happened to Yehuda and why. When he received the diagnosis of carbon dioxide necrosis, everything became clear. Due to the paralysis, Yehuda's diaphragm was compromised. Normally, when one breathes, one inhales oxygen and exhales carbon dioxide. Yehuda was unable to take deep breaths, causing dangerous levels of carbon dioxide to build up. Despite his oxygen levels being normal, the carbon dioxide was compromising his thought processes.

I felt relieved and vindicated: I was not crazy; there was, indeed, something wrong with him.

Yehuda was treated and released on condition that he use a BiPAP every night. The BiPAP would do the work for him that his diaphragm could not. I was relieved that we now knew what had caused all that stress. I regretted all the time wasted, and celebrated having the real Yehuda back. But even though I had him back mentally, I lost another part of him to his BiPAP. Once he was "tucked in" for the night, we could no longer communicate.

Making a Move

We had to move out of our two-story split-level home on Ardell Grove. Living in that house was bordering on impossible. Due to Yehuda's mobility issues and caregiver needs, it seemed like adults, kids, caregivers, and friends were forever colliding with each other.

We needed a live-in caregiver, but did not have the extra room for one. Yehuda needed specialized therapy equipment, but we did not have the space. Rooms that theoretically could have been converted were on floors that were inaccessible to him.

We had tried mounting a shelf in a linen closet and removing the door for Yehuda's voice-activated computer. That was impractical, as the software picked up all of the noises around the room and could not isolate Yehuda's voice. We even tried using the garage, which was attached to the house and could be entered through a small mudroom. That also had glitches. There was a small step Yehuda could not navigate. He would have to go out of the house and be wheeled to the front of the garage. In addition to this being a nuisance and impractical, the garage was not weather controlled—too hot in the summer when we initially tried it, and definitely too cold in the winter. It would also mean I would not be able to park our van inside. While in New York a garage is considered a luxury, Ottawa's winters made one a definite necessity.

Intellectually, I was very aware of the need to move, but my brain was not in sync with my heart. I could not bridge that gap. I really did not want to move. I wanted to stay right where we were. I wanted to turn back the clock. I was not ready to give up the past. By moving, I would be admitting that Yehuda's needs were too great. Moving would make it real. Leaving 28 Ardell Grove would be admitting that life had changed and would never go back to normal.

In June 2011, we had purchased a home several blocks away, on Roselawn Court. It needed modifications and alterations, which its layout made very doable. We had walls knocked down to create an open-concept layout, among other renovations. Two of the most important rooms to be included in the newly finished basement were a bedroom for a caregiver and a therapy room for Yehuda. An elevator was installed to provide access. This room was outfitted with a ceiling track lift and a hospital bed, as well as two large therapy machines (a standing machine/tilt table and a hand bike for aerobic exercise). Yehuda's computer would also be in there.

I was encouraged to take part in decorating our new home to my taste, to spend money to fix it up in the way that would make it most appealing to me. The kitchen had to be gutted, and since I would be the one spending the most time in it, it should reflect my needs and taste. By the time we finally moved in the following summer, even I had to admit that the kitchen really was beautiful!

Once we moved in, unpacked, and got our bearings, we relished our newfound space. Yehuda could now navigate the wide corridors and doorways in his power wheelchair. He could join us in the kitchen, the living room, and the dining room—rooms which, in our "upside-down" house on Ardell, were on the second floor and inaccessible.

Moving day, summer 2012. An accessible home
opened up new doors of opportunity for Yehuda.

CHAPTER TEN

You're Lucky If...

O UR NEW REALITY BROUGHT US IN CONTACT WITH MANY new people holding various job descriptions. We did not always know what their responsibilities were. Our learning curve was steep, sometimes dangerous, sometimes humorous, but always memorable.

Managing the Managers

I had assumed that the role of a case manager was to facilitate helping the family with specific needs and goals. Well, in the case of some of them, I assumed wrong.

When it came time to start discussing Yehuda's discharge from Ottawa Rehab in the spring of 2011, I hosted a meeting at my house, around the dining room table, during which I observed the case manager and the director of the care agency plan out an entire schedule of care. Not once did they include me by asking what I wanted or needed. It was not until they had scheduled everything in a completely senseless way that I burst out crying. They finally let me tell them what I had envisioned and had to rearrange the whole schedule. The case manager had the effrontery, on the way out, to say to me, "I'm so sorry that this conversation was so distressing for you." I was so mad, I could not even respond.

Sometimes we felt we would manage a whole lot better without a case manager. As we tried to explain numerous times, we are not stupid; we are university-educated, successful teachers, raising a large family. We are quite capable. We suffered a trauma the likes of which we never imagined—let alone experienced—before. That is the part we need help with—nothing less and definitely nothing more.

Upon questioning one case manager as to why she kept recommending a particular agency to us if each worker we tried was less qualified than the previous one, she answered, "Well, that agency is cheaper; I was trying to save you money." Thanks, but no thanks. How about you listen to what our needs are and help us to fill that void? That is what you are getting paid to do. *We'll* worry about our money and how we want to spend it.

There were some who really meant well. However, their experience with a client who had needs as high as Yehuda's and with equally high goals was not as great. It made for some frustrating times. Often, we felt as if we were asking for someone to reinvent the wheel. Was Yehuda the first person to need a wheelchair? Was he the only one who wanted to be able to communicate hands-free, who required a call bell? The obstacles were great. One by one, we set out to defeat them.

We asked for help identifying agencies to reach out to. A kind woman came to our home with a directory. It was dated 2008—two full years prior to the accident. When I questioned the relevance of the book, the woman chuckled. "Well, actually, it's from 2003! I filled in the other half of the three to make it look like an eight, two years ago!" No, not funny at all.

Then there was the woman who arrived with various pendants. These were alarm systems that a client could push to alert someone in the event of an emergency, the same product you hear advertised on the radio for elderly people living alone. The only way to use these pendants is to push the button with a finger. Yehuda had lost his fine motor skills and could not move his fingers at all. The meeting was a complete waste of time. Once again, I questioned the case manager. "Did you even bother to find out information about the product before you sent the sales rep to our home?" She had not. Finally, I went to Home Depot and bought a wireless doorbell kit. I brought it to the rehab center and asked them to modify it so Yehuda could hit the large button with his fist.

Our nerves were already stretched as taut as a rubber band. These situations added much unneeded stress to our already compromised existence.

Caregivers?!

I tried to find books about what life as a quadriplegic was like for the person and the family. There were not many, and I was less than impressed with those I read. One line, though, stuck with me. It was a line about caregivers: "You're lucky if they don't kill you and you don't kill them." As time went on, I started to understand exactly what it meant.

We were lucky in that we had several very good, qualified, caring, and sensitive helpers. It took a long time, though, to get it right. Especially in the early days when we would have preferred to have a live-in caregiver, we did not have the space or accommodations to make that feasible. Instead, we were at the whim of agencies, or others whom we hired privately.

Time and again we would go through the process; interviewing candidates, explaining the job, training them—only for them not to show up, quit, or otherwise not work out. It drained the already limited amount of energy we had left.

Until the accident, Yehuda and I had each other to rely on—we were each other's support team. We complemented each other with our strengths and weaknesses. We did not need help, nor did we want anyone else in our inner circle. Having a caregiver meant opening our circle.

Unfortunately, there was no other option. Especially at the beginning, Yehuda's needs were too great and I was already stretched thin by my responsibilities. As time went on, we were able to decrease the amount of outside help, but we could never get rid of it entirely. I cannot say that I ever stopped seeing the caregiver as an interloper, but I did learn how to ignore the constant presence.

Watching my ever-capable husband having to rely on others for help was painful. For example, before he got the power chair, if he wanted to get from point A to point B, someone had to push him. During mealtimes, he had to be fed. He also could not dress himself.

The first time Yehuda came home for a visit, for Shabbos Chanukah, 2010, we had to figure out the logistics. Where would the caregiver go? What would her duties be? What tasks did we want only family members to perform? Could we trust her with our precious husband and father? Would she know what to do?

Meeting and training caregivers involves tremendous emotional strain. You have to open yourself up and be vulnerable to a complete stranger, who is going to be taking care of your loved one. There has to be a high level of trust. The caregiver learns the medical history pertinent to the patient's care. She becomes part of the family—but is not family. It is a delicate balance—to include but exclude. Hopefully, the caregiver quickly learns how to be unobtrusive and give the family their space, to disappear when not needed. Some learn faster than others. Some never learn.

We ran into several of those over the years.

One of Yehuda's first caregivers was overly eager to meet our children. My nieces and nephews were also visiting that weekend. She loudly shared just how much she loves children, how many she had, and gave a very detailed explanation as to why she does not have more. This conversation took place within earshot of the children.

My home is my island, my oasis. It is where I shelter my children and protect them from influences I deem improper. I do not have control over what goes on outside our walls. I cannot always prevent what they see and hear when they are out and about. But inside my home, I can—or should be able to. I resented when caregivers exposed our children, in our home, to inappropriate subjects; for bringing in the outside world. Our children were raised without television for a reason.

It was of prime importance to maintain Yehuda's dignity and respect for him as head of the family. The children understood that their father needed care and that there were times he could not be disturbed. But there was no need to go into detail about the care he received. We specifically requested that caregivers use tact and discretion when speaking about Yehuda in public areas of the house. If they had a concern as to his health or care, they were to ask me to come to the bedroom and discuss it. No matter how many times we stressed this, some just could not get it.

One caregiver, a nurse, yelled up to me in the kitchen to ask me a question. When I reminded her of the rule and told her we do not speak about Yehuda's care in front of people, she looked at me and said, "I didn't realize that the children are 'people.'"

Yehuda was always meticulous about his dress and appearance. He made sure to be neat and presentable at all times. When he became paralyzed, it became even more important to him that he look put-together. He always wore a dress shirt, tie, and suit pants—just as he did before the accident. His physiotherapists would tease him that he was the best-dressed client they had. It took time to train caregivers on what looking presentable meant.

Over the initial months following the accident, Yehuda lost a lot of weight. Never having been too large to start with, this was a concern. In order to make sure he received enough calories to supplement his slowly growing appetite, the doctor advised him to drink nutrition shakes. These are not the tastiest beverages, but Yehuda knew he had the option to drink the chocolate-flavored version, which he found more palatable.

One morning, the caregiver requested chocolate syrup on behalf of Yehuda to mix in with his shake. I was surprised by the request, so I went in to check with him. Yehuda showed me he was drinking a vanilla shake and it tasted awful. I wondered how we had mistaken a vanilla-flavored can for a chocolate-flavored one. I assumed it must have been left over from a previous batch. The chocolate syrup did not seem to disguise the taste at all.

I went back to the kitchen to resume the task I was in middle of. It was then that I noticed an open can of concentrated baby formula on the counter. Realization dawned on me, and I raced back to Yehuda and the caregiver.

"Is this what you gave him?" I asked incredulously, waving the can in front of her. Sure enough, the caregiver had fed Yehuda undiluted baby formula. No wonder it tasted disgusting! Not just that, but the first ingredient listed was lactose—and Yehuda was lactose intolerant. Thank G-d, he did not react to it. I am not sure why.

Yehuda had his blood pressure taken at several points during the day. It was important to be sure he was at or near baseline to prevent an AD episode. One morning, I received a message from my fifteen-year-old daughter. The caregiver had just left, as his shift was over. He asked her to relay to me that her father's blood pressure was higher than it should have been. This is considered a medical emergency, and I should have been notified immediately and personally!

It was at times like these that I wished I could do it all and not have to depend on others. But that would have been impossible.

In rehab, Yehuda was given methamphetamine for pain management, and even after discharge, he relied on it to manage his pain. As a controlled substance, it is only available from specific pharmacies, prescribed by specific doctors, at very specific intervals.

One time, when I called the pharmacy to have the prescription refilled, they encountered a glitch and could not dispense it due to an error on their part. I was beside myself. There was no way Yehuda would be able to get through the night without his dose. As it was, some pain existed even with the meth.

"Isn't there anything at all you could do for us to obtain the meds?" I asked the clerk.

There was not.

"But the error is on the pharmacy's part, not mine," I reasoned, trying to remain calm. "Can't you do anything?"

"No, sorry, there's nothing I can do."

"Well then, what should we do in the meantime?" I was starting to feel a bit hysterical.

"Why don't you try Tylenol?" the clerk suggested brightly.

Tylenol? *Tylenol?* Seriously? I was flabbergasted.

"Sir, are you a pharmacist?"

"Yes, ma'am, I am."

"Well then, how can you possibly tell me to give him Tylenol? I might as well give him a lollipop—it would be just as effective! IF TYLENOL WOULD WORK, HE WOULDN'T BE TAKING METH!"

Finally, the pharmacist somehow figured out how he could obtain a minimal dose that would get us through the night—and deliver it, too.

Advocate, advocate, advocate. This was my hardest job—to stay firm and insistent, yet polite, to make sure Yehuda's needs were met.

Once, I was advising a hospital social worker of an issue I was trying to prevent. She kept reassuring me that things would proceed smoothly and urging me not to be concerned. I began to detail for her a whole list of prior discharge scenarios that had gone awry. Her jaw dropped in disbelief. "Don't you ever curse?" she asked. I explained to her that no, we never curse. We were not brought up like that. Such words are not part of our vocabulary—ever!—no matter how trying, stressful, or demeaning the situation. And, yes, being dependent on others is often trying, stressful, and demeaning.

Yet, despite all these challenges, we must have been doing something right. Uncle Moishe told me that one of Yehuda's nurses said, "I feel privileged to work here. And you know what amazes me most about this incredible family? You know what blows my mind? It is such a happy home!"

Our family, September 2013.

The following are a few accounts of true events. They are horrific, but hilarious at the same time. Until now I was loath to share these stories because I focused on the horrific aspects instead of the hilarious. However, time heals, and now I can actually find the hilarity in what occurred.

So here is a behind-the-scenes peek of the true and terrifying accounts of what it is like to depend on others. My hope is that you will get a kick out of these stories!

There were the unfortunate times when my aides (PSW's—personal support workers) left before their duties were over, or never showed up at all. For example, there was the time that one individual called at 7:00 a.m. (when her shift began) because it suddenly occurred to her that it was her anniversary, and she refused to work on her anniversary! One question we had was that she was not married, so we were dumbfounded as to what the anniversary was of!

Then there was the PSW who, after accepting the job, called to say that it suddenly occurred to her that she has young children (and she never leaves her children with babysitters), so she was unable to honor her commitment!

A PSW who was hired to work for us on Sundays called in sick on three consecutive Sundays when it was too late to find a replacement. We surmised that she had found a different job. Or perhaps she was not interested in fulfilling her commitment to us!

Next, we have the story of the PSW who needed to attend to something "important" and therefore found it necessary to run out without a word that she was disappearing on us. Trouble was that not only was her shift not over, but that she left me, an immobile person, unable to call for help, alone. It goes without saying that with me being respirator-dependent, this was a bad move. When my wife called her on it, she just said, "Hey, what's up?"

To which my wife immediately responded, "Your job is!"

But the kicker was yet to come.

We posted an ad in an online site describing the job requirements. Of course, my requirements are quite detailed and extensive. Can you believe that the same individual responded, saying that she had experience with the exact same requirements we were looking for? She was perfect for the job—which she was just fired from!

Then we had the twenty-seven-year-old PSW whom we hired for Sunday. She was only too happy to take the job. After going through the rigorous training days (at our expense), she carried out her duty once before informing us that she could not honor her commitment. You see, her mother suddenly forbade her from coming on Sundays!

We must not forget the experienced PSW who got "fed up," threw down his exam gloves, and angrily marched out of our house, never to be heard from again! I guess he cracked under the pressure!

Now it's time for the face cream episode.

At a certain point, we decided to go a step up from PSW's and engaged the services of a full-fledged nurse. We were hopeful that she would have more common sense, which apparently is not very common. Sadly, we were disappointed once again.

There was a point in time that my face was dry, requiring face cream. Thankfully, my face cleared up. The highly recommended nurse, without consulting with me, sought out my wife and asked her where the face cream was.

My wife asked, "Does my husband need face cream?"

The nurse responded, "I didn't ask him."

Well, I didn't.

The nurse returned to me and asked me if I needed

face cream. I replied that my face had cleared up, so I no longer needed the cream.

At that point, she returned to my wife and told her that she had to buy more face cream!

My wife, getting exasperated, asked the obvious question, "If my husband said that he doesn't need the cream, why should I buy it?"

To which the nurse replied, "Because you don't have any!"

My wife, by then totally dumbfounded, said, "If he doesn't need it, why should I buy more?"

The nurse and my wife went round and round, with the nurse demanding that more be bought and my wife replying that there was no reason to buy more.

We learned from this episode that even nurses can be on a completely different planet!

On the topic of uncommon sense, we had the individual who switched into extremely thick goggles when he worked. When asked about this unusual custom, he explained, "They make me work faster."

Different places of origin apparently have different ways of doing things, at least according to one of our PSW's. We used to keep the key to our prior house in our mail slot. This individual called fifteen minutes after her shift was to begin. She was exasperated after looking everywhere for the key. We reminded her that we kept the key in the mail slot.

To which she responded, "What's a mail slot?"

When we explained what a mail slot is, she explained, "Oh, I see! In your culture you have mail slots!"

The uncommon sense is not limited to PSW's and nurses. My very own doctor, upon reporting that my blood work came back with elevated levels of potassium, asked if I was eating too many bananas!

We wanted to inform him that bananas would clog my feeding tube![1]

So there you have it! The woes of relying on others. It takes all types!

From the Rolling Rabbi blog, "What Is It Like to be Dependent on Others?" April 24, 2015

---

1. This incident occurred when Yehuda was once again respirator-dependent.

CHAPTER ELEVEN

Our New Normal

The Command Center

O N THERAPY DAYS (NEARLY EVERY DAY), YEHUDA WOULD BE escorted to the basement by his caregiver. It did not take long for the room to be dubbed his command center. Mostly, it looked like a study or home office, with shelves of teaching books and supplies and a desk lining one wall, his computer on another, hospital bed and hand bike on the third. We hung up his *semichah* certificate, his college degrees, and his awards. That left two bare walls.

From time to time, Yehuda was asked to speak via Skype to different classes in various schools. Sometimes he even managed to go teach for an hour or so in person. It meant so much to him to be able to teach and share his story. It was very meaningful for me, too—my husband, the teacher, was still able to be a teacher. He could still do that.

I got this bug in my head: Let's see how many places call to ask him to speak and let's keep track of it. Certainly, if one Chofetz Chaim branch asked, others would, too. With many branches throughout the United States, the invitations could add up.

I had seen a picture of a real command center—a military one—with a huge map on the wall and different colored pushpins stuck into multiple locations. What they represented, I had no idea, but the concept was clear. I had to buy a huge map of North America. I would hang it on the wall and every time Yehuda spoke, we would put a pin in that location.

For the time being, we assumed that any talks or speeches would be local. It had not yet entered our minds that he would actually be able to travel out of Ottawa. Going to shul was complicated enough. Teaching a class at Hillel Academy or the JCC added its own set of challenges. We thought we were stuck in Ottawa forever. We would never travel again to visit family, take road trips, or go on vacations. It was simply impossible and out of reach.

That all changed when Yehuda received a phone call from Rabbi Yochanan Kuhnreich, the principal of Beth Jacob D'Rav Hirschprung of Montreal. Our daughter Asna would be graduating in June; could Yehuda please come and address the graduates?

We had not given much thought yet to the logistics of attending this graduation. Would I be going by myself or would Yehuda come along? Certainly, he wanted very much to be there; the question was, could he get there, and how? Montreal is about a two-hour drive from Ottawa, close enough for an able-bodied person to go out to dine or shop. Could Yehuda's body tolerate being in a car for two hours, participating in the graduation, and then heading home later that same evening on another two-hour ride? What about his meds and night-time routine? If interfered with, would there be complications?

We discussed these questions with Yehuda's therapists, who were thrilled with the idea and encouraged us. It was definitely doable with the proper preparations. Having not left Ottawa in nearly two years, we found the prospect both exciting and frightening.

Slowly, a plan unfolded. We would book an accessible hotel room, rent a hospital bed, and book an extra room for the caregiver who would accompany us. But there were too many details, too many what-ifs. We were afraid that if we forgot something or something went wrong, we would miss the graduation. That would be devastating! The plan then expanded to include a trial run. Yehuda and I would go to Montreal on a random night prior to the graduation to make sure everything went smoothly. If not, well, at least we would learn what to do better for next time.

With hope in our hearts and a justifiable dose of trepidation, we set off for Montreal. By the time we left the house with all our gear, it was nearly lunchtime. We soon had to pull over to the side of the road for Yehuda to have his lunch and meds. Schedule and routine were very important in keeping him safe and healthy. I admit to being annoyed at having to pull over and spoil the feeling of freedom by being reminded of the reality.

Baruch Hashem, both the trial run and the actual trip went off without any glitches at all. Our therapists were waiting at home with bated breath, expecting a call from us at any minute about some scenario that needed troubleshooting, or worse—a crisis of some sort.

Instead, Yehuda successfully imbued the graduates with a lesson for life. In his address, he discussed how *Chazal* mandate that a person who loses a parent and simultaneously acquires an inheritance is obligated to recite two blessings, *"Baruch Dayan Ha'emes"* for his loss, and *"Shehecheyanu"* over his newfound wealth.

"Clearly," Yehuda pointed out, "it's entirely possible that the very same incident, essentially tragic, is a cause for a blessing of gratitude as well. And so it is with each and every experience and encounter in life: there is always a reason to say thank you."

And thank Hashem we did! We had traveled (twice!) to Montreal, survived to tell the tale, and were eager to do it again. There was now a pushpin on the map: Montreal!

Rochester was the next city to earn a pin. This trip was Yehuda's first time back since the accident. It was a chance for him to thank the community for taking care of us in the weeks following the accident. We were starting to believe that there was, indeed, life beyond Ottawa.

Ahuva and Sandy

One beautiful day in the summer of 2012, my sister Ahuva called.

"Shaindel, are you alone?"

What a strange question. "Not really," I replied guardedly. "I'm in the kitchen."

"Can you go someplace else?"

"Sure, give me a second."

What was going on? I hurried downstairs to the command center.

"Okay, I'm ready to listen. What's up?"

"I'm getting engaged. Tonight! To Avromi Vegh!"

I shrieked with delight. "Ahuva! Ahuva! Ahuva! You know what that means? It means we can all go to your wedding!"

Had my sister gotten engaged any time during the previous two years, I do not know if or how I would have been able to go—certainly not the first year after the accident. And there was no way Yehuda could have participated. But now, it was a whole different story. We had already been to Montreal and Rochester. It was only a matter of logistics. We could make this work!

I ran upstairs to whisper the exciting news to Yehuda. Ahuva wanted the kids to be surprised. They would find out later that night. Yehuda beamed when he realized he would be able to participate.

There was a lot to organize. We needed to discuss arrangements with the therapists. We also had to speak to the caregivers—who would be available to accompany us? Asna was leaving in a few short weeks to attend seminary in Israel; we had to make plans for her to fly to New York as well. Ahuva and Asna are very close, more like sisters than aunt and niece. Besides, if our "whole" family was going to the wedding, then the "whole" family had to be there! This would be our first New York trip since the accident; we were venturing farther and farther away from home. We wanted to debut as an intact unit. We had suffered a trauma but would come out on top.

The wedding was set for Thursday, October 25th. I would drive down to New York with the children and Jenny[1] would come along

---

1. Jenny, who was Yehuda's student in Torah High, came straight from school for several

to help me. Yehuda would fly with his caregiver Moe. Asna would fly directly from Israel to New York.

We would all stay at the home of our dear friends, Rabbi Meir and Yosefa Glazer. They had an accessible room on the main floor of their home—or so they told us. The part they left out was that they built it especially for us! They put up drywall to enclose a large area of the living room—and this became the accessible room. They had the walls painted and hung pictures. At the time, we had no idea of the extent of their preparations to host us.

We timed the trip so that I would get to New York before Yehuda. The Simes, Vinitsky, and Glazer families assembled outside to await his arrival, and neighbors from up and down the block joined us,

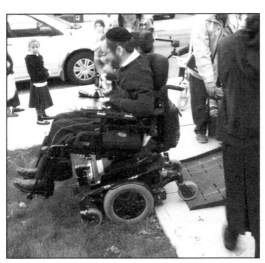

many bearing signs: "Welcome to New York!" As Yehuda wheeled himself down the ramp of the accessible van, he declared, "Touchdown!" An eruption of cheering, clapping, and hooting ensued. Once again, Yehuda did not let quadriplegia stop him.

The wedding was beautiful. We graciously accepted the blessings and good wishes of all

Touchdown! Arriving in Queens on his first international flight post-accident.

hours several times a week to help me after Nochi was born. She became my right-hand woman and loved the children as much as they loved her. When she got married, even my mother came in from New York to celebrate. Yehuda was thrilled to attend her wedding. We hosted an NCSY Torah High *sheva brachos* for her and Yisroel in our home. Yehuda programmed a meaningful speech to present from his eye-gaze computer and had us all in stitches as he shared recollections of good times spent together.

who were touched to see us. At the *badeken,* Ahuva motioned for Yehuda to come forward to give her a *brachah.* The tears began to flow—tears of gratitude for having reached this day, tears of prayer and hope that Yehuda would be able to bless each of our children on their wedding days.

We danced the night away. As the band struck up the lively tune of Shlomo Carlebach's *niggun "Neshamah,"* my feet moved of their own volition. That song was one of my favorites, and Yehuda had bought me the CD as a birthday gift. Since the accident, I had not been able to listen to that song. I hid the CD in my closet. It was too painful, as it reminded me of life "before" and all we had lost. That night, I was able to listen to the music and put my heart and soul into dancing. I could feel some happiness again.

As we prepared for Shabbos and *sheva brachos,* we heard ominous weather reports. A major storm was in the forecast. Hurricane Sandy was due to hit the region within seventy-two hours.

My mind began to work overtime. What would a hurricane mean for us—our drive home, Yehuda's flight, Asna's flight...? WAIT! What if we lose power? Yehuda's special air mattress and BiPAP machine were electric. People tried to reassure me. "Queens won't lose power. All power lines are buried underground." But I could not take any chances. This was Yehuda's health and safety that were at possible risk.

We got in touch with our friend Sruly Perkal, a one-man *chessed* organization who would give the shirt off his back to anyone in need. He is the kind of guy who seems to have anything you need that you never thought you would need. He reassured us that he had not one, not two, but several generators at his disposal. Should power go out, all we had to do was call. My mind was temporarily put at ease. Somewhat. We would have to sit tight and see what developed.

On Sunday, Yehuda arranged to speak in the yeshivah. Rumors were circulating that all flights were being canceled in anticipation of the storm. Assuming these reports to be true, Asna accompanied Yehuda to his speech while I took a much-needed break. Within a short time, however, we found out the rumors were baseless and Asna's flight would be leaving as scheduled. Our hopes for an extension of her visit were dashed. Someone drove to pick her up from yeshivah to prepare for her flight. As I drove her to JFK airport, I scanned the skies for signs of the impending storm. It had started raining, but nothing terrible. Asna's flight turned out to be one of the last to depart. One by one, flights—including Yehuda's—were being canceled.

There was no way I would be driving home through a storm, and I would not leave Yehuda behind without knowing when or if he would get a flight back. We settled down in anticipation of an extended visit.

Fortunately, our neighborhood was not seriously affected. The power stayed on and we enjoyed time with family and friends. An impromptu reunion with Yehuda's students was arranged and made complete with a heartwarming *kumzitz*.

Luckily, Moe was in no rush to get home. But Jenny was under intense pressure to return to school. She contacted her university professor to apprise him that she was stranded in New York City due to Superstorm Sandy. Not at all impressed, he threatened to fail her for nonattendance. I felt awful. I had asked Jenny for help and now she would suffer serious repercussions. Fortunately, the professor was eventually persuaded to back down.

The storm subsided over the next several days and we tried to make plans. The airline was not forthcoming as to when they could rebook Yehuda's flight. We did not have the luxury of simply taking any available flight. Timing was an important factor, as was the size of the aircraft, which would have to accommodate the wheelchair.

The only option was for someone to drive Yehuda home. Avrohom Dov had rented an accessible van to transport Yehuda from the airport and then again to and from the wedding. Under the assumption that we would not be using it again for several days, the van had been returned. Now, it would have to be rented again—which was easier said than done. Even after the rental was finally secured, there were some technical difficulties. The van needed gas. Most gas stations for miles around were out of gas. For those that had a supply, there were long lines of cars looped around the neighborhood, waiting. One could only hope there would be enough gas left for us! At a minimum, there was an eight-hour drive ahead. Yehuda would need to stop several times to prevent pain flare-ups. Whoever was driving him would have to sleep over in Ottawa to rest up for the return drive. One-way rentals to Canada are costly and there was no return flight to rely on.

We called our friend in Ottawa. "Harry? We have a huge favor to ask. Could you please drive our van from Ottawa to Syracuse? Avrohom Dov will drive five hours north. If you could meet Yehuda in Syracuse, it will only be a ten-hour trip for Avrohom Dov instead of sixteen."

"Of course, of course. You know I would do anything to help out."

Once assured that Yehuda had a safe way to get home, I packed up and prepared to leave.

Never ones to let weather get the better of us, this became the first of several trips to New York.

Stopover in Syracuse

It was early March 2012, and Malka was now in tenth grade. Her school in Rochester, Ora Academy, was having their semi-annual mother-daughter *melaveh malkah*. Malka asked if I would attend. I was terrified. It would be my first time leaving Yehuda. Should I really be going? How could I go? How could I not? I vacillated between feeling I was abandoning Yehuda and his needs and not being there for Malka and her needs.

In the end I felt Malka needed her mother. I began making plans to spend Shabbos in Rochester with the children. I arranged for several of Yehuda's friends to spend Shabbos with him in addition to the nursing care.

Once I was already planning, I had an idea. The route to Rochester passes through Syracuse. Would it not be a nice idea to stop into Crouse Hospital with the children, especially Nochi? I would be able to thank the staff for the expert care they had provided us. Would they not be touched to see eighteen-month-old Nochi as a precocious, healthy toddler?

I looked through my mounds of paperwork for Janet Press's business card. Janet was the Perinatal/Obstetrical Coordinator. I emailed her to let her know I would be driving through town and would love to see her and her staff.

As expected, Janet was thrilled with the idea. It was unlikely that all my nurses would be there at the same time, but I could leave a note for those on a different schedule. The children and I prepared a gift package for the staff—a beautiful box of chocolates, a copy of the article in the *Ottawa Citizen* by Andrew Duffy about Yehuda, a picture of Nochi, and a thank-you card.

We set out on the three-hour drive to Syracuse. Thankfully, the weather cooperated and the trip was uneventful. We were greeted with smiles and hugs. One by one, the nurses came over. They wanted to be sure I remembered them. I had no choice but to say that of course I did—even if I did not. How could I disappoint any of them?

One nurse in particular was extremely insistent. She was the one who had pushed me in a wheelchair to visit Yehuda several days after his surgery and I had been beyond grateful to her for arranging it. Two of the nurses, Nancy and Zeeve, were not there. I was disappointed, as I had really hoped to see them again. Nancy and Zeeve had joined us for our Shabbos Kiddush and Havdalah while I was hospitalized.

The visit was a morale booster to the nurses, who do not often receive the appreciation they rightfully deserve. It was a boost for me to be able to share with them how far we had come since the initial trauma and fear of the unknown.

On a personal level, the trip was an eye-opener for me. I learned I could trust others to keep Yehuda safe. It was important for me to accept that it was okay to take a break sometimes and take care of myself. Without self-care, there would not be strength to take care of others.

It would take some more time for me to internalize this message.

COR Speech

Several weeks before Pesach of 2013, Yehuda received a phone call from Rabbi Sholom Adler of the COR[2] in Toronto. His brief conversation left me curious as to the purpose of the call.

Yehuda explained that Rabbi Adler was arranging his yearly pre-Pesach seminar and was looking for an inspirational speaker. He had heard about the challenges Yehuda was going through and wanted him to come to Toronto and address the participants.

"What did you tell him?" I asked eagerly.

"I thanked him for the invitation, but declined," he said.

I was horrified. What a fantastic offer! Why would he turn it down? I took a deep breath. "Why?" I finally managed to ask.

It was not the speech that concerned him, he explained. That part was easy. But he was afraid. How would he get to Toronto? Where would he stay? Who would take care of him? Fear of the unknown was now paralyzing him further. I reminded him that he had already traveled to Montreal to attend and speak at our daughter's graduation. Why was this any different?

Back in Syracuse when we first learned of his paralysis, I was asked what his profession was. When I said teacher, the doctor was relieved. "Well, he could still do that," he said. "He will still be a teacher and a husband and a father. I'm just glad you didn't say truck driver." I had held on to that sliver of hope as I tried to wrap my head around my new reality. Yet now, here he was, ripping away the very hope I was clinging to.

You can still be a teacher. Do it! You have to go!

I discussed my thoughts with a mentor. How could I phrase my opinion in a way that would not seem accusing, challenging, or dismissive of his fears (which I thought were irrational)?

---

2.   Kashrus Council of Canada.

A day or so later, Yehuda and I discussed the idea again. The therapists were on board and agreed to help. We decided that if we could work out the details, he would really like to do it. But had Rabbi Adler already gotten someone else to speak? As I held my breath, Yehuda quickly called to tell him he would reconsider. A huge grin broke out on Yehuda's face. Rabbi Adler was understanding and offered to help him in any way he could.

Yehuda was going to Toronto! A pushpin for the wall!

Conflicting Events

A few weeks earlier, Malka had called home with exciting news: Ora Academy would be putting on their bi-annual production of drama, song, and dance. Malka had been chosen for one of the main parts. It would be taking place at the beginning of March.

"Mommy! Will you come watch me perform?"

"Yes. I am not sure how it will work out, but, yes, I plan on coming."

Should I go? Could I leave Yehuda with others to care for him?

Again, I felt Malka needed her mother. I would have to trust that Yehuda would be taken care of. And then he got the invitation to go to Toronto! I quickly realized I would be unavailable to go with him, as I was already booked to travel to Rochester for Malka's performance that very same night. Yehuda's friend Gavriel was eager to help out. He agreed to drive Yehuda and his caregiver to and from Toronto—at least four and a half hours each way!

Yehuda was pleased with the arrangements. The trip turned out to be a huge boost to his confidence. It goes without saying that his presentation was very well received and made a lasting impression on those who attended. The entire journey—without a trial run, without me—went off without a hiccup. A whole new world was opening up before us.

The *Chizuk* Wall

In addition to pushpins in the map, we now had Asna's graduation invitation and a flyer advertising the COR speech as souvenirs of success. What better way to maintain that *chizuk* and focus on goals than to frame these items and hang them up? Thus, our *chizuk* wall was created. Any time there was an article about Yehuda in a newspaper or magazine, it was framed and hung on the wall. Any time Yehuda or I spoke, the flyer was framed and displayed. Thank goodness for Dollarama!

In my speeches, I have explained how I used the *"chizuk* wall" for exactly that: *chizuk* (encouragement). Displaying all those mementos was not a display of *ga'avah* (pride). (Okay. Maybe a little.) The impetus came from a sense of purpose, of fulfilling our roles. What did Hashem want of us? What was His plan? We did not know. But we knew that if He put us in that situation, we had to use the situation to its fullest. When we saw we had a purpose and our story had meaning and could give meaning to others, it gave us a shot in the arm to help us keep going when the going got tough.

Our *"chizuk* wall." Success breeds success. We had to start a second wall.

CHAPTER TWELVE

The Rolling Rabbi

I N August 2013, Yehuda embarked on a new venture. Eager
to reach out to others, he started writing a personal blog called
"Rolling Rabbi." In it he shared his story, nuggets of Jewish wisdom,
and his views on life. This endeavor reinforced his sense of mission and
purpose.

Yehuda became a whiz at using his voice-activated
computer system. Being able to blog opened up a
whole new world of reaching and teaching.

MY STORY
August 2013

We now know that the daily challenges that come our way are guideposts along our journey. They are meant to teach us something. But the wisdom of three years has given us an understanding that our journey is a marathon, not a sprint. Unlike an illness, where the patient can see some light at the end of the tunnel and a return to their prior state of health, what we are facing is a non-ending new reality. Everything we had thought of as permanent and unchangeable was suddenly ripped out from under us, in an unforgiving moment. Now, many things must be different, but we fight to keep them normal. We accept that things are different, but somehow, they must stay the same. At the same time, many things that we took for granted before the accident we will never underestimate again.

AN OVERWHELMING RESPONSE
August 25, 2013

If you are reading this—it means you have heard and are interested in perusing this blog. Did you know that there are many others like you? I launched this site on Friday at 12:30 p.m. and the last time I looked at it before Shabbos (five hours later) there were close to eight hundred respondents!

Since then, this trend has multiplied upon itself many times over, thanks to the magic of cyberspace! By now (Sunday afternoon) there must be around two thousand interested parties.

Amazing! And most humbling.

So I want to thank each and every one of you. You have given me a tremendous amount of *chizuk* (invigorating inspiration). I can see so much good coming from this new endeavor. I have so much to enlighten and share with you. And I am sure that you will do the same for me.

HELP ME OUT!
August 29, 2013

Your views in sheer numbers have been completely overwhelming! In under a week there have been well over three thousand hits! Unbelievable!

Your comments have been insightful, meaningful, and inspirational!

However, only a tiny fraction of viewers have sent in comments. How unfortunate!

I would love to hear how you heard of my blog. Do you know me from the past? What made you interested? Will you please leave me a comment?

I'm SO intrigued by who you are and where you live. What's your background? Do we share anything in common? Have we crossed paths?

So—let's hear from you! And let's all grow together!

PRE-ROSH HASHANAH BOOST OF INSPIRATION
September 3, 2013

I fondly remember a powerful thought from my great *rebbi zt"l* in advance of Rosh Hashanah.

As we know, Hashem sits in judgment on the awesome day of Yom Hadin (the Day of Judgment). The fate of every human being for the coming year hangs in the balance. Prosecuting angels face off against defending angels, and Hashem weighs every single action of each person. A most terrifying image.

Suddenly, as the prosecuting angel gets up to present his case, he stops short, paralyzed with fear. He hears the shrill sounds of the shofar on earth, and in a state of confusion, he panics, rendered powerless to perform his job. He assumes that the shofar blow he hears is the shofar blast announcing the coming of Mashiach—which triggers an end to his existence (*Talmud*; *Rosh Hashanah* 26a).

The thundering question is: We blow the shofar every single year. And every single year this trick works to stymie the prosecuting angel. Assuming the prosecuting angel is incredibly adept at his job, how could he be so gullible year after year?

The simple but astounding answer is: True—the prosecuting angel is wiser than we could ever imagine. He could never be tricked twice, let alone thousands and millions of times. It is we who are jaded, lulled into a sense of false security, believing that our redemption is unrealistic or far away at best. After all, if the repentance of our pious ancestors was insufficient to bring about the redemption, how ever could we contemplate doing such a thing?

The Chafetz Chaim addressed himself to this quandary. He taught that all the pain and suffering of our people throughout the ages, every drop of blood, sweat, and tears, are cumulative. Each one is counted and weighed by Hashem. Therefore, it is specifically we who can tap into that enormous collective power by telling Hashem that although our own merits may fall short to actualize the redemption, consider our meager efforts in combination with our entire history's phenomenal efforts—for we are indeed one people—and finally bring an end to our exile!

Yes, indeed—the prosecuting angel has the proper perspective. He does understand just how close Mashiach is. So he gets flustered every single year when he hears the shofar blowing, understandably anxious that it spells his doom. It is only because we lack the keen insight of an angel that we could never internalize on an emotional level just how imminent our redemption truly is.

That being the case, can you imagine the power of a little bit of extra effort on our part? It could actually tip the scales in our favor, and answer our prayers and hopes of final redemption in our days.

SIMCHAS TORAH—BE A TREE HUGGER!
September 25, 2013

I remember a cute and memorable *mashal* (parable) from my *rebbi* in high school at WITS in Milwaukee.

It says in *Mishlei* (3:18), *Eitz chaim hee lamachazikim bah*—"She is a tree of life for those who grasp on to her." The subject of this verse is the Torah. We sing this as we return the Torah to the holy ark after reading from it.

Two questions are blaring. First, how is the Torah comparable to a tree? Secondly, why is this true only for those who grasp on to the Torah? If the Torah is comparable to a tree, wouldn't this be so regardless of who may be holding on to it?

A *mashal*: Imagine being swept along a choppy and dangerous river. The current is so fierce that you cannot stay afloat. Every time you manage to come up for a breath of air, you are pulled down under the furious waves. So, you fling and flail your arms and legs, desperately trying to swim across to dry land. But to no avail. Every incredible effort you make is met with an equally incredible counterforce. As your strength wanes, the high winds and choppy waters make your efforts meaningless. You just cannot deal with the pain it takes to face the relentless pressure that is forcing you down.

Suddenly, when you have all but given up, you see just ahead a long and sturdy tree trunk that has fallen right across the river. You know that if you can muster enough strength to reach up and grab hold of that solid tree trunk you will survive. But do you have it in you? Do you have the courage that it takes? Can you possibly tap into a flicker of hope that resides in the deepest and darkest part of your inner self? Can you ignore all distractions and intrusions, and only focus on your salvation—the rock-solid tree trunk?

The tree is the Torah. The rocky and stormy waters are all of life's distraction—everything that pulls us away from being all that we can and should be. Living a Torah-true life means holding on tightly to the most solid base that exists.

So let us rejoice! Always remember the gift we have been given! It gives us the power and energy necessary to reach our ultimate potential. Look ahead and never look back!

TRUE TESTS—MORE THAN MEETS THE EYE
October 14, 2013

...In *Pirkei Avos* (5:3) Avraham is praised for conquering ten tests; however, the Mishnah does not delineate what the tests actually were. Fortunately, the Rambam and others inform us what each test was.

- #1 — Leave your homeland for an unspecified place.
- #2 — The famine in Canaan immediately upon his arrival.
- #3 — The abduction of Sarah by Pharaoh, King of Egypt.
- #4 — Battling the four kings.

#5 — Having to take Hagar as a wife.

#6 — Circumcision at the advanced age of ninety-nine.

#7 — Avimelech, King of Gerar, kidnapping Sarah.

#8 — Expelling Hagar from his home.

#9 — Expelling Yishmael from his home.

#10 — *Akeidas Yitzchak* (the Binding of Yitzchak).

A blaring question screams out at us.

To qualify as a test, a challenge must be a choice or a decision. Imagine walking down a path which splits off in two directions. In such a case, you have a choice to make—will you choose the left, or the right? A conscious decision is called for. After recognizing that a choice of action must be taken, then deliberating the pros and cons of each, it is up to you to take the plunge and accept the consequences of your decision.

Now, let us take another look at Avraham's ten tests. Which of them qualify as true tests?

Numbers one, four, five, six, eight, nine, and ten certainly are conscious choices that Avraham made. He alone made these decisions, and he alone would have to live with their consequences.

However, number two was a famine that just happened. There was nothing at all for Avraham to choose. Likewise, numbers three and seven were incidents that happened *to* him, not *through* him... The question is, why were these three considered tests?

Apparently, a test is much more than being faced with a choice. A test includes being hit with a situation or a challenge that cannot be foreseen, an overwhelming and crippling fork in the road that cannot be avoided. And the test is, how will you react psychologically and emotionally? How will you live your life in acceptance of this new reality that was forced upon you? How much fortitude do you have, deep inside, to face up to the next challenge that confronts you? Will you be crushed or strengthened? Crippled or invigorated?

And maybe, just maybe, that is the greatest challenge of all!

CONTINUE PRAYING FOR ME?

October 15, 2013

Why is there a question mark and not an exclamation point in the title of this post?

Because a few people have asked me lately whether they should continue saying Tehillim on my behalf or not. After all, it has been over three years since the start of my journey.

I shall never forget the outpouring of love and prayer from acquaintances and people I will never know. There were prayer rallies all around the world, as well as mitzvah campaigns which were initiated by dear friends. And who could ever forget all of those wonderful people who dropped everything and ran to our assistance and support?

But now that I am stable health-wise, is there still a need to keep it up? Do I still need people's prayers?

Let me share with you a memory from my yeshivah days. For many years, the entire yeshivah said Tehillim for one of the members of the *hanhalah* who had undergone multiple organ transplants, and it was a very scary time. For the first year or so, we said Tehillim every morning after Shacharis. However, after that critical stage, we began to say Tehillim only a couple of times per week. Although he was not as energetic or strong as before, we did not keep up the practice every single day.

Why not? Prayer always has an effect, and he could use all the help he could get!

As I understood it, Hashem desires full-hearted urgency as the fuel for our prayers. Once prayer becomes routine and empty of meaning, the experience becomes worn out and flat. So we prayed for our dear *rebbi* once in a while so we would not become complacent in the endeavor.

In addition, I would never ask for prayers in the first place. It feels a bit unusual to ask another person to pray for me. If it moves you and it feels fresh, I suppose you would have no other choice than to spill out your heart in pleading with Hashem to help me. On the other hand, if it becomes a scripted and expected prayer, perhaps you ought to consider praying on a less regular schedule.

DO YOU HAVE A PASSION FOR PLEASURE?
October 20, 2013

Ahh! Pleasure... The feeling of complete muscle release. Having no worries, clearing your mind from the whirling hurricanes in your head and heart. Total and absolute relaxation.

In my "new life" I have become accustomed to a lack of many creature comforts—simple things like collapsing on a couch or having sufficient breath to sing a song.

With this background, allow me to share the difference between a tzaddik and a *rasha*.

The final entry in *Midrash Tanchuma* teaches that a *rasha* is considered to be dead, even while he is still alive. Why? Because he sees the sun rising and setting, yet he fails to say the appropriate blessings. As well, he eats and drinks, but he neglects to say the correct blessings.

Not so a tzaddik. Everything he tastes, hears, and sees motivates him to say a blessing.

The question lurking beneath the surface is, had the Mishnah not been written, we would have assumed that a tzaddik is differentiated from a *rasha* by a wide schism. A tzaddik performs the greatest mitzvos, while a *rasha* commits the greatest *aveiros*.

The difficulty is blaring. While the Mishnah teaches us a significant difference between a tzaddik and a *rasha*, namely, that a tzaddik says more blessings than a *rasha*, we know that a much wider demarcation lies between them. Doesn't a tzaddik perform inspiring mitzvos, such as saving a life or teaching Torah to the multitudes? And doesn't a *rasha* commit horrible *aveiros*, such as extinguishing a life or robbing the life savings of a friend? Surely the Mishnah should choose matters way above and beyond the recital of blessings!

Apparently, the Midrash is not trying to teach us what a tzaddik and a *rasha* **do**, rather, who they **are**. The very definition of a tzaddik is one who recognizes and appreciates the environment around him. When he sees the sun rise or the sun set, he bursts forth with blessings, thanking Hashem for the incredible gift of day and night! When tasting delicious ice cream, he spontaneously erupts with a blessing, thanking Hashem for sensitive taste buds!

Not so a *rasha*. His behavior upon seeing or tasting the wonders of "nature" is indifferent, much like a stone—unmoved and unfeeling to the phenomenal stimuli all around it.

Life is not so much about *saying* blessings, but rather *living* blessings! We are practically drowning in the treasures and luxuries from Hashem, sent directly and specifically for each one of us. So let's soak it up! There is no end to how much goodness we can absorb!

OUR DUTY IS NOT TO ACHIEVE,
BUT ONLY TO DO AND TRY!
October 24, 2013

This was a common idea that my *rebbi* charged us with. This week's *parshah* (*Chayei Sarah*) sheds light on this fundamental principle.

A monumental midrash (*Bereishis Rabbah* 61:6) as elucidated by my great *rebbi*:

There was once a king who had a beautiful orchard. He entrusted a loyal servant with its care. One morning, the gardener found two trees that were intertwined. One tree bore luscious and nutritious fruit. The other tree bore rotten and poisonous fruit. Since they were intertwined, it was impossible to care for one without automatically caring for the other.

The gardener was confused. "If I water the good tree, the poisonous tree will also be watered. If I don't water either tree, the good tree will also die. What should I do?"

Then, he settled his mind. "I am but a worker here; whatever the owner of the orchard desires, he shall do. I am only flesh and blood. I fulfilled my obligation. Whatever the owner of the orchard chooses, he will do himself."

The Midrash compares the intertwined trees to Yitzchak and Yishmael, the sons of Avraham Avinu. At the end of his life, Avraham wanted to bless Yitzchak. The dilemma he faced was the same as the gardener's. If he only blessed Yitzchak (the good tree), Yishmael's (the poisonous tree) feelings would be hurt. If he were to bless both, it would bring terrible poison into the world. Yet, if he were not to bless either, the blessing to Yitzchak would be lost.

Now, let us keep in mind what this blessing

represented. The future of the entire Jewish nation rested upon this blessing. It was this blessing that would be passed down from Yitzchak to Yaakov, and from Yaakov to his children. And do not forget that Yaakov and Rivkah risked their lives to obtain this blessing. As well, Esav, a hardened criminal, cried bitterly when he realized that he had lost this blessing!

Considering all of this, how could Avraham nullify the destiny of the Jewish People just because he was worried about hurting Yishmael's feelings? Wouldn't the entire future history of our nation take precedence over the feelings of one wicked man?

Avraham understood that halachah did not permit him to mistreat anyone *even if* the eternity of the Jewish People was hanging in the balance.

Apparently, Avraham's example teaches us that we are only temporary, hired help in this world, contracted to do the will of Hashem—and nothing more! Much like the gardener, Avraham threw up his arms and ceded control. He said, "I am only flesh and blood. I live my life, and I do as much as I possibly can. And I am satisfied with that. If more is left to be done, I will not be burdened by that. I will leave that up to Hashem (the Owner of the orchard)."

As my *rebbi* always used to say—"If Hashem wants more than I can do, He can do it *without* me. And if Hashem does not want it, it will not get done even *with* me."

So let us keep in mind what Alfred Lord Tennyson said, "Ours is not to reason why. Ours is but to do and die."

CHAPTER THIRTEEN

Family and Friends

YEHUDA LOVED LIFE. HE WAS SPONTANEOUS IN SHARING that love with his nearest and dearest. It came across as love and care for his family. We felt safe in his presence. And he knew how to have—and create—a good time. In fact, our family memories are replete with the fun we shared in our pre-accident life.

Family Fun

The kids knew that if they wanted something, Abba was the one to approach. One specific story stands out in my mind.

We were out in the car, running some errands, and had to stop for gas.

"Mommy, can you buy us a chocolate bar?"

"A chocolate bar?" I repeated. "What are you talking about? This is a gas station, not a candy store. In the gas station, we buy gas, not candy."

"But Abba does!"

Ha! The cat was out of the bag. Yehuda loved chocolate and Yehuda loved his children, so chocolate at the gas station it was.

And no, they were not able to convince me. I left such indulgences to their father.

Their father came up with plenty of oddball ideas of his own.

It was a long summer evening.

"Quick!" Yehuda told the kids. "We're going out. Everyone get into pajamas!"

Go out? Get into pajamas? What was he thinking? Always a stickler for routine, I implored Yehuda to stick to our schedule so I could get the kids to bed in time. He assured me we could manage to do both.

"But what's the deal with the pajamas?"

"It'll be fun," he said.

Pajama clad, Yehuda and the kids climbed into the car as I (still dressed!) slowly trailed behind—and off we went to a drive-through car wash. As the rainbow-hued suds swished across the car, the kids shrieked with laughter and we sang songs at the top of our lungs.

Another time, Yehuda decided that we all needed a change of scenery. We quickly packed pajamas and a change of clothes and drove to a hotel ten minutes from our house. As we got there, we realized that if we hurried, we could still make it downtown in time to watch the sound-and-light show on Parliament Hill. We rushed into the car yet again and made it in the nick of time, just as the music began to play.

Every summer, Yehuda had the same goal: This would be the year he and Shmuly would bike downtown and back along the city's scenic Ottawa River Parkway bike paths. It was sixteen miles from the start of the bike path to downtown, and we were about six miles away from that. It was fun to humor and cheer them on, despite finding them practically passed out on the deck, not having gone nearly as far as they had hoped.

When the children were old enough to attend summer camp, it was Yehuda who would drive five hours south to pick them up when the session was over. This was also his way of spending quality time with them on the way home by taking them tubing down the Delaware River, or camping.

Our old home on Ardell Grove backed to a huge empty field. Yehuda would grab a football and call whichever kids were around to come join him in a game. Calls of "Hike!" and "How about them Vikings?" wafted through the kitchen window as the kids dashed after the ball.

You could take Yehuda out of Minnesota but you could never take the Minnesota out of Yehuda.

Mini Minnesota Vikings, Purim 2010.

Our construction-themed costumes, Purim 2013. Our *mishloach manos* were labeled with a thank-you note: "The construction is over, we're all moved in. Thanks for standing by us through thick and thin!"

We loved to dress up for Purim in matching costumes. Of course, we were all Minnesota Vikings one year, complete with hand-painted purple Vikings logo T-shirts made by Asna. Yitzchak's costume was crowned with a plastic Vikings hat. One year, we were a banana bunch with the Chiquita banana logo. We continued our tradition even after the accident. The first Purim after we moved into our newly renovated home on Roselawn, we were construction-themed.

Other years, we were the Rockin' Rollin' Simeses, and the Simes

Mimes. Our friends eagerly anticipated the great costume reveal. It is amazing what 2-for-$7 T-shirts from Michaels can do for morale.

Chanukah had its own fun. Motza'ei Shabbos Chanukah was reserved for a family party—no students, just us. This was the night we fried latkes, played dreidel, and handed out gifts to each child. But first the kids would huddle outside our locked bedroom door, listening to the crinkle of wrapping paper and trying to guess what might be in the boxes—all the while reminding us that we had had many days and nights before and on Chanukah to wrap the presents; why did we have to keep them waiting? The suspense was "killing them"!

We would finally emerge from our room, laden with piles of presents. In age order from youngest to eldest, the gifts would be distributed in a pompous and suspense-inducing ceremony. Each child in turn had to stand on a chair. Yehuda would play the sound track of the "Rocky" intro—and only then could s/he begin to unwrap the package. Most times, we were successful at choosing an appropriate gift. Occasionally there were tears of disappointment, or frustration due to the lack of batteries. Originally, I thought gift-giving should be delayed until a child was old enough to understand what a gift was. Yehuda felt it should be done regardless of age. He always wanted to give and make others happy. Of course, once I heard his reasoning, I agreed. That is how even the youngest kids became the proud owners of some new toy or game every Chanukah.

The accident did not stop him from spending time with us. In fact, it became more important than ever. We cherished the time we were able to spend together.

When Yehuda was physically up to it, we based our schedule on his. Supper was at five every evening. He would sit in his place at the head of the table and ask the kids about their day. Following his routine from before the accident, he would think of a number from one to ten, and whoever guessed it had the first turn. This continued until everyone got to share. After supper was homework time. Based on the needs of the children and Yehuda's abilities, we would divide up the responsibilities.

Elisheva doing
homework with Abba.

Chan doing homework
with Abba.

When he was feeling strong and his pain could be kept at bay, he would join us on outings on Sundays or days off. Spring was the easiest—no snow to make maneuvering the wheelchair nearly impossible, no cumbersome outdoor gear to keep him warm. Summer was second best. As long as he was well hydrated and out of direct sunlight, Yehuda was able to take the kids to the playground on his own to watch their antics and athletic abilities. When Shmuly or the

Yehuda taking the kids to the park.

Fun at the park.

Have wheels, will travel!

girls were home from yeshivah or school, we would venture out a little farther. On one such occasion, Shmuly drove Yehuda and the kids to Parc Omega, a safari drive-thru in Quebec. Other times we went to Gotta Paint, a paint-your-own-ceramics crafts store. Yehuda wore wrists guards to stabilize his hands. By placing the paintbrush in the wrist guard, he was able to move his hands to choose paint colors and paint. He surprised me with a hand-painted spoon rest.

Sometimes friends would drive him to events. Yehuda and the younger boys had a great time at the Museum of Aviation.

Strawberry picking at one of Ottawa's berry farms. Yehuda appreciated the beauty of nature even more after the accident.

The Museum of Civilization was another favorite destination.

Lichvod Shabbos Kodesh

Shabbos was Yehuda's day to shine and express his gratitude to us, both before and after the accident. From our very first Shabbos as parents, he kept the tradition of saying *Birkas Habanim*. As the family grew, it became an even bigger highlight of the week. Yehuda would close

Yehuda with the kids at the Canada Aviation and Space Museum.

his eyes, place his hands on the head of each child in turn, and bless them all. Once they reached toddler age, they would pop out of their seats and run to stand by Yehuda. They knew that for *brachos*, the order went from oldest to youngest. Sometimes one of the munchkins would sneak in and cut the line. With a smile, Yehuda would motion to him or her to go back and return soon. As they got a little older, Yehuda added another tradition; he would take a few moments to whisper a sentimental message into each child's ear, followed by, "I'm proud of you." The children glowed as they walked back to their seats, feeling like a million dollars.

After the accident, Yehuda could no longer raise his hands. The children would go to him, place their heads in his lap, then take Yehuda's hands and gently place them on their heads. The youngests learned how to flip over the lap tray of the wheelchair, climb up on Abba's lap, put their heads down and place Abba's hands on their heads. Sweet little nothings were whispered in their ears.

When Shmuly and the girls were away, they would call in every Friday for their weekly *brachah* and message, taking into account the three-to-six-hour time difference. If Yehuda was in the hospital, we would go to him, not leaving without a blessing. After he was trached and could no longer speak, they would go up to him and wait silently until he motioned with his eyes that he was done, then drop a gentle kiss on his head.

In our home, the song *"Eishes Chayil"* was sung with a unique twist. We had first seen it at Mom's cousins' Shabbos table. After singing the first words, *"Eishes chayil mi yimtza*—A woman of valor, who can find," Walter would turn to Malka, his wife of several decades, and say, "Well, I found her!" Yehuda did the same every week. Every week he professed that I made the best chicken soup he ever tasted. He then described Mr. Black Beard, an iconic figure who spent Shabbos at his parents' home. As a child, Yehuda was convinced that the old man used black shoe polish to dye his beard so that he would look younger. Mr. Black Beard slurped his soup—proclaiming *"Lichvod Shabbos Kodesh"* before each slurp. Yehuda encouraged us to enjoy our Shabbos food for the honor of Shabbos—minus the slurping, of course.

Another favorite Shabbos story was that of Dave Brenner. Dave grew up in an irreligious home. After his first year of college, he began to search for the meaning of life. He backpacked through country after country, ending up in Israel, where he took a few months off to study Judaism. Dave was enthusiastic, but his parents were opposed. Upon his return home, they forbade him from keeping Shabbos. He tried anyway, but it was just too hard to do it alone. He sat down with his family to watch a late-night talk show. The guest was teaching the host, Dave, the phrase *"Shabbat shalom."* As the show came to a close, the camera zoomed in on the guest, who was saying goodbye to the host: *"Shabbat shalom,* Dave!" Dave Brenner was transfixed; all he heard was *"Shabbat shalom,* Dave!" reverberating in his head. Within days, Dave Brenner was back in Israel. From then on, we would wish each other, *"Shabbat shalom,* Dave!" every Shabbos. In time, it morphed into a salutation regardless of the day of the week.

Every other week without fail, on Friday afternoon, I received a flower delivery with a personalized card. This never failed to remind me of the Friday after we were engaged: Yehuda had flown off to Israel to spend Pesach with his family and would be gone for twenty-two days. The doorbell in my parents' home rang. It was the florist's delivery man dropping off three dozen red roses with a card attached to each dozen. I was touched, yet also let down. I suspected that Yehuda had arranged a delivery for each of the three weeks he would be gone and the flower shop erroneously sent all three at once! At the coaching of my mother, I called the florist to explain my disappointment. The manager was completely apologetic, full of good wishes for a long and prosperous marriage, and assured me that they would send a dozen flowers at their expense on the next two Fridays.

Yehuda loved gadgets. One day he arrived home from work carrying a huge box. He called everyone to gather round as he unveiled the surprise. It was a juice maker. (When he was growing up, Yehuda's family had a juicer and he wanted to share the experience with us.) From another bag, he pulled out oranges—odd shaped ones with blemishes and bruises, perfect for making fresh-squeezed orange juice. He demonstrated how the machine worked and put the kids in charge of making juice for Shabbos. Every week brought another surprise in the form of fruits to add to the concoction.

The cold winter Friday nights were graced with a different brew— tea essence. Yehuda would combine several tea bags from various boxes of different flavors. Needless to say, some varieties fared better than others!

These experiences made Shabbos our favorite day of the week. Yehuda and I would often ask the children: "Who can guess my favorite day of the week? Shabbos! Who can guess my second-to-favorite day of the week? Friday! Which day is the hardest day of the week for me? Sunday! Why? Because it is the furthest from Shabbos!"

When I got married, the song I chose to walk down the aisle to was *"V'zakeinu L'kabel Shabbosos"*—Make us worthy of welcoming Shabbos with great delight, enjoying wealth and respect, and free from too many transgressions. I wanted to build a home based on the foundation of Shabbos and enrich our lives with family and friends.

Though our stream of weekly guests had to stop after the accident, it was our fervent wish to be able to resume hosting at some point. It was during those years that the words, *U'virtzoncha hani'ach lanu Hashem Elokeinu shelo tehei tzarah…* — "May it please You, grant us rest, with no trouble, unhappiness, or weeping on our day of rest," were uttered weekly with great intensity. Please, Hashem, keep Yehuda safe. Do not let there be an emergency or a crisis—not on Shabbos!

Gifts and Surprises

Yehuda loved to surprise me. In 2013, three years after the accident, he arranged a present for me for our twenty-first anniversary. It clearly took a lot of coordination, determination, and effort on his part and on the part of his friends who had to make all the preparations on his behalf. All I knew was that I had to get dressed up and drive Yehuda and me to the Casino du Lac-Leamy. We had to be there at a specific time. When we announced ourselves at the front desk, we were directed to the elevator and told which room to go to. By now, my curiosity was at its peak. We found the designated room and knocked on the door. The door opened and music began to play. Our friends, professional musicians, were playing the violin and the cello. Yehuda had given them a list of our favorites, and now they serenaded us, starting with the songs that accompanied us as we walked down the aisle at our wedding. It was touching and meaningful. I felt like a queen.

Two years later, the plan was so original that I almost ruined it completely. The doorbell rang, which in and of itself indicated something unusual. Most people, especially caregivers and therapists, just knocked and walked in. I was occupied with the kids and sent someone to open the door.

"Ma, someone is at the door for you. He said he's here to paint."

"Here to paint? Are you kidding me? Paint? Now of all times? Here of all places? Do I look like I ordered a paint job? Tell him no thank you. It must be a solicitor."

"But Ma, he says he was told to come to this address."

"Come to this address? Believe me, the last thing I need on my head right now is a paint job."

I walked to the door to send him packing. He kept insisting he was told to come. Meanwhile, Yehuda was smiling broadly and motioning toward his eye-gaze computer. The kids asked him if we should have the man come in to explain what was going on. Yehuda shook his head up and down. After going in circles for a little while longer, we finally put the pieces together. Yehuda had a friend hire this man to do a caricature of us for our anniversary. The painter had come to paint a picture of us, not to paint our walls! I went to change into portrait-appropriate attire. The kids gathered around as Yehuda and I sat still as can be and watched our portrait come to life.

Even when he had a hard time communicating verbally, his message was quite clear: I was important to him and he treasured me.

> Yesterday was our twenty-third wedding anniversary! Thank G-d!
>
> For this auspicious occasion, I hired an experienced painter to come to our house and create an image of my wife and myself. The question arose whether he should paint me in a wheelchair or not.
>
> I am interested to know what you think about this dilemma and why.
>
> From the Rolling Rabbi blog,
> "The Survey," June 30, 2015

Anniversaries were not the only time he surprised me. One day, pre-accident, he came home with a box—it was a sewing machine. One of his colleagues had won it in a raffle. As a professional seamstress, she already had a state-of-the-art unit. Yehuda knew I had always wanted to learn to sew. Especially with a growing family of mostly girls, sewing could come in handy. How complicated could it be to sew a skirt? Think of all the money I would save! Yehuda always encouraged me to follow my dreams; this time he found a way to make it a reality. He bought me the sewing machine and a colleague of mine offered to give me lessons. I made matching skirts and coordinated outfits for the five girls. How proud I was to take them to the Loblaws photo studio to capture it for the camera! As my skills progressed, Yehuda purchased various sewing supplies to help me along.

Another time, it was a wooden case of new silverware to be used for Shabbos. He became a member of the store's club membership. With every purchase, a hole was punched into a marked card toward earning prizes and rewards. Yehuda was certain he would punch his way through the card. He probably would have.

Friendship

Yehuda cultivated close relationships with friends. Although many considered him their teacher and mentor, he also enjoyed having a wholesome good time with them. Rabbi David Rotenberg described Yehuda's love of magic tricks and sports.

> When we first got to know the Simeses, and had the pleasure of sharing occasional Shabbos meals together, it somehow came up that I did card magic. At the time, the kids were quite young, and yet, even though they were excited to see some tricks, their reaction came nowhere close to the absolute glee exhibited by their father. He would often keep his cool during the trick, but as soon as I found his card, or made the other ones turn blank, or whatever that day's effect was, he would lose his mind with bewilderment. Soon, he started yelling *"mechashef!"* any time I finished a trick, which I took as a particularly hilarious backhanded compliment, to think he was so impressed by my sleight of hand that he would accuse me of performing some sort of forbidden dark magic. In later years, I knew that if I was coming to visit after not hanging out for a while, and especially if he was in the hospital, I needed to be prepared with at least one good trick.

> I remember one day when Rabbi Simes was at the Queensway

Carleton, and I was coming to help with *tefillin*. I arrived outside of ICU visiting hours, so I played the clergy card. "Yes, I'm here to visit with Rabbi Yehuda Simes," I told them. "I'm also a rabbi, and I need to assist him with his prayers." Well, when I got into his room, he was extremely happy to see me, but admitted that he just was not up to putting on *tefillin* at that time. He did, however, beckon me closer to surreptitiously ask if I could show him a card trick. I then drew the curtain for some privacy while we did our "super spiritual rabbi stuff," worried the entire time that a nurse would come in and discover that I had snuck into the ICU outside of visiting hours, claiming to be a rabbi, just to show my friend a magic trick.

Although there are a number of special memories I have of my friendship with Rabbi Simes, perhaps the one that I'm most proud of is the time we went to the Senators game against the Minnesota Wild. I honestly don't remember how it came up, but somehow we got it in our minds that we wanted to go to a hockey game together. Obviously, it was the first time since the accident that he would be doing anything at all like that, but we were determined to make it happen. Although I knew that the arena was wheelchair accessible, he wanted to make sure that we wouldn't be sitting in what he called "the corral." So I called the arena, and after speaking with a few people, I figured out an alternate spot for us to get accessible seats. I also checked the schedule, and discovered that his hometown Wild were coming to town on a weekday night in November. After confirming the date together, I bought us the tickets…and also made a couple of special arrangements.

In the weeks leading up to the game, any time we saw each other or corresponded by email, he would make sure to…talk about how the Wild was going to win. In the days before the game, I came over to learn how to get him in and out of his special van. The Friday night before, the Sadinskys were over for

Shabbos. When they found out about the plan on Sunday, they immediately tracked down and bought him a Minnesota Wild jersey to wear to the game. Having split allegiance between the Wild and Senators, he also wore a Sens cap a cousin had given me, and I had given to him. The days before the game, our wives spoke about what his favorite treats were, and mine went and bought all sorts of snacks to assemble us each a take-out container packed with candy. He could barely stop eating Tootsie Rolls the entire game. By luck, a group from Machzikei happened to be at the game the same night, and when people heard that we were there, several members of the Jewish community swung by to say hi and to hang out with us either during the game or intermission.

During the game, he seemed to be having the time of his life, and whenever the Wild scored, cheered heartily... At the start of the third period, I  revealed the biggest surprise of the night. I told him, "I hope you don't have plans on rushing home at the end of the game." Thanks to a contact... we were going to get to meet a couple of the players. He couldn't believe it. After the game, which the Wild won, we got escorted down to the players' family and friends meet-and-greet area, and we met a few players, took some pictures, and got some autographs. It was amazing.

While he was at the game—and I experienced this with him on a number of other occasions—he was so present in the moment,

just enjoying himself, and just wanting to be "one of the guys."
Afterward, he wrote a whole post on his blog about the fun time
he had…but he was also able to turn his experience into an
entire lesson on what life is really all about. I suppose that that
was part of his *gadlus*, and it is something that I try to emulate.
He went to that game because he wanted to. It was fun. He was
never "above it." He enjoyed it in every way. But afterward, he
didn't just reflect on the entertainment factor; he made sure he
could use his experience as a way of inspiring or teaching others.

CHAPTER FOURTEEN

Planning Our Dream Trip

J UST BEFORE ROSH HASHANAH OF 2013, BECKY CALLED FROM Israel with exciting news. Her daughter Osnat's engagement to Shay Meyerovich was official! How quickly time had flown! How could the baby born a month after Yehuda and I got married possibly be old enough to get married herself? It made me feel positively ancient. We discussed when the wedding would be—likely Chanukah, where the couple would live, and a myriad of other details.

When I hung up the phone, a hundred thoughts were racing through my head. *I am going to that wedding! I am going to that wedding! I don't know how. I'll need to figure out the details, but I am going. Someone needs to be the Simes family representative, and who deserves this trip more than I do?* But one thing was certain: I was not going to tell Yehuda anything until I had it all figured out. No sense in scaring him or making him unnecessarily nervous about my going too far away. I would explore all possible scenarios, analyze what Yehuda's care involved, which parts normally involved me and whom I could trust to take over for me. Not only I would have to feel secure; obviously, Yehuda would have to feel protected as well.

As I toyed with the idea, an inner voice kept whispering that it was wishful thinking. But I continued wishing and thinking. *Could you imagine going to Eretz Yisrael! All by yourself! To recharge your spiritual batteries, to* daven *at the Kosel and Kever Rochel, to dance at your niece's wedding! To travel on an airplane for ten hours all by yourself! To enjoy a weeklong vacation from all responsibilities! To do what you want, when you want, without having to watch the clock...* The more I thought about it, the more I envisioned myself on that trip of a lifetime. It certainly seemed like a lifetime since the last time I was there. Every day since the accident seemed like another lifetime, with crisis after crisis and constant adjustment to new degrees of normal.

Yehuda could be told none of this until all the details were organized. As I had already learned from our previous trips together and my quick trips away, there were loads of details. Was I being completely unrealistic? I called Fraidel and told her I had a secret to share and would need help. She agreed that it was a great idea and that I should definitely go. Maybe I was just engaging in selective hearing, as she was usually supportive of my crazy ideas.

My secret was safe. It was mine to distract me and give me what to look forward to as I got ready for the Yamim Nora'im and Sukkos.

> I have an ENORMOUS announcement to make. But first, allow me to give you a bit of an introduction.
>
> I have experienced quite a few life-altering events over the past three years. A few examples come to mind.
>
> Surviving a crash that should have killed me, according to natural law. Weaning off of my tracheotomy, and being able to breathe once again. Extracting my feeding tube, and being able to swallow once again. Feeling a pin prick, and finding sensation once again. Moving my arms with a slight flicker, and recognizing movement once again. Building up my tolerance for sitting upright, and enjoying posture once again. Strapping into my tilt table, and rejoicing over standing once again. Actualizing an adventure to New York City, and learning that I can travel once again.
>
> Truthfully, it would be impossible to list my many

mind-blowing accomplishments, because there would be no end. Indeed, Hashem has blessed me every step of the way!

Now, about two months ago, my niece in Israel got engaged! She is the daughter of my eldest sister. An incredible girl linking together with a fantastic guy! Their wedding is scheduled for December 9th.

Concurrent with that, a dream has been brewing in my mind. The seeds of this dream were planted ever since I was born. My family ingrained within me a love for the Land of Israel. My parents yearned to settle in our Holy Land. And they happily sent my three older sisters to live there, knowing full well that the most they would ever see them would be the summertimes—until they themselves could move there.

Their dream finally became a reality when I graduated high school. My parents held a huge garage sale, ridding themselves of sentimental attachments, and separating themselves from the community that they loved—all for the privilege of rebuilding their lives in Eretz Yisrael. So my parents and I packed up and made *aliyah*. It was then that our entire family was reunited for the first time since I was six years old, firmly rooted on holy soil.

The next three years were a glorious time in my life, living and learning in the Land of Israel. It was a singular uplifting experience in my life.

A few years later, my wife and I began to build a family. I kept Israel in the forefront of my bedtime stories and reminiscences. I, just like my parents, wished to keep the flame burning in the hearts of the next generation.

We visited Israel a few times as a young family. As the years went by, I occasionally traveled there to visit family for special occasions.

Just over three years ago, I promised my wife a trip to

Israel. It would be my eighteenth wedding anniversary gift. A dream vacation, just the two of us, without the kids (eight at the time). By then, it had been thirteen years since my wife had been back to Israel. Just the thought of it brought goosebumps.

Then Hashem showed us who the true party planner was. Because of the "accident," we were forced to take a three-year hiatus from our vacation plans. A three-year time period when it was out of the realm of possibility to even imagine embarking upon such a journey. The obstacles and impossibilities are too numerous to enumerate.

Suddenly, my niece became engaged. I was finally at the point when I was physically and emotionally prepared to make my dream a reality. The engagement triggered electrifying thoughts of, "I will NOT live the rest of my days without visiting Israel again. I will NOT live the rest of my days without visiting the Kosel and our holy sites again. I will NOT live the rest of my days without visiting the graves of my parents again."

So, ignoring all of the "impossibilities," I triumphantly announced to my extended family, who were with us for Sukkos, that I would be going to Israel for the wedding.

From the Rolling Rabbi blog, "On
Eagles' Wings," November 3, 2013

Our sukkah was full of my family enjoying a beautiful daytime Yom Tov meal. The sun was shining and, for Ottawa, the weather was perfect. As we enjoyed our soup, we engaged in some pleasant conversation. The conversation turned to Osnat's wedding. Yehuda looked up from his soup. "I'm going," he casually announced. "When I go to the wedding…"

I do not remember the rest of his sentence. There was complete and stunned silence as everyone froze with their spoons in the air. My heart started palpitating. *Well, there goes my vacation!* I nervously looked over at Fraidel, who looked back at me with equally shocked eyes. This could not be happening. *How on earth does he think he is going to the wedding? Just who does he think will be taking him? Me? Exactly how is that going to work? That would be all work and no vacation. This is not happening. Nope. Either I'm going by myself or not at all. Going together would be way too much work and effort. Just getting into the car is an ordeal!*

I looked over at Yehuda and repeated what he had just said. "When you go to the wedding…?"

"Yes," he beamed, "when I go to the wedding. Didn't I tell you I decided I was going to the wedding?"

I shook my head from side to side. "No," I replied, "you didn't tell me. You must have forgotten to mention it."

Everyone laughed and started discussing the trip to Israel. Trying to remain calm distracted me from hearing the rest of the conversation. When the meal ended, Yehuda got ready for a nap. He joked and laughed with excitement. Inside, I was crying, but I did not have the heart to disappoint him. So much had been taken from him—would I be the one to wrest this opportunity from him as well? I told him I was already planning on going and had not wanted to tell him yet. I needed time to make arrangements so I could present him with a solid plan of action.

> One by one, we conquered each item on the list. My physiotherapy has increased in intensity.
>
> All of this insane planning and prepping had been kept under wraps since Sukkos, because we didn't want to get sidetracked by an avalanche of well-wishers and cheering on.
>
> Until...
>
> NOW!!!

The time has come to officially and unhesitatingly shout, at the top of our lungs, that for once and for all, we are making the enormous and colossal journey of a lifetime...

We are going with Hashem's help to the land of our fathers...

THE LAND OF ISRAEL!!!

D-Day is December 4, 2013! As of today, thirty-one days!

May all of our hearts' desires be fulfilled by Hashem, speedily in our lifetimes!

From the Rolling Rabbi blog, "On Eagles' Wings," November 3, 2013

Hello everyone from the freezing and frozen land of the Eskimos,

Okay guys—you better be sitting down for this one! I don't think I've ever made an announcement even remotely close to what I'm about to say.

Now, don't start jumping to conclusions (conquer your urge to read the end of this email). I'm not talking about measly things such as phenomenal amounts of time I spend standing or ridiculous increases in numbers of speeches and teaching. Or even Uncle Harvey and Aunt Margie's visit to us this coming Sunday. All that may be true—and yet, they pale in comparison to what I'm about to shout at the top of my lungs.

But first, some background. I've always had this dream of living in Israel. That's why I didn't think twice when our parents took me with them to settle there. Indeed—I happily sacrificed everything that I held near and dear to my heart just to have the privilege of making that dream come true!

And even when I felt compelled to return to America for a short two-year stint to earn a bachelor's degree—it was always my intention to return to Israel forever.

How could I leave behind Daddy's tears when we landed at Ben-Gurion? How can I forsake my old stomping grounds on Rechov Hamapilim? All the ups and downs with Mommy—my nightly visits that I was too embarrassed to share with my friends.

And of course—the mama hens Becky and Judy, who cared for me and guided me through a most difficult time of my life. A turbulent downswing when I felt all alone and with nowhere to go. I just wanted to be normal—like all my friends. Why must I be the only one saying *Yizkor* when the rest of the yeshivah packs out? Why must I be the only one saying Kaddish? I felt such pressure—and it was only the homes of Becky and Judy that kept me at peace.

Well, the next eighteen years were a fairy tale—as you all know. Suddenly, yet another overwhelming challenge/opportunity. So, for the last three years I've clenched on to that dream—never daring to let it go.

And now—a brand-new opportunity! Yes, indeed—sometimes what you wish for is what you get!

It may be that it took the engagement of a special young lady to get me going.

The dream began taking shape. Slowly but surely the steps began to actualize. Obstacles? To be sure! But without obstacles to smash through—we would not be who we are today!

It's a new reality to embrace and conquer! So here we go!!!

Put on your crash helmets! Securely fasten your bulletproof vests! Pull up your army boots! Because what I'm about to say is liable to completely blow you right out of your house!

Steady now—hold on tight! This is no time for feeble hearts or weak internal systems!

WE ARE COMING! YES, IT'S TRUE—WE ARE COMING! I WILL NOT GIVE IT UP! I WILL NOT LIVE THE REST OF MY DAYS WITHOUT SEEING THE LAND AGAIN! NOTHING CAN POSSIBLY HOLD ME BACK. NOT NOW AND NOT EVER! QUADRIPLEGIA? HA—I LAUGH IN YOUR FACE. DON'T EVEN THINK OF HOLDING ME DOWN! I AM SO DRIVEN YOU COULDN'T POSSIBLY BELIEVE!

I always promised Shaindel a trip for only the two of us to Israel. In fact, it was only the unfortunate occurrence three years ago that momentarily got in the way. Momentarily, I say—but not forever! I WILL MAKE THIS COME TRUE WITH HASHEM'S HELP!

From the Rolling Rabbi blog, "Surprising
My Family," November 7, 2013

Without exaggeration, hundreds of details needed to be worked out. Many of them involved the help of our therapists who alerted us to their existence. All I could think of were the arrangements we needed to make to get to Montreal, Toronto, Rochester, and New York. Would Yehuda's doctors agree to this crazy idea? Would our health insurance plan cover him overseas? As far as I could see, he definitely had a "preexisting condition"!

I called the insurance company. They assured me that as long as Yehuda was given medical clearance by his doctor before we left, he was considered healthy. In the event of a medical emergency, he would be covered. Go figure. That was the first time in three years that I heard the words "quadriplegia" and "healthy" in the same sentence.

Next: Would his doctor allow it? Well, considering that Yehuda had a long list of doctors, it was hard to know which of them needed to be consulted. We started with his physiatrist, Dr. Vidya Sreenivasan, who was absolutely ecstatic about the idea. She was overjoyed to see Yehuda moving on with his life and adapting his dreams to his new physical reality rather than letting his limitations define him. In fact, she was so certain of this, that she wrote a letter to our insurance company explaining why this trip was so important to him therapeutically. Based on this letter, the insurance company agreed to cover the complete cost of his ticket.

One office visit was a source of great mirth to us…okay, maybe gallows humor. We asked the doctor a general question: "Is there anything we should know before we go?"

The doctor said, "Let me check my database and see." He logged on to the Canada World Health website. Apparently, there was an outbreak of polio in Israel—some infiltration in the water system or something—and the public health department was recommending that everyone who went to Israel or the Middle East get a polio vaccine.

When you hear polio, what do you think? Paralysis, right? So I said, "Good! Let's make sure he gets that one! We wouldn't want him to be paralyzed!" The doctor regarded me quizzically while I stifled giggles.

When we got home, we told the kids, "Guess what, guys! Good news! We found out today that Mommy and Abba have to get a polio shot because we're going to Israel and polio could cause paralysis. You know, it's very dangerous."

So they said, "Oh yeah, good thing Abba's getting that one."

I said, "Yeah, and I'm going to get it too because we don't want to play bumper chairs."

"You know, Ma," one of the kids said, "we're morbid sometimes."

"We're not morbid," I answered. "We're just laughing at ourselves."

I think humor was a huge factor in helping us cope.

One more doctor needed to be consulted: Dr. Douglas McKim, the respirologist. After examining Yehuda and setting up a series of appointments to track his health, Dr. McKim gave us the go-ahead to book tickets. The condition was that Yehuda had to follow very strict protocols while traveling, and especially on the airplane. We could not believe our ears! This could actually happen!

Booking tickets when traveling in a power chair poses a whole slew of issues. We had to determine the exact weight and dimensions of the chair to be sure it could fit onto the aircraft. We had to find out exactly what kind of battery is used, as some are banned from aircraft. At which point in the journey would the wheelchair be taken from us? When it was taken, how would we get Yehuda out of the chair without the help of our ceiling track lift which hoisted him up into the air? Once he was out of his wheelchair, how would he get into a seat on the airplane? His wheelchair was equipped with a specialized air cushion which prevented him from getting pressure sores. Individuals who are paralyzed and cannot move themselves run the risk of skin infections. How would we prevent that on a ten-hour flight?

> My Trusty Helper.
> It's the substitute for my mobility—in a very real way, an extension of my own body. The inspiration behind the title for this blog.
> Should it break down or malfunction in any way (as happens on occasion), I become literally powerless, with no destination in sight.
> Leaving it out of my eyesight causes me extreme panic.
> A very precious commodity indeed!
> What am I referring to?
> My power chair, of course! (Never to be confused with an electric chair!)
> So here I am—conceptualizing traveling together with my faithful "friend." How will I bring it with me? It certainly won't fit under the seat ahead of me, nor in the overhead storage area! And sitting in it will not be

an option, because it would block the aisle. I can just imagine all of the passengers climbing around, over, and under me in order to get to the bathroom! No, no, no! Not happening!

What actually happens is, the airline personnel supply me with a "transfer chair." This is a mini manual wheelchair in which they pull me onto the actual aircraft. My preassigned helpers manually transfer me (a "pivot transfer") into this miniature chair from my own power chair. After pulling me up the aisle and settling me beside my preassigned seat, I'm blessed with another manual transfer so that I gracefully land in my seat for the next ten hours.

Back to my power chair, which was left back at the cargo door. Problem—the maximum height allowance is thirty-one inches. The back of my chair? Forty-two inches. So, after investigating various options, the best method will be for my wife to dismantle the entire back of my power chair. The now disassembled chair is ready to be loaded onto the plane, together with the other cargo.

All of these things must be accomplished within five minutes. They load us first, under the impatient stares of the airline personnel and who knows how many passengers.

I can just picture the scene: Numerous airline personnel barking instructions, reminders, and orders. A few hundred passengers, including nervous fathers, pulled-in-many-directions mothers, rambunctious children, and aloof businessmen.

Talk about pressure!

But maybe there is a lesson in all this. About how to keep our wits about us even when the world is crashing down around us! How to remain cool, calm, and collected when intense pressure threatens to take us over!

The key is, place your trust in Hashem, and then, trust yourself. Trust that you have what it takes to banish your fear and to hold tight to the immense strength within you!

From the Rolling Rabbi blog, "Turning the Cumbersome into Cruise Control," November 19, 2013

Who would provide care for Yehuda during the flight and once we got to Israel? It took a long time to train a new caregiver on the specifics needed for Yehuda's care. Given the experiences we had in the comfort of our own home, it was harrowing to think of having to train someone new in a foreign country. The fallout could be deadly.

We discussed our trip with Carol. Carol was one of our first caregivers and had proven herself to be one of the very best ones we had. While she was not a nurse, she had more common sense than most of the nurses we dealt with. She was super sweet and easygoing. Carol became very close to Nochi, often taking care of him at night when he was an infant so I could sleep. She agreed to go on the trip with us, obviously at our expense on top of her pay. Her one condition was that we had to take her to see the "Crying Wall."

Becky and her husband Moti took care of accommodations and equipment rental on their side of the Atlantic.

Yehuda's therapists designed a rigorous schedule to get him fit, trained, and in shape for the journey. Yehuda was psyched. He crashed his records and was in the best shape physically, mentally, and emotionally.

I just wanted to fill you in on today's breakthrough! I was doing my normal cycling routine, but I didn't quite have it today—I think I might be battling a cold (for me—a real battle!).

Whereas normally I would quickly get onto the tilt table for some energetic standing/power exercising, we took the time for range-of-motion stretches. My physiotherapist began by twisting my hand into pronation (regular for you—but upside down for me) and holding...

Suddenly, I noticed a DEFINITE FLICKER in my fourth digit!

My physio was astounded! This was a case of new recovery!...

But what practical use is there in having a flickering finger when somebody squeezes my wrist in an unnatural hold?

You see, this just might define a brand-new frontier! Because a flicker today may be a movement tomorrow! And a movement tomorrow may be connected to another movement the next day! And the end of this frontier just might be...

AN ABILITY TO PICK UP THINGS!!

Take today as an example...

I was at a kiddush in shul, and as usual, there were various pretzels and yummy chips. For a fleeting moment, the thought crossed my mind, *How aggravating it is to wait for someone to hand me a few crunchy treats. If only I could turn over my wrist and pick up a couple...*

Frustration resolved!

And then, I began to think. This mirrors life itself.

When we make a small movement toward the performance of a mitzvah, it will lead us to a larger movement. Before you know it, we will be able to connect it to another movement. And after a while of growing and climbing upward, we will grow into completely different people!

Indeed, one tiny step in the right direction leads to

a much larger stride. As our rabbis teach us, *Mitzvah goreres mitzvah*—"One mitzvah leads to another."

Always keep at the forefront of your mind the significance of tiny steps. They may not seem like much today, but they will inevitably lead to bigger and greater things in your bright future!

From the Rolling Rabbi blog, "My Amazing Recovery," November 16, 2013

The salvation of Hashem comes in a blink of an eye. This was a common saying of my great *rebbi, zt"l*. He would often quote the Radak (Rav David Kimchi) who explains this beautiful idea.

Are we saying that Hashem's salvation arrives so quickly as to be compared to the swift shutting of an eyelid?

But, when Hashem's salvations come to deliver us from pain and sorrow, they always arrive on target, exactly when and where we need them.

What, then, is the use in learning about the alacrity of Hashem's rescuing us when we truly need Him? There is nothing novel or unique about this teaching!

Apparently, teaches the Radak, this verse about the similarity of a salvation to a blink of an eye, is informing us *when* the salvation finally arrives, not necessarily *how*.

It doesn't come soon after a challenge presents itself. There's no such thing as a "quick fix." Overcoming a challenge *requires* a lot of soul searching and introspection. For example: What is my challenge coming to teach me? How can I grow and become a better person, not *in spite of* my trial, but *because of* my trial? Why am I not changing into a stronger and more fortified individual?

"I'm not learning a thing and I'm not changing at all. I'm not growing or becoming any greater than I was before." This sense of hopelessness and helplessness is called *yiush* in Hebrew. It's when you have totally given up all hope of digging out of your unfortunate situation. It's when you look at yourself in the mirror and say, "This is me, and I'll stay like this forever. I can't, and I won't, ever change."

At this point, you are at rock bottom—all is bleak and dark. Nothing or no one could possibly help you.

Suddenly, without warning, there is a flash. A striking light that urgently lifts you up, and shouts at you, "Get going!"

This is what is meant by *the salvation of Hashem comes in the blink of an eye!*

This powerful idea came to me yesterday when I was pounding the cycling machine. About three weeks ago, I set a goal for myself. The longest I could imagine staying on the bike was twenty minutes, i.e., approximately one thousand revolutions. I had set this lofty goal to be accomplished by the time we left for Israel (December 4th).

Last week, I was far from my goal. The whole week I was weakened by a stomach bug. The most I managed to cycle was only for about five minutes.

And it's true—I felt a total sense of *yiush*, a dreadful feeling of regression. The finish line seemed unreachable. I was crushed by an image of a steam roller, flattening every last vestige of will and drive.

Then, out of nowhere, I reached sixteen minutes on the bike!

The very next day—eighteen minutes!

And then, the smoke cleared completely. I felt as though Hashem was holding my hand and pulling me beyond my outer limits.

At nineteen minutes, I felt a second wind! Struggling just a bit, I crossed over my long-awaited goal, the goal that appeared unattainable just a few days prior.

Twenty minutes came quickly. However, I did not stop to celebrate. Instead, I turned up the speed—pounding, churning, rocking. I could not stop; I would not stop! Nothing or no one could hold me back!

Smashing through just beyond twenty-one minutes, I looked back and thought, *Gee—that was easy!*

In a blink of an eye, Hashem's salvation cut through my *yiush* and made me forget the difficult road I had traversed.

Share this lesson with me! Remember, it's not over— UNTIL IT'S OVER!!!

> *From the Rolling Rabbi blog, "The*
> *Salvation of Hashem Comes in a Blink*
> *of an Eye," December 1, 2013*

This is it! ... We leave to the airport in just a few hours! A quick thought...

This afternoon, my family attended a Chanukah luncheon at my kids' school. At the end of the program, the principal asked me if it would be okay if he wished my wife and me mazel tov over the microphone on account of our trip to Israel tomorrow.

I said, "Sure!"

Now, you have to understand that everyone in that room already knew about our plan to travel to Israel. So when he announced, "Mazel tov to the Simeses upon their upcoming trip to Israel!"—no one noticed or even raised their eyes! There were no standing ovations or shouts of joy! No one rushed over to give us hugs and high-fives! Finally, after three and a half years, we no longer enjoyed "celebrity status." We were finally privileged to become "regular" and "normal"—just like everyone else!

That is...

UNTIL WE GET TO ISRAEL!!!

From the Rolling Rabbi blog,
"It's Zero Hour!!" December 3, 2013

CHAPTER FIFTEEN

Our Unforgettable Israel Adventure

Our Israel trip empowered us with so many important lessons!

Before our trip, I felt like I'd plateaued in terms of risk-taking and my comfort level. But I knew that if *this* trip would be successful, my comfort zone would expand exponentially, and I would be willing, ready, and able to take on virtually all of my dreams!

So I did what I could to prepare for this colossal adventure. This included spiritual as well as physical preparation.

Spiritually, I slowed down on my daily prayers and really concentrated on the meaning of each word. I wanted to be totally focused when I got to the Kosel (so I would block out all distractions and intrusions to my concentration). After all, who knew the next time I would ever be back again?

Physically, I pounded away at my cycling machine (I killed my previous record the day before we left by racking up over thirty minutes with *no* breaks!). As well, I worked like crazy by sitting on the floor for as long as I could to strengthen my trunk muscles.

Yes, indeed—I was in tip-top spiritual and physical shape. I felt as though *nothing* could stop me from experiencing Israel to its fullest!! I never felt more in control and on top of the world!

I also took all possible precautions when it came to the actual twelve-plus-hour journey. My traveling aide and I practiced and fine-tuned manual transfers from my power chair into a regular chair and back again from a regular chair to my power chair (mimicking the actual transfers I would make from my wheelchair to my airline seat and vice versa). We over-practiced and over-trained these procedures at least twenty times!

As well, I worked with my physiatrist (a spinal cord specialist) to coordinate my many medications with my "inner plant" and the havoc the seven-hour time change may cause on my system. For weeks before our departure, I selectively ate like a champion, and I ensured that I took my necessary vitamins and supplements.

I also ordered a special air cushion to sit on while sitting on the airline seat, in order to prevent fearful and devastating pressure sores.

We anxiously and excitedly counted down the days until D-Day! We just couldn't believe that the trip of our lives was taking place imminently!

I reasonably thought that I prepared for every eventuality, and that I had everything under control.

Or, so I imagined...

Departure date finally came! We raced to the airport, arriving well in advance of our departure.

From the Rolling Rabbi blog, "Our Amazing
Trip to Israel, Part One," December 30, 2013

Shaindel's Israel Trip Diary

Tuesday/Wednesday, December 3/4, 2013

Today is the day! Can't believe it has finally come! The kids are all packed up; we're mostly packed, have to throw in last-minute stuff and prepare some food...

The kids are excited. Nochi has so much "clotheses" to go to a lot of friends' houses. The kids got special treats in their lunches today... We actually got out of the house on time, taking pictures of the kids with all their stuff. They've gone in to say goodbye to Abba. ...

Pulling in at the airport... Unload onto the carts, take some pictures, get some name tags... Off to the gate we go. Waiting. I can't sit down, will be sitting for the next twenty-four hours; no thanks. Carol is waiting there already. Went through security pretty easily. After holding out my arms and getting patted down, I go check on Yehuda—he's getting patted down too—they wish him a happy Chanukah and off we go.

Almost time to board, we'll be first. Help! How do I get the chair back off? Stay calm and think. Carol does a great job transferring Yehuda. I focus on finding my wrench and screwdriver. Luckily, there are a bunch of mechanical people there so I show *them* what to do!! That was easy. Onto the plane we go, step one.

Flight goes well... In Toronto, we wait for everyone to get off the plane. Crew is really nice; they ask if I want to take a picture in the cockpit. Sure! I'm not allowed to tell Air Canada so I won't put it on the blog.

The wheelchair is back, got to put it back together again. Problem is, we used cable ties to hook everything together and we don't have scissors... They find us something and off we go. Apparently, it's a ten-minute walk to the next gate. We don't have to find our luggage. It will hopefully meet us in Israel.

Toronto's airport is beautiful. Of course, ours is the very *last* gate number, but it's corded off. They're not opening it yet, so we wait one gate over... They open our gate. I go to the counter lady to tell her we will need assistance. No problem, they'll call us when they are ready.

The gate area is starting to get fuller. I can't sit down, too jittery... A woman comes over and starts schmoozing with us—great. I'll bet she's going to sit right next to us on the plane. Within five minutes we know her whole life story. She asks Yehuda some kashrus questions and we part ways. Not for long; she joins us as we wait.

They are ready for us! At least I don't have to take off the backrest or the headrest. This is easy. Everyone is so friendly and telling us to take our time. As we board, we see these space-age pods—that's the best word I can use to describe them. Each section is on the diagonal—a cushioned seat, footrest, water and other treats—with its own curtain. I want one of those. For $3,000 it can be ours! Each, that is.

As Yehuda is being transferred, we see activity going on, on board. People getting things set up, etc. I hear a crew member tell another, "The pilot doesn't want anyone on board yet—there's mechanical trouble." I'll pretend I didn't hear that. Yehuda is so occupied. Okay, we're on; I set up the BiPAP and organize our paraphernalia so we don't have to get up and down too much. I'm by the window, Yehuda has the aisle. I jump over him anytime I want to get out.

> Everything flowed like a well-oiled machine. We were called to board twenty minutes before the rest of the passengers. The transfer from my power chair to the airline transfer chair went flawlessly, as did the transfer into my seat. Actually, this was the first obstacle that I overcame, because para- and quadriplegic individuals routinely receive bulkhead seating, in order to afford them the space they need for their transfers. However, this was not a possibility for me, because I had to stow my BiPAP machine (my respirologist nearly canceled the trip until I guaranteed him that I would not fall asleep without putting on my BiPAP and its mask) and

its ten-pound battery beneath the seat in front of me. As such, I had to take a regular seat, with its tiny space behind the seat in front of it. This made the transfer a lot more harrying...but we got it done with surprising ease!

This would turn out to be the first of *many* situations beyond my comfort zone. I went with it, and said goodbye to my fears!

From the Rolling Rabbi blog, "Our Amazing Trip to Israel, Part One," December 30, 2013

Shaindel's Israel Trip Diary

Some time later the crew comes to us... "There is some minor issue with the plane, but it's better not to fly it—safety first!" Of course, we just want to get there in one piece. Off we go, undo all our stuff, repack our carry-on, get Yehuda transferred. Luckily, they hadn't taken out the wheelchair just yet in case this would happen. It was waiting on the deck thing. Problem with the cable ties again with no way to open them... One of the flight attendants had a manicure scissors in her bag...

Went out to the gate, everyone was shocked to see us. "Where have you been?"

"On the plane!"

"No way! Well, it's better than sitting out here," they said. Of course, our lady friend rushed over to see how we are.

So there we sat, relaxed and comfortably ensconced in the metal container that would miraculously (recklessly?) fly about 35,000 feet above solid ground. No problem...

As my wife and I chatted and laughed about the crazy preparations that went into this unbelievable adventure, the head official of the airline crew suddenly appeared, with his eyes looking dejected, and his head lowered to the ground. He reluctantly informed us that there was a mechanical problem with the plane. It became necessary to ground this plane, and to locate another one to carry us to our destination.

So there I went again—another transfer from my airline seat to the tiny transfer chair provided by the airline. Followed by yet another transfer from the transfer chair to my own power chair. At least there were no passengers impatiently waiting for me to complete this lengthy procedure!

We were delayed for two hours in the Toronto airport. With $10 food vouchers in hand, we aimlessly roamed the airport. Before long, we came upon a food stand. To our amazed delight, the store contained an entire array of fresh glatt kosher meat sandwiches!! Coming from Ottawa, this certainly threw us for a loop!

We found a place to sit and thoroughly enjoy our scrumptious kosher meal, provided courtesy of Air Canada!

From the Rolling Rabbi blog, "Our Amazing Trip to Israel, Part Two," January 5, 2014

Shaindel's Israel Trip Diary

As we watch, another flight begins boarding—there was a line of about ten old people in wheelchairs. I asked Yehuda if he could get on line with them and I'd take a picture. He didn't think it was so funny… Back to the gate to eat and wait. They said 8:10 p.m.—I was suspicious that we'd end up there all night. Once you pass a certain time, they need a new crew… Our lady friend came over to assure us that she spoke with the crew to ensure that they hadn't forgotten about us and would indeed take care of us and get us onto the plane when they were ready. I sensed at this point that it was going to be a l-o-n-g flight and a l-o-n-g wait.

Before long, they told us they were ready for us again. They woke up some captains who could fly this aircraft and they were somewhere in the building. As soon as they were done switching all food and essentials onto our new plane, we could get on… They kept apologizing about the wait, so we asked if they could make it up to us and bump us up to better seats. Unfortunately, they are not allowed to do that. But since the flight was empty, they said they could block off a row of seats each! Reorganized all our stuff. Set up the BiPAP with battery and cords. Got meds, gum, and headphones ready. People started boarding. I held my breath; our lady friend went past us. Finally, take-off. 10:00 p.m…. Guy in front of me proceeded to lean all the way back…

The time seemed to fly by, and before long, the passengers for our flight to Israel were called up to the gate. However, this time we were not graced with prior boarding. So we had to squish in line with the other passengers, and conduct the manual transfers with our fellow passengers all around us! No problem…

This time, the transfer to my airplane seat did not go as smoothly as the first. But it worked—and we were off!

My job was to stay awake as long as possible, because I definitely did not want to wear the mask with the clumsy BiPAP machine. Unfortunately, I only lasted about two hours, and as I blissfully fell asleep, I put on my mask, closed my eyes, and fell into a deep sleep… dreaming about the pending adventure of a lifetime. The last two hours were definitely the longest of the entire trip. Emotions such as excitement, anticipation, and disbelief flooded me! I still could not believe that we were soon to touch down in ISRAEL!!

Truly, nothing less than a dream come true!

As we landed and taxied on the runway in Israel, we broke down in tears; tears of gratitude mixed with excitement...yes, indeed—we had done it, we were back again, at LONG last!!

From the Rolling Rabbi blog, "Our Amazing Trip to Israel, Part Two," January 5, 2014

Shaindel's Israel Trip Diary

Viewing Eretz Yisrael from the sky was just unreal. As we got closer, I couldn't contain myself anymore, getting ready to land, closer, closer, and bump! Clapping! Tears were streaming down my face. I made no attempt to stop them. *B"H*, we have arrived! We said our goodbyes to the people disembarking and a final farewell to our lady friend. Of course, I told her about the blog and told her to spread word of it to others.

We were helped off the plane, but not before a crew of Hebrew-speaking people swarmed on board to clean up. Oh, so exciting to be surrounded by Hebrew—yay—we are home! The little wheelchair they brought us was rickety, with no seat belt at all. They had to hold Yehuda on… I went to put the wheelchair together again—but again, those cable ties with no way to open them. But the ingeniousness of Israelis—one guy held on to Yehuda, the other guy used a lighter to burn it open! At that point, we got him into the wheelchair. We were on a metal platform that was lowered and pulled on a little car thing to take us to the terminal. A ramp was lowered and Yehuda's chair rolled onto the ground of Eretz Yisrael. Touchdown!

We followed a security officer to customs, breezed right through and went to baggage. Two pieces were already there, got the other, one to go. Waited and waited. A London flight was using the same carousel. Yehuda suggested that maybe someone had taken our suitcase off on the other side. Sure enough! There it was—okay—out we go! Open the doors—to Becky, Moti, and Hillel Waxman. What an exciting commotion and reunion.

Went to where the rental van was waiting. It's a nice new white van, Mercedes. Apparently the only one of its kind in Eretz Yisrael. In Israel, disabled people get FREE cars every three years! We opened the trunk and…there was about three inches of space. The only thing that could fit was one carry-on and Yehuda's chair cushion from the plane. It took a long time to figure out how to use the ramp. It's not as easy as ours but luckily, for old times' sake, it has tie-downs on all four sides, not a locking system. There's room for two passengers in the front, wheelchair in the middle, three in the back—if you don't have any luggage!

Becky and Carol went home with Rabbi Waxman. Moti drove Yehuda and me home… Got to Efrat and had to figure out the ramp all over again. It folds in/up/down, pretty crazy. Judy and Nahum met us there. Brought a delicious hot supper. Apartment is set up so sweetly. Nice and cozy. Learned about the button for the *dud* to warm up the water… Finally went to bed.

Friday, December 6/Shabbos, December 7, 2013

Slept until 10:30! *Davened* Shacharis outside overlooking mountains, beautiful view! Yehuda had physio with a great person.…

In Israel, the girls go to shul Friday night more than Shabbos day. Osnat was having six girls sleeping over for her *Shabbos kallah*. They came into shul[1] like a queen and her followers, adorable… Beautiful *davening* and singing. My *neshamah* was soaring.

Moti spoke for a few minutes before Ma'ariv, welcomed us… So many people came over to welcome us. There's a huge poster in the lobby advertising Yehuda's speech next Motza'ei Shabbos.

Yehuda was up for a few hours in the middle of the night, not feeling well, nauseous and secretions. Finally fell back to sleep. I told him we'd go together to shul… But I fell back asleep until Judy came at 11:30.

---

1. Just like Dad and Mom Simes, Moti and Becky had a shul in their home. In 1999, a formal shul was built and dedicated in memory of Yehuda's parents amongst others.

The Tiferet Avot shul in Efrat.

"Wake up!!" Lunch at shul. Minchah at 1:15. Yehuda had an *aliyah* and *bentched Gomel* for flying.

Went back for a nap. Ma'ariv about 5:15/5:20. Yehuda not feeling so well. Wheezing. Nahum came to check on him. Lungs are clear but wants him on antibiotics, nebulizer. Yehuda won't be going to Ramat Beit Shemesh to speak as planned—so I go instead. Hadn't really intended to speak there but Yehuda felt really bad and I didn't want to miss it. Had second thoughts when I got there and the room was full of people and I didn't recognize anyone. Gave them time to finish their Tehillim so I could review and calm down. ...

People were crying, great feedback after. We estimate 130–150 people. The room was full and saw people upstairs... Lots of people came over after... Got tour of the yeshivah, it's beautiful... Came back to Efrat about 12:15/12:30. Yehuda started meds, had physio. Supposed to rain tomorrow. Not sure about the schedule. We're supposed to go to Har Hamenuchos and the Kosel.

Sunday, December 8, 2013

Well, looks like the jet lag has caught up with me. Couldn't fall asleep until about 3:00 a.m. and tried to go back to sleep at 7:00.

Yehuda won't be going out today. It's really raining... I will be going with Becky, Osnat, and Judy to Har Hamenuchos and then to the Kosel.

I see a lot of interesting things on the way. The electric train, Angel's bakery—boy, does it smell good! You could get fat just by smelling it...

It was emotional at the *kevarim*. Becky invited Zeide Yitzchak and Bubby Asna to the wedding—put an invitation on the *kever*. She spoke about their too-short lives but how much they accomplished. That they had such a beautiful relationship is evident in the relationships of their children and she hopes Osnat and Shay will also be as lucky. I feel so bad that I never really knew them... I asked them to watch over Yehuda and take good care of him. He was so young and they didn't get a chance to raise him—he needs them now—and to watch over their grandchildren whom they would be so proud of. We were all crying.

To the Kosel. We drive through Geulah and Me'ah Shearim. I can't wait to go—hustle and bustle, interesting things, seminary girls walking around...

We park in a lot called Mamilla... Now I'm getting completely overcome. I have been waiting for this for so long. Judy helps me tear *kriah*. The plaza is empty so I zone in on one spot and go straight over. Tears are already streaming down my face. Once I get to the Kosel, I start crying like there's no tomorrow. So much is going through my mind.

When I calmed down a bit, I said Tehillim and *davened* Minchah, put *kvitlach* in the wall cracks for our students. I don't want to leave but we must. We walk back to the car in the rain—good for Eretz Yisrael, bad for the hairdo. Good thing I brought another...

On the ride back to Efrat, we found out that Yehuda needs an x-ray. Going to Hadassah Ein Kerem. Nahum spoke to a pulmonary specialist who will be waiting for us. We waited in the hospital from

5:00 p.m. to 1:30 a.m. to be admitted… Hospitals will be hospitals. They run on their own time frame.

It was sensible for us to stay in Efrat, since two of my sisters and their families lived there. We enjoyed our first evening in Israel, eating delicious food and catching up with everybody. What a delight!

On Shabbos, an ominous sign appeared on the horizon. I began to feel ill and weak. More significantly, my breathing became labored and raspy—a hint that dreaded pneumonia was brewing.

In my condition, I cannot cough (without the external assistance of "breath stacking"). Thank G-d, I am at the stage that I can clear my throat on my own.

You probably don't think about the great gift of coughing, which clears your throat and lungs from secretions. For three months after the accident, it was necessary to perform suctioning to accomplish this objective. They did this by removing my trach from my throat and inserting a long tube through the same hole. As they threaded the tube down my trachea, a machine suctioned out my secretions. This procedure was very uncomfortable—even painful. I dreaded the numerous times during the day when I had the urge to cough or clear my throat. Someone had to quickly call the nurse to suction me, while my eyes teared and I tried to hold myself together. And then, I shut my eyes as the nurse suctioned out my secretions. The machine screamed with every productive output.

So, the next time you cough, say a prayer of gratitude to Hashem! And NEVER think that coughing is just a "given" in life.

From the Rolling Rabbi blog, "Our Amazing
Trip to Israel, Part Three," January 21, 2014

The ominous sign led to the inevitable. By Sunday morning, my LVR (lung volume recruitment) plus abdominal thrusts were assisting me with productive secretions mixed with blood. (LVR refers to the introduction of massive bursts of air through my mouth, via multiple compressions on an LVR tube—otherwise known as breath stacking). Since I am vulnerable to pneumonia, I have often experienced rumbling airways and large secretions. But I've NEVER seen blood mixed with secretions!

I immediately called my brother-in-law, my in-house doctor, and informed him of the unfortunate turn of events. He ran over, and after a quick checkup, determined that I had to go to the Hadassah emergency room, with expedience.

Generally speaking, pneumonia lands me in the hospital for approximately two weeks. This would definitely put a damper on our vacation, not to mention missing the whole point of the trip, which was my niece's wedding...

We went into emergency mode. More importantly, we threw our arms up to Hashem, and tapped into our inner strength and *bitachon*.

After many hours, the doctors determined that it would be necessary to admit me into the hospital.

What a downer! Admittance into the hospital ALWAYS sets me back. Without an air mattress (which requires being turned in my bed every three hours) or physiotherapy, and hospital surroundings (all doom and gloom), it always takes me a couple of weeks to regain my spirit and strength.

Now, I want to share something with you. Before our trip, there were quite a few things that we were concerned about. I spoke with a close friend of mine, who happens to be a quadriplegic as well, to hear his experiences when he traveled to Israel. He opened my eyes to the risks involved, and he also calmed me with tips to overcome these risks.

Thankfully, Hashem was with us every step of the way. Not one single inconvenience or let-down that we could have anticipated took place. Every single thing flowed smoothly!

Except for out-of-the-blue pneumonia!

Remember, for this trip I was in tip-top physical, spiritual, and emotional shape. I'd never felt better nor stronger. We were completely psyched and prepared.

And yet again, we learned who is *really* in charge. Hashem was there to remind us that we can never think that we are in control of our destinies. Just when we were at great risk of falling into that trap, Hashem caught us in His loving arms and vividly reminded us that only He holds the cards!

In the end, I was admitted on Sunday night. I will not go into the Israeli hospital experience right now, except to say, it served as an intensive lesson into the inner psyche of the Israeli and Arab mentality. In fact, nationalities were blurred—I actually asked a gentleman to put *tefillin* on me, and when he expressed his cluelessness as to what *tefillin* were, it became clear that he was an Arab!

I struggled through a restless night. Finally, the next morning came. This was it—MONDAY! The day of the wedding! And here I lie, feeling sick and short of breath. Of course, tensions were high. How could the wedding go on without me? After all, I was the side show to the bride and groom!

> *From the Rolling Rabbi blog, "Our Amazing Trip to Israel, Part Four," February 2, 2014*

Shaindel's Israel Trip Diary

Monday, December 9, 2013

The day of the wedding… Put together my wedding stuff and some of Yehuda's stuff. The plan is for him to leave for the wedding and go back for more IV and observation… Walked up the hill to the hospital. I thought I was in decent shape but I was breathing hard. Judy said it's the climate. I hope so! Went 'round and 'round up escalator through beautiful shops—soft yogurt, bakery—but had to keep going. Up elevator, down escalators. "Go straight, turn right, turn left, near the door, all the way to the end…" Got the grand tour. Finally found floor four, room ten, a four-bed ward. Dr. will be free at two after meeting to speak to Nahum and make a plan for what goes on next.

Dr. will let Yehuda out for three hours. Need oxygen. Called Rabbi Hillel Waxman to arrange it. The administrator of his yeshivah is head of Hatzolah… Some complications back and forth, deciding what to do. Dr. said can go, but waiting for Dr. note that didn't come. Shortness of breath—maybe can't go.

> Team Simes went into high gear! My hospital room became the control center of a flurry of activity, with the ultimate goal of getting me to the wedding! My brother-in-law Nahum, the doctor, spent most of the day by my side. By the minute, he monitored my condition and relayed the information to my doctor. My wife and sister served as my executive assistants. They fetched the hard-to-find nurses and manned (womanned?) the phone!
>
> As the day wore on, my oxygen saturation level increased, and I displayed an improved disposition. We all began to pray harder. By midday, my brother-in-law began to believe! By introducing increased amounts of oxygen, the objective began to take shape!
>
> Now we had to get the doctor's approval to leave the

hospital and attend the wedding. His agreement was—negative! He felt I was just too ill to leave the confines of the hospital.

Meanwhile, we had to secure the use of an oxygen tank, in case I would end up with a leave of absence from the hospital. We tried various organizations, but none of them were agreeable to lend us one on short notice. Again, we hit a roadblock...

Suddenly, I was struck by a flash of inspiration! One of my closest friends lives in Beit Shemesh, and he has connections with a volunteer ambulance service. Perhaps he could convince them to lend us enough oxygen canisters to last for three hours—the maximum on which we figured my doctor would allow me to leave the hospital.

As the time for the wedding inched closer, my oxygen levels were still erratic. My brother-in-law (father of the bride) kept urging us to go ahead. Double pneumonia? Reduced oxygen levels? Tied up in the hospital? "Who cares?" he asked. "You came halfway around the world for this wedding of the century! You didn't let anything in the world stop you! You came SO far! Just get up and get out of that hospital—575 people are expecting you!"

Well, as I've grown used to, *yeshuas Hashem k'heref ayin*—"the salvation of Hashem comes as quickly as the blink of an eye." The oxygen canisters arrived just in time! My own oxygen levels leveled off in the nick of time! My brother-in-law ran to the phone to update my hospital doctor!

Immediately, we called for nurses to unplug me from my IV and to get me dressed. After waiting for about five minutes, my "team" frantically ran through the hallways to grab any available nurse.

Guess what? The hallways were EMPTY! Not a soul in sight!

(Danger—the following paragraphs are not intended for the faint of heart...!)

At that moment, we could sense the end zone! The quarterback (that is, Hashem) just executed a perfect hand-off to us—and we were ready to blast through the defensive line!

My brother-in-law did the prep work, as my wife organized the oxygen and power chair. Within ten minutes, I was ready to go. However, as I lay in my hospital bed, we realized that we had to leap over the final hurdle!

THE TRANSFER!!!

But at Hadassah Hospital there are no ceiling or mechanical lifts—all transfers are done by hand! This was *way* out of my comfort zone—just contemplating an unpracticed transfer sent shivers up my spine! And this would be performed by two unlikely characters... my brother-in-law and wife!

I frantically pleaded with my wife, "You guys don't know what you're doing!"

She immediately looked me straight in the eyes and responded, "WE'RE THE ONLY ONES WHO KNOW WHAT THEY'RE DOING! So take a deep breath and saddle up for the ride of your life!"

She took the top, my brother-in-law took the bottom, and they swung me into a sitting position. Then, with incredible fluidness and grace, they scooped me up and dropped me down into my power chair!

TRIUMPH! A perfect landing!

That last minute taught me a tremendous lesson: Never be afraid of things that are in the realm of possibility. Now I always say a prayer before undertaking difficult challenges, and I feel more deeply that Hashem is always with me.

What a shot in the arm! I was charged and super anxious to free myself from the restricting grips of Hadassah Hospital, if only for three hours.

With reckless abandon, we ignored the stares of the hospital staff and rushed into our accessible van. The marriage ceremony was set for 7:00 p.m., and we sped toward the hall at 7:15. The groom's father was shouting, "Let's get the ceremony underway! We have nearly 600 guests who are getting restless!" To which my brother-in-law shouted, "Keep singing, keep singing! Louder, louder! They are on the way, it's only a few minutes now!"

The truth is, as much as we raced toward our destination, and my brother-in-law held off the crowd, nothing could be done to alter the decree of Hashem. What was destined to happen at a specific time could never be changed, whatever efforts we made.

As the saying goes, "Go with the flow!"

From the Rolling Rabbi blog, "Our Amazing
Trip to Israel, Part Four," February 2, 2014

We knew we were getting close to the wedding hall when we heard the thunderous singing and stomping. The entire wedding took place under an enormous tent. As we pulled up, the tent was aglow with throbbing *simchah*, and its walls seemed to pulsate with the beat of the music.

We were totally geared up to explode into the tent. We pulled right up to the tent's entrance, lowered the van's ramp, and I blew out of the van. One of my close friends grabbed the oxygen tank and ran behind me. I was mobbed by family and friends, and they pulled me right into the *badeken* hall.

The sea of people split, and I, together with my entourage, raced up to the *kallah*. Her father was just finishing his blessing for her, and then people all around motioned to me to step up and bless my niece. As tears poured down my face (and I imagine down the faces of many others), words of blessing and hope poured out of my lips. As I cried out these words, my niece's head was bowed.

Next stop—the *chuppah*! They had set up two separate ramps to reach the elevated *chuppah*. Each ramp was angled at a very steep slope, and I needed two guys behind me to push as I drove up at full speed.

Now, for some background. Before I got sick with pneumonia, my sister (mother of the bride) asked me to recite the seventh blessing of the *sheva brachos*. This particular blessing is commonly referred to as the "singing *brachah*." This is because a cantor is often chosen to chant/sing this blessing. If no cantor is present, a close relative or friend with a beautiful voice is honored with this blessing. It is considered a great honor to receive this *brachah*.

I, however, deferred to someone with a sweet singing voice. You see, this has been a source of frustration for me, because before the accident, I loved to sing at joyous occasions and around the Shabbos table. Of course, this love of mine was lost with the onset of my paralysis. I no longer have sufficient lung capacity to produce the rise and fall of a melody. So, I rely on others to carry the tune, and I try to keep up—somewhat similar to my life in general.

My sister countered that all I'd need to do was to start off singing at my own pace, and the massive crowd would accompany me. Ha ha, funny joke! I could just imagine starting off, and the crowd being so stunned as to be speechless! I pictured in my mind standing up, in front of nearly 600 people, and ending up reciting instead of singing... Another brother-in-law of mine offered to assist by singing the *brachah* quietly and I would follow along. I declined—either I would do it myself, or I wouldn't do it at all.

We hadn't finalized before I was admitted to the hospital, so I assumed that my sister would give me one of the shorter *brachos*—especially considering that I still had pneumonia and I was coming straight from the hospital!

I sat there, enjoying each *brachah* one by one, and was stunned when they called ME up for the final *brachah*!

Apparently, even when we're confronted with something difficult, we can step up to the plate if we have the right motivation. In this case, my motivation was not disappointing all the people who were counting on me. So it's all about finding the right motivation to push you through the moment!

In the end, without any hesitation, I drove up to face

the bride and groom. Someone held up the cup of wine, a second person put a card with the words in front of my face, and a third person put a microphone inches from my mouth.

I struggled to sing the first phrase; there was *silence* from the crowd. I continued on to the second phrase... utter silence!

Suddenly, the band started to play rousing music. That's all the crowd needed—the place erupted with blasting singing and clapping! Of course, it didn't hurt that I had a powerful microphone against my lips! It was truly a memorable moment!

There was enough oxygen in my tank for three hours. So I stayed and danced up a storm!

It was humorous to see the guy carrying the oxygen tank behind me; if I stopped too short, he would crash into me. And if I drove too quickly, the cord would yank my head backward!

And there's another lesson for you. There must be complete unity and cooperation in order to achieve success in any endeavor. One person must not advance quicker than his partner, nor may he advance any slower.

Think TEAMWORK, TEAMWORK, TEAMWORK—and you'll never go wrong!

From the Rolling Rabbi blog, "Our Amazing Trip to Israel, Part Five," February 6, 2014

Shaindel's Israel Trip Diary

Tuesday, December 10, 2013

Went to Hadassah to pick up Yehuda. Discharge at 4:00.

Wednesday, December 11, 2013

Woke up for 8:00 a.m. bus to get to the Central Station for a bus to Kiryat Sefer [to give a speech]. Pouring, pouring. Missed it. Was waiting on the wrong side of the street. Crossed over, nearly missed it. Got on the Kiryat Sefer bus, but it was the "wrong" one. Got off... my friend Mirel came by taxi to get me. Around twenty women at my speech.

My nephew Asa picked me up, went to *sheva brachos...*

Want to do Kever Rochel and Geulah tomorrow. Snowing!

Thursday, December 12, 2013

Well, the snow came. Even by Ottawa standards, it really did snow. I acted Israeli—put bags on over my shoes to go out. Looked gorgeous.

Tunnel roads are closed. Figured I might as well get gifts and treats here in Efrat in case our Geulah expedition gets pushed off. All stores are closed. Walked up to the shopping center... Only a grocery store was open. Tried to find Israeli treats—more American stuff than in Loblaws! I walked back with my package... Got back and found out the tunnels are open. Rabbi Waxman will come get us and take us to Yerushalayim after all... Change of plans; too many trips back and forth with threat of roads closing again. Supposed to get colder and be worse tomorrow...

Around 7:00 p.m. we suddenly realized we hadn't eaten supper and were starving. We were wondering why no one came by. They probably thought we were in Yerushalayim; I hadn't told them we didn't go. Called Nahum, he said there's tons of food. Turns out *sheva brachos* had been relocated to Judy…

It was nice until they started praising me. I felt I had to respond. Told Osnat and Shay that as long as your husband is the center of your world and you stick together, nothing in the world can stop you. *Brachah* that they should be the center of each other's world… Osnat and Shay came back to see Yehuda and we watched wedding pics together. Couldn't get through all 4,000 of them! Michael came by. Finally, getting ready for bed—power went out! Came on a couple of hours later, off and on again. Hope it stays warm!

Erev Shabbos, December 13, 2013

Michael came to do *tefillin*. Said Becky and Moti still don't have power… Trying to get someone with a 4x4/SUV to shuttle people from Ramat Beit Shemesh to here for Shabbos. People are afraid they'll get stuck. WARNING: Attention Vancouver residents! The Simeses are invited to Vancouver in May—expect weird and wacky weather conditions. The Simeses bring it wherever they go. NY—Hurricane Sandy. Efrat—largest snowfall since 1958!

…Shoveled with Michael and Nahum. Helped set up at hall. Snowed until 4:00 Minchah. Covered path. Snowed till late.

Motza'ei Shabbos, December 14, 2013

Yehuda spoke. People came to hear him from all parts of Efrat. The speech was amazing, even though they had to change the venue due to power outages. All were very impressed with his message of hope, optimism, and purpose. Women came over to me afterward to talk about our experience. Shay uploaded the speech so we could have it to listen to and share with others.

Another foot of snow! Reshoveled again to get home. In Yerushalayim, 35,000 homes with no power.

Sunday, December 15, 2013

Today is supposed to be our last day here. We leave tomorrow. Roads are pretty icy. Spent a very long time shoveling out the van and bringing it up the hill. Rachel and Michael got out and went to camp out in the airport until their flight at 6:00 a.m. Monday. We are thinking of going to RBS or Tel Aviv to camp out so we can be closer to an open road to the airport. Tel Aviv hotel three thousand shekel! We'd have to leave here at 9/9:30 a.m. to be there by 10:30; flight 12:40 p.m. Turns out the roads are open... It's so beautiful out, really warm and sunny. People all over. Weather forecast shows it will be above freezing overnight, so roads shouldn't freeze. Decide to stay put.

Well, guess what? They closed the roads, can't get out. It is freezing. Won't be ready to leave at 9:00 a.m.! Now what? Can't get through to Air Canada. Finally, a guy says we could change but we'd have to pay because flight is still on. Explain the conditions but he's not authorized... Travel agent in Netanya finds out that our flight was canceled—due to snow in Toronto! Ha! Ha! *B"H* we didn't go camp out! They rescheduled our flight to Tuesday at 9:00 a.m. Can't do that unless we sleep over somewhere, and even then it's crazy. Next flight is Thursday, same time. We can change for free because of the cancellation. Yay!

Monday, December 16, 2013

Now I'm going stir crazy. Great to be in E"Y, but want to be doing E"Y things. Otherwise, feel bad about missing kids. The van is in good shape in a good place. Finally decide to get out. Go with Becky and Moti to Malchah Mall. Looks like everyone else in Yerushalayim had the same idea.

...Bring home burgers and chicken for dinner; don't have time to eat there because roads will be closing at 6:00 p.m. due to cold. Can hardly see any snow in Yerushalayim. Lots of downed trees. As soon as we exit tunnels and checkpoint, it's another world—like Canada.

Getting Yehuda ready for bed—notice toes on right foot are crazy

swollen and puffy. Take pictures for Nahum; he's in Yerushalayim—
slept over to be at work. Make plans with Rabbi Waxman to get picked
up around 2:00 p.m. to go to Kosel and Rav Avraham Kanarek...[2]
Waiting to hear about toes.

Tuesday, December 17, 2013

Well, verdict is frostbite or lack of circulation; kind of
confusing. Can't be colder here than in Ottawa, have had TEDS
[thromboembolism deterrent stockings] too tight before. Has to
elevate and keep warm.

Must go to Kosel today. Now 11:45 a.m.; power went out.

Bought some beautiful things here as gifts for hosts, drivers, and
Tefillin Brigade.[3] Got some nice things for family and kids, too. Making
all sorts of arrangements for the kids for the next few days. Shmuly is
home until Tuesday 8:00 p.m. so kids will be with him. Need someone
to move in with them. They're starting to feel unsettled. Devorah
wanted to know which *week* I'm coming home. Nochi wants a pink
present.

The power went back on. It's 11:50 a.m.

---

2.   Harav Avraham Kanarek was born in Leipzig, Germany, and learned for a few years in
Belgium. At age fifteen, he went to learn in Kamenetz under Rav Baruch Ber Leibowitz *zt"l*.
With the onset of World War II, Rav Kanarek traveled with a group of Kamenetz students
who had joined with students from Mir Yeshivah. He did not follow the Mir to Shanghai,
as his family had procured visas to go to America. In the US, Rav Avraham joined Yeshiva
Chofetz Chaim, led by a young Rav Henoch Leibowitz. He moved to Eretz Yisrael in the
1970s, becoming Rosh Yeshivah at Yeshivas Chofetz Chaim in Yerushalayim. He passed
away in 2020.

3.   The *Tefillin* Brigade was the way we fondly referred to the dedicated men who had a
rotation for nearly seven years to come put *tefillin* on Yehuda every single morning. They
helped him put on his *tallis* and *tefillin*, *daven*, and turn the pages of his siddur when he was
not able to on his own. Whether Yehuda was home or in the hospital, they came, rain or
shine, in the brutally cold winter or sweltering summer.

Later...

Yehuda was able to visit CCJ [Chofetz Chaim Jerusalem]. He was eager to see his *rebbeim*. As we were parking in front of the yeshivah, we saw Harav Avraham Kanarek being escorted by Rabbi Haim Alcabes, gingerly holding on to his arm to maneuver around the snowbanks.[4] What *chizuk* it was for us to see the efforts that this *gadol* went through to give *chizuk* to his *talmid*! Yehuda spoke to the entire student body. Rav Kanarek said that it was he who gained *chizuk* from Yehuda and not vice versa!

Being in E"Y has really been a dream come true. When we were first making the plans, it seemed so overwhelming and like a once-in-a-lifetime experience. You do it one time and that's it. But I would definitely do it again. I thought that what I needed was to sit at the Kosel for hours on end and

At Yeshiva Chofetz Chaim in Yerushalayim. Yehuda derived immense *chizuk* from his *rebbi*, Harav Avraham Kanarek.

A dream come true! Finally at the Kosel!

daven there so many times; to go to Kever Rochel, etc. Apparently not. I shoveled snow in the streets of E"Y. How many Jews over the centuries would have given up everything to be a street sweeper in

---

4. At the time, Rav Kanarek was ninety-two years old!

E"Y! Well, I did that. I wasn't planning on really speaking here—I did that, too!

I'm realizing more and more that Hashem is in control and that's all there is to it.

Wednesday, December 18, 2013

Today is our last day here for real, unfortunately. Rabbi Waxman can pick us up around 2:00 p.m. to go to Kever Rochel, but I don't want to spend my last day in the apartment waiting. I decide to go to Yerushalayim to go to the Kosel one more time. It took much longer than usual. Waited for number 1 bus to Kosel. Starting to feel like a seasoned traveler, until I watch the young mothers get off the bus carrying their babies, pulling out the strollers from under the bus and setting them up again. Of course, everyone helps!

I *daven* really hard at the Kosel; I don't know when I'm coming back.

Kever Rochel is totally unrecognizable; we are in the middle of a huge fortress. I'm trying to picture where I am standing in relation to the road that we used to drive on before they built the tunnels. I can't imagine it. I wasn't prepared for how emotional I would be... When I got to the words about *"choleh"* I lost it, then about kids, totally depleted! But so cleansing. I hope those *tefillos* go high. ...

Back to apartment to pack. We say our tearful goodbyes to those we won't see in the morning.

Thursday, December 19, 2013

Up at 6:30 a.m., don't want to leave but feel like there's a lot to do. Of course there really isn't, just last-minute odds and ends. Go to the corner *makolet*... I also wanted to take a picture of the sign behind the counter—it's reminding the workers to deal honestly with their customers, because [in the Next World] they will be asked if they were honest. I want to show the kids that it's not just what we learn about, it's a real way of life.

Becky and Moti and Judy come to get us ready. Driving to the airport, getting warmer and warmer, less and less snow. We see the bend in the road where we stopped to feed Asna eighteen years ago. See where David and Golias fought. Get to airport toasty warm... Say goodbye to the van. Everything seems under control; check in, get ready to board. For some reason, I didn't bother to check the itinerary to see what time we land in Toronto. Apparently, it takes twelve hours, my oh my! I think I'm going to go stir crazy... We land in Toronto 6:15 p.m. local time. Our connecting flight is at 8:00. Looking forward to being home early.

They can't find the wheelchair. Well, it's not really lost, but it's taking a long time. As time ticks by, we realize we are NOT making the 8:00 p.m. flight, nor the 10:00 p.m.—that one is ten people overbooked already.

Get the chair, go through customs, get the suitcases, check in the suitcases. Try to get on a flight. Unfortunately, the next one with room for us and the wheelchair is at 12:15 a.m. The airline representative feels bad for us so we get bumped up to business class, get $10 food vouchers and permission to go into the lounge. ...

Having a relaxing time in the lounge. Suddenly, realize we have a flight to catch—better find Gate D36! We get there; it opens at 11:30 p.m., forty-five minutes before the flight. There are only two people in sight. Two more come and insist that this can't be the right place because no one else was there. Sure enough, they changed the gate to D51! What a nice stroll forty minutes before the flight!

Where is Carol? Try calling but can't get through. We start going, there is no D51. Finally, they announce F51=D51. I should have known. Still no Carol; they were paging her and paging her. We decide that we are NOT missing this flight no matter what. With help from a flight attendant, I get Yehuda out of his chair—good thing I "practiced" with Nahum at the hospital.

On this trip, we experienced so many cases of getting the *refuah* before the *makkah*! Because Yehuda didn't feel well, I went to Ramat

Beit Shemesh to speak. While there, I got a grand tour of the yeshivah, including the room where the administrator—who is also the coordinator of Hatzolah—stores the oxygen tanks. When we needed oxygen to get to the wedding, we knew whom to call! Similarly, when we wanted to leave the hospital to go to the *chasunah*, there was no one to help with a transfer, and no lift. Yehuda wanted to wait for people who knew what they were doing, but very smoothly, we told him that WE ARE the people who know what we're doing! Well, now that I'm "experienced" we could get on the plane; we got the aisle seat but the arm didn't go up and down so we had to lift Yehuda up and over!

Packed flight. Everyone wants to go to Ottawa at 12:00 a.m.! Go figure! We're just stopping for a brief de-icing. I guess I fell asleep because next thing I knew, it felt like we were crashing. Actually, we were landing; it was about 2:00 a.m.—wow! Can't remember the last time I stayed up and out so late at night!

The waiting game begins again. Get the chair, get the luggage, get a cab. A van pulls up—no ramp! No prob! The middle seat is taken out, the guy pulls out a foldable ramp like we have at home and props it up against the car! By now we feel like real hotshots, no lift, no accessible van, we can do it all, we're invincible.

We get into the house at 3:00 a.m. Sleep fast—the kids will be up in less than four hours to see us. Home sweet home.

We may have only traveled six thousand miles away but it was worth more than that in terms of courage, inspiration, dedication, and hope for the future! I've talked about my metamorphosis; I think this was another part. I left a pack of outer shells behind, packs of insecurities and fears. I have what I want and need—my husband, my kids, my family, all of the extraneous stuff will NOT bother me. I will not allow it to stop me. Our life is ours and ours alone; no one can get in the way if we don't let. I feel like I'm ready to walk into the sunset to a bright future. Unpredictable, but bright. *Chasdei Hashem ki lo samnu!*

CHAPTER SIXTEEN

Two Steps Back

YEHUDA WAS HAVING A HARD TIME RECOVERING FROM THE overseas expedition. We assumed that in addition to the normal (and not so normal) exertions of travel, he was still recuperating from his bout of pneumonia and its attendant hospitalization. He was fatigued and lacked his usual energy level.

Weeks turned into months. Yehuda was often unwell and was hospitalized several times. He was treated and released time and time again, but the cause of his lingering malaise remained elusive.

During one hospital stay, the attending doctor noticed an arrhythmia on the heart monitor. Further testing revealed that Yehuda had had a cardiac incident. He was transported to the Ottawa Heart Institute where he had four stents put in—one of his arteries was 99 percent blocked! We teased him that a score of 100 percent is not always a good thing and to please stop striving for "perfection."

Once again, he was released, but episodes kept occurring. The frequent and lengthy hospital stays were frustrating and draining for him and the family.

One Shabbos afternoon, Yehuda began to show signs of sepsis. We called 911, confident in our diagnosis. We had already had plenty of experience with his symptoms and what they represented; a UTI that had gone septic and was causing confusion.

The paramedic team arrived quickly and began their assessment. Based on his EKG, they determined he was having a heart attack. Shmuly and I looked at them in disbelief. Impossible! He had had four stents inserted just a few months ago—how on earth could he possibly be having a heart attack? We firmly insisted that this was not the case. In no way were the symptoms indicative of a heart attack!

The paramedic insisted that they would be transporting him to the Ottawa Heart Institute. Again, I firmly declared that Yehuda could not be having a heart attack. Instead, he must be transported to our local hospital, Queensway Carleton, where he had an extensive history and they knew him well, inside and out.

My request was overridden by the paramedic's supervisor and we were transported to the Heart Institute. As soon as we were brought in, the doctors took one look at his EKG and declared, "This man just had four stents put in; he is *not* having a heart attack. That would be medically impossible."

Vindicated again—but my worries were not over. Now that we were in the Heart Institute, protocol declared that Yehuda had to be transported to the nearest hospital—the Civic, which was right next door. We could not get permission to be transferred to Queensway Carleton. I desperately wanted to get Yehuda seen by his usual medical team. Once I realized this was not going to happen, I tried to pacify myself. Perhaps, under the scrutiny of different eyes, we would finally get to the root of Yehuda's illnesses.

As the staff in this hospital was new at treating Yehuda, I had to educate them as to his needs, abilities, and lengthy past history. They tested him for all kinds of ailments. They even put him in quarantine for tuberculosis—which, of course, he did not have.

Once again, after being treated for some time, he was discharged. Once again, I was taking him from doctor to doctor, describing what was going on and trying to get some answers. But there were no answers. Yehuda was getting weaker. Exercises he was once able to do well were becoming more challenging. Even driving his wheelchair became a great effort.

After a trying five weeks, most of which were spent in the intensive care unit of our local hospital, I am now home and better than ever!

I cannot thank all of you enough—I know that your prayers had a great impact upon my recovery. Thank you for following along and taking action when it was needed!

On the topic of prayer, I would like to share something with you.

Did you know that every prayer is answered? And that the answer is ALWAYS "Yes"!

Think of it much like a river or a lake. Imagine that the sun begins to beat with unbearable heat, and the waters evaporate into rain clouds. The soil directly beneath the clouds is parched and thirsty for water. However, the clouds yield no rain or relief from the oppressive heat. Instead, the wind comes, and blows the clouds to a completely different area. In that area, there is no river or lake to produce rain clouds, and thus, no possibility of life-sustaining rain. In this new location it begins to rain, and the vegetation in this place is nourished and sustained.

The people in the first place wonder, "Where's the rain? Why must we suffer without life-sustaining vegetation? Weren't rain clouds just above? Why did the wind come and blow them away?"

The people in the second place exclaim, "Thank G-d for the rain! It's so wonderful—we don't even have any water source to produce rain clouds! Hashem must have used the wind to bring us the rain clouds!"

It's the same thing with our prayers. Hashem soaks up and "uses" EVERY prayer. Indeed, there is a positive answer for each and every one. And if at times it seems that we're not receiving what we asked for, perhaps Hashem is "using" our prayer for someone who needs it more than us.

*From the Rolling Rabbi blog, "I'm
Home, Thank G-d!!" April 2, 2014*

I'm tickled pink to be back on the computer! As well, I'm overjoyed to be in touch with my dear friends who are reading this!

Now that the weather is getting warmer (finally!), I can look back at my toughest four months post "accident." It was a winter full of hospital admissions for pneumonias, cardiac and respiratory illnesses. This weakened my body and my spirit. It would be accurate to say I was racked with pain and I ended up with a decreased range of motion.

I'm now looking forward to a road trip to Queens, New York, for Shavuos! I will be staying for ten days with one of my closest friends, a five-minute walk (or should I say sit?) from my yeshivah! I can hardly wait for this incredibly inspiring and invigorating experience!!

Until next time, all the very best and BE ALL THAT YOU CAN BE!!

*From the Rolling Rabbi blog, "I'm
Back in Touch!" May 19, 2014*

Marilyn's Doorbell

We were in Queens for Shavuos, staying with the Glazers, and I had settled Yehuda in his bed for a nap. I set up the call bell and Yehuda tested it out. All was in working order. I wished Yehuda a restful sleep.

Some time passed and I realized I had not heard Yehuda call me. I hoped that meant he was sleeping soundly. I went to his room, slowly and quietly turned the doorknob so as not to disturb him. I tiptoed in and took a peek. Yehuda was lying there wide awake, looking distraught and clearly uncomfortable. He reported that he had been ringing and ringing but no one had come to his aid. We had not heard the bell. What could have gone wrong?

Several hours later, Marilyn, the Glazers' elderly neighbor, came to the door. She was frantic.

"Yosefa, Yosefa! Someone is playing a mean trick on me! It's terrible! I don't know what to do!"

"Marilyn, what is it?" Yosefa asked. "What kind of trick? You are such a nice lady. Why would someone try to hurt you?"

"But someone is. My doorbell rang, so I went to the door to see who it was. Yosefa, no one was there. No one! It kept happening, again and again and again! The doorbell rang, I went to check, no one there. I went back to what I was doing. Ring again! Oh, Yosefa, what should I do?"

Realization slowly dawned on Yosefa. Marilyn's doorbell rang yet no one was there. Yehuda rang and no one came... We did not know whether to laugh or cry!

Recently, someone asked me, "How do you blog?" After all, I don't have use of my fingers—so how can I type? For that matter, how can I compose using Microsoft Word, send emails in Gmail, navigate Skype, and utilize Google?

Am I dictating to someone else, and letting them do the work?

Actually, I tried that once upon a time. It was way too tedious and taxing. I found that I could only accurately express my thoughts by interfacing directly with the computer—without any intermediaries muddling the process.

Thus began a painstaking search to regain a major

piece of my freedom and independence. Before my accident, beyond being hooked to the numerous slips of paper that filled my pockets, I was downright, deeply dependent on them for the smooth functioning of my days! But now, after losing the ability to keep track of my coming and going, and having nothing to rely on except my faulty memory—I felt totally lost.

I enlisted the help of my occupational therapist. Together, we set up a computer workstation that was wheelchair accessible. ...

I was advised to get for myself a "head mouse." I bought a camera that I mounted on top of my computer monitor, and by sticking a metallic sticker on the bridge of my glasses, I SHOULD have been able to SIMPLY stare where I wanted to "click," and BLAMO—I could click away! Or, so they said...

In reality, I became riddled with pain because it was necessary to stare (glare?) at each icon for about three seconds. This caused massive spasms and pain in my neck and shoulder blades. Of course, I was told I would have to practice again and again to build up my endurance. You know what kind of advice that was? BAD ADVICE! The pain just grew and grew...

After beating my head against the wall for about three months, I finally worked up the courage to decapitate my head mouse. I had to believe there was a better way.

I then engaged the services of a computer nerd (i.e., a technologically savvy professional) who led me through a few dead ends, until one glorious day I finally washed my hands of every external device. At long last, I settled on the simplest method of all...voice recognition software. I bought a program called "Dragon." My Dragon roared into my life and completely set me free!

Although he wasn't easy to tame and train, I finally grabbed him by the horns and rediscovered the beauty of the spoken word!

The final obstacle was how to enter my Microsoft password, since Dragon couldn't open without it. After being stuck for over a month, I rediscovered the uniqueness of the human face! My computer nerd (now a computer geek) introduced me to the final piece of my blogging journey...face recognition software!

Having learned a couple of memorable lessons about the incredible power of our words and our faces, I was all set up and ready to roll.

And that's how Rolling Rabbi was born!!

From the Rolling Rabbi blog, "How Do I Blog?" June 23, 2014

The response to my blog has been nothing less than remarkable! The storm of interested people who expressed their eagerness to learn and grow simply overwhelmed me!

Because of the blog, I suddenly found myself in a unique position. A position that I had never dreamed of. Although I grew accustomed to touching the lives of my students in Ottawa, I never imagined reaching the masses through my computer!

I always said that my "accident" created more than a few good aspects. In short, it forced me to reconsider my role in the world. Before my life change, when it came to accepting roles outside my comfort zone, I preferred to defer to others more qualified than myself. The problem with that? I could always find someone out there more experienced or well-trained than I. But seared into my mind was the rabbinic imperative to "*Be a man where there are no men.*" That powerful motto was always the driving force which pushed me to seek and discover untrodden territories—places where my contribution would be most impactful. The greatest impact is achieved where others are not stepping up to the plate, either because no one else is around, or because the people available are ill-equipped to execute the mission. So I navigated my way through life, cautiously tiptoeing in shallow waters.

Suddenly—*blamo*!! In a flash, I was thrust into the limelight, emboldened to come to grips with my new identity. It was necessary to recognize the undeniable fact—no one on the face of the planet was even remotely similar to me. Even among spinal cord injuries, I am absolutely unique because by all "natural" accounts I never should have survived the initial injury.

I then came face to face with the stark reality that I, no more and no less than anyone else, am a one hundred percent unique individual. Indeed, no two people in the world have the same strengths and talents, nor identical weaknesses and failings. Therefore, their mission statements fit their own particular "inner laboratory." This is a truism that only came into sharp focus after I endured the "catastrophe" four years ago.

All of this is a long-winded way of expressing my gratitude to all of my viewers on the one hand, and, on the other hand, to express my wonderment and curiosity at the number of my followers.

Did you know that you could receive notification by email every time I post an entry to my blog?

Just become a follower of mine, and let's march together into the bright future!

From the Rolling Rabbi blog, "20,000 Views and 'Only' 133 Followers?" July 8, 2014

Imagine the method by which a father teaches his son to walk. He steadily distances himself from his son by incrementally stepping away from him, and he encourages his son to consistently put one foot in front of the other. The son continues to walk a little more... and a little more...until he needs no more help at all from his father.

What's going on in the son's head as he endures this procedure?

"I just want to get close to my father! Why must he torture me so? Every time I get close to him, he distances himself from me!"

But his father knows better. He knows that the best way to train his son to walk independently is to position himself just beyond his son's grasp—but within his reach!

With this parable, we can gain an inkling into the purpose of our challenges. They are placed before us as opportunities for personal growth. Every time we seem close to reaching our potential, we get further away from getting there. That's because we have grown that much stronger. So the bar of excellence is raised even higher—indeed, beyond our grasp, but within our reach!

From the Rolling Rabbi blog, "Why Do Challenges Come Our Way?" July 10, 2014

CHAPTER SEVENTEEN

The Longest Stay

HOSPITALIZATIONS HAD BECOME MORE A MATTER OF "WHEN" than "if." One night, as I was putting Nochi to sleep, I said Shema with him and then, "Good night, I love you, I'll see you in the morning."

To which my little boy replied, "Not if you bring Abba to the hospital in the middle of the night." No, our newest normal was definitely *not* normal.

Nochi drew a picture of his Abba.

Over time, we learned that being admitted to the ICU did not necessarily indicate a dire emergency; sometimes it was precautionary. Yehuda tended to desat[1] quickly and without advance indication.

Once, while he was in a regular ward, I arrived to visit him moments after his caregiver—whom I had hired to be there when I could not—had left. When I entered, I found him hyperventilating. He had no way to call for help and no one noticed he was in distress. I had suggested during several previous admissions that he should be in the ICU due to his paralysis and respiratory issues. At the time, the staff felt it was unwarranted; it would obviously be more cost effective for them to keep him in the regular ward. But after the distress incident, the staff agreed it was too risky for him to be left unattended.

It took years until the younger children realized what an ICU really meant. We were all gowning up to visit Yehuda during one of his many hospitalizations. He was on contact precaution due to some infection he had. The smaller kids could not understand why the gowns were so huge on them—why did the nurses not just give them gowns that fit? Well, because children do not usually visit the ICU. Really? We come all the

Yehuda had a knack for finding the humor in his situation. Shown here with a matching Build-a-Bear friend. The bear was nicknamed "Paw," the westernized name for father. In due time, Paw received a wheelchair of his own.

---

1. Suffer a decrease in blood oxygenation concentration.

time—why not others? Because the ICU is for very, very sick people; it is a special part of the hospital. For our children, the ICU was a positive place—parties, the birth of a sibling, spending time with their father, watching videos, Abba getting treated so that he would get better and come home.

Triple Whammy

Because we knew Yehuda so well, we were highly sensitized to the subtle changes he displayed. We had all become experts at reading his face, his grimaces, his spasms, the flare of his nostrils, as signs that his condition was about to deteriorate. Even the children could tell when something was wrong.

On Tuesday, July 8, 2014, Christina arrived to be our live-in caregiver. She was a sweet, caring, sensitive woman who came to us from the Philippines via Cyprus. She took an immediate liking to Yehuda and was eager to care for him. I was relieved that I finally had a helper I could count on. Little did I anticipate just how much help we would need!

The first weekend she was with us, Yehuda had very alarming and distressing symptoms that once again necessitated a call to 911 and a hospital admission. I took Christina along in the ambulance. I thought it would be important for her to see what happens on the ride and how to explain the situation to the nurses in triage at the emergency department. After the initial intake assessments and routine blood work, we got Yehuda settled in the ICU.

He was treated the way we had become accustomed to, with broad-spectrum antibiotics pending the results of blood cultures which would determine the specific infection. Results slowly started to come back. Yehuda had not one, not two, but three full-blown infections! The infectious-diseases specialist was very puzzled: One of the three was specific to the Middle East—how could someone in Ottawa have caught that? The puzzle was slowly pieced together. Yehuda most likely had picked up MERS (Middle East Respiratory Syndrome) at the hospital in Israel. It had been incubating for the last few months and had only now become detectable. I questioned the doctors as to why there was not a better way to detect what was causing the strange symptoms from which he had been suffering for months. Once again, they explained to me that because his body is so sensitive to every change, it reacts immediately to everything that attacks it.

We were warned that Yehuda was in serious condition. Each of the three superbugs was very dangerous in and of itself. Hearty, strapping men could succumb to any one of them. Yehuda had not one, but three potentially fatal infections. He was not strong. He had had numerous infections and illnesses over recent months. Following each setback, he never quite bounced back to his previous level of health. The illnesses were compounded and building upon themselves. Damage had been done.

Three days later (Tuesday, July 15, 2014, which coincided with 17 Tammuz, an ominous date on the Jewish calendar), I received an urgent phone call from the hospital. "There is an emergency. Come quickly!"

I informed the kids, raced out of the house, and drove like a maniac to the hospital, 2.6 miles away. Praying the whole time and not knowing what was going on, I was in a panic.

I ran up to Yehuda's room and was buzzed into the ICU immediately. The staff was waiting for me and explained what had happened. Yehuda had had a cardiac arrest. His heart stopped. He coded. In essence, he died—again. Thank G-d, they were able to bring him back with CPR. My arms and legs shook as I took in the information and realized how close I had come to losing him. Again.

The doctor gently explained that Yehuda was very, very sick, that he had never been this sick before, that there was really no way yet to know what would happen to him. Brain damage might have occurred as a result of oxygen deprivation. He may or may not recover. The next twenty-four hours were critical. If there were any family members who would want to say goodbye, now was the time for them to come.

"Should I call my son to come home from camp?"

"I would if I were you."

"My children at home, too?"

"Yes."

"His siblings?"

"Yes."

"Mine?"

"Yes—and any friends who would want to know."

This was it, then; this was the moment I had been dreading and hoping to avoid since the accident. How do you tell your children that their father might die? How do you bring your children to say goodbye? How do you say goodbye? What do you say?

Nothing, nothing at all, can prepare a person for this. In a daze, I called my son to arrange for a ride home from camp. I called Yehuda's sisters to advise them of the situation. Becky asked if we had made burial plans. Their parents were buried in Israel. There is a strong tradition to be buried in Israel. Is that what he wanted? Truthfully, I do not think we discussed it too much post-accident; it was a conversation I never wanted to have. I could not say the words out loud. I hoped that as long as the words remained unsaid, death could not become a reality. My husband might be sickly for the rest of his life, but he would never die. Dying was not an option. No, it was not an option but a huge fear, the elephant in the room.

I had to compose myself and process this new reality before going home and collecting the children.

I arrived home to find them in a very bad state: hysterical, fearful, wanting answers. As gently as I could, I explained to them that Abba had had a cardiac arrest and what that meant. I explained that the doctors were able to get his heart to beat again. Unfortunately, his body was very, very weak from fighting so hard against all the infections inside him. Hashem is the One Who decides who will get well and who will not. Right now, we do not know what Hashem will decide.

As long as I live, I will never forget the look in Chan's eyes when I put her to sleep and she said, "Tell me, Mommy, will Abba die?" As I returned her gaze, my heart shredded. "I don't know, Chan. I don't know."

"With Rabbi, Only G-d Knows"

We arranged shifts among the family for the next twenty-four hours. The children spent time with Yehuda and talked to him. Relatives came as well. We camped out in the family lounge of the ICU until the initial danger passed, at which point we were hopeful that he would improve and we could put this entire episode behind us. This was his second near-miss, not counting the accident itself. I asked a doctor what his chances were. Humbly, the doctor responded, "I can give you textbook answers. I only know what the statistics say, but with him, with Rabbi, only G-d knows!"

Strep B can cause severe damage to a compromised individual. We received a call from Health Canada that as family members who had come in close contact with Yehuda, we were at risk—albeit a slight one—for catching the infection and passing it on to others. I was asked if there were any others who had cared for Yehuda in the days leading up to his diagnosis. When I replied in the affirmative, I was told that all of us—family members and caregivers—had to go to a doctor immediately to be checked for signs of the infection and given a prescription for an antibiotic. Whether or not we were infected, we had to take the medication prophylactically.

It was quite a scene as ten of us piled into the doctor's office. The staff had been given advance notice by the Health Department. Ten prescriptions later, we walked over to the pharmacy to collect the medication. Back home, vials were lined up on the counter for those taking pills and one shelf on the refrigerator door was dedicated to liquid medication.

We made a great show of all of us taking our medication several times a day. To my frustration, Yehuda's caregiver, who was also notified by the Health Department, sent me a very angry email blaming me for putting his health at risk. I had to politely explain that no harm had been done to him. In fact, he was actually quite safe now that he was on antibiotics. We were all in the same position. There was no evil intent to poison him.

Once again, I was struck by the absurdity of my life. My husband might be dying, yet I still had to put up with caregivers and their shenanigans. If "all" I had to do was deal with Yehuda, that alone would have been a handful and then some. To also have to deal with the "extraneous" people in my life, who were, in theory, supposed to be making my life easier, was a difficult challenge indeed. Perhaps, if he had had the decency to express concern for Yehuda, I might not have reacted so strongly—but I doubt it. There were simply too many years of pent-up frustration.

New Kids' Picture

Our family (okay, me) is very into pictures. I do mean very. From the time Shmuly was born, I dragged, bribed, and cajoled my family to go for a yearly family portrait. We have them all hanging on our walls. In fact, a guest once remarked, "Look! Your house doesn't have any rabbi pictures, no artwork—just your kids!" When Malka was born and we spent an hour shifting under bright lights, trying to get three kids to smile at the photographer, Yehuda declared that he would never be doing that again. From now on, kids only. That worked well for a few years. A few portraits later, Yehuda was wondering why we were not in any of the recent pictures. Should a family picture not have the whole family in it? Once again, we joined in the fun.

We had a stack of pictures that accompanied Yehuda on his hospital admissions—we hung them up all over the room. It reassured us that we were still connected, and reminded the staff that not only was he their patient, he was also our beloved husband and father.

As a display of affection, support, and encouragement, the kids now decided it was time for an upgrade. They planned a coordinated color scheme and went to our backyard to take an updated family picture. They asked me to be in it. I could not. We cannot have a family picture with just one parent in it. It's either both parents or neither. I could not handle the thought of a one-parent family.

The picture came out beautiful. We printed it out to display in Yehuda's room. At the same time, the kids uploaded the picture to a website that makes photo gifts. The site transformed the picture into a gorgeous flannel blanket. At some point, we made a matching pillowcase to go with it but it somehow ended up in the hospital laundry, never to be seen again.

Yehuda was so touched by the gift. It was also a great conversation piece among the staff who would come in to visit and check it out.

Here Comes Our Favorite Rabbi!

Even before this current hospitalization, Queensway Carleton had become our "home away from home." I cannot even count how many times we went there for medical care. Sometimes Yehuda's condition was treatable in the emergency room and we would go home after several hours. Other times, he needed further treatment, observation, or other intervention. We knew that being admitted was always a possibility, but it was not what we looked forward to. We were always apprehensive when heading to the hospital—not because we were afraid of the care Yehuda would receive, but because we dreaded the separation. We could not bear for the family to be apart. Yehuda hated to be away from us. He garnered strength from being surrounded by those he loved and who loved him. He thrived in the environment where he could still be himself—making a difference to us, to our friends, to our family, to our community.

When going to the hospital, the primary focus was on getting him well enough to go home. Other issues had to be relegated to the sidelines. Admission to the hospital always entailed some sort of physical setback by the time he was discharged. The longer the stay, the longer it took to catch up—the proverbial one step forward, two steps back. Any gains Yehuda made came about through intense effort and sheer determination. It was painful to watch him go through the same processes again and again and again. But he never let feelings of frustration get in the way of his interactions with the staff. He deeply appreciated the care they gave him and made sure to express it often.

Yehuda was likely the most popular patient in the hospital. When we would show up in Emergency, the nurses would exclaim, "Rabbi, what are you doing here again?" "Rabbi, you look too good to be here." "Rabbi, you look a whole lot better than the last time you were here! Must not be too bad." If admitted, the charge nurse would welcome him with her booming, "Here comes my favorite rabbi!" and he would be greeted in the ICU by all the nurses in turn. We knew most of them by name. Even the ones who were not assigned to him would stop by to catch up. They all knew the goings-on in our family. We would tell them that while it was nice to see them again, we would rather meet them in the supermarket.

In order to gain access to the ICU, one has to call in to the nurses' station from outside a locked door. After the visitor identifies himself and whom he is visiting, a nurse buzzes him in. The kids loved that job—get upstairs to the second floor, wash hands with sanitizer, call in to the nurses, and resanitize. It was a drill they were used to. The youngest ones would say, "Hi, I'm here to visit my Abba," and the door would pop open. When I called to be let in or for the nurse to check on Yehuda, all I had to do was say, "Hi, it's Shaindel." We were on a first-name basis. Even in other parts of the hospital, we were often greeted by various staff members who recognized us.

Respirator-Dependent Again: Preparing to Come Home

Due to the cardiac arrest, Yehuda was once again respirator-dependent. We hoped that just as he had been able to wean himself from it in 2010, he would do it again now in 2014. Yehuda was willing and determined to make this happen; however, his body simply could not do it. The numerous pneumonias and respiratory illnesses had damaged his lungs. Scar tissue made it harder for them to work at the capacity they were used to. His doctors tried multiple times, for short increments of time, to have him breathe on his own. They would wait and try again several hours or days later. Yehuda managed for very short intervals but could not get past a satisfactory margin. The doctors advised us that it was not safe. We would have to leave that goal behind us, unaccomplished. It was painful.

Being respirator-dependent is a fancy way of saying that Yehuda was on life support. His lungs were still working but with a great deal of help from a machine. This would complicate his being able to leave the hospital and live at home. It would also entail a much higher level of care at home than before. In fact, the length of his stay in the hospital was determined mainly by our ability to get things ready for him at home. Technically, he was deemed "healthy" long before he was actually discharged.

The respirator Yehuda was using belonged to the hospital; at home he would need his own. As we have socialized healthcare, we had to apply to a ventilator equipment pool to receive one. Until they were able to locate one, he would have to wait in the hospital. I was desperate to get him out—mainly because the longer he stayed in the hospital, the greater his risk of acquiring another infection. As we always said, "A hospital is no place for a sick person."

I decided to take matters into my own hands and find a respirator, no matter how much it cost. But where would I get one? I immediately thought of our friend Sruly Perkal, who had reassured us, during our Hurricane Sandy adventure in New York, that there was no need to worry about a possible loss of electricity, as he happened to have several generators available.

I called Sruly. "Do you have a respirator?"

"I don't, but my next-door neighbor does!"

I knew I had called the right guy. He was able to put me in touch with someone knowledgeable about the ins and outs of obtaining a respirator. I was pleasantly surprised to find out that they were not nearly as expensive as I had imagined. Our motto has always been that health and life are worth every penny. This would be the best investment of our funds.

But as I continued my research, I was appalled to find out that buying a respirator would not help us. Only the vent pool was licensed to service and maintain the safety of respirators. If we took another route, we would have no insurance coverage or backup for the machine. It would be useless. So close…yet so far. The wait continued. We had to use the time wisely. I and all our caregivers had to be trained in the proper usage of respirators—RT101—or RT for Dummies. Yehuda's life depended on us knowing exactly what to do, how, and when.

Being respirator-dependent once again precluded Yehuda from being able to eat. We had to plan for long-term tube feeding. The proper food, dosing, and schedule had to be worked out. The staff worked with us to make a plan based on his anticipated schedule at home.

Many lengthy meetings and consultations were held before Yehuda could be discharged. I felt I was already quite experienced with what we would need to make the transfer as smooth as possible. At the forefront of my mind was the emergency call bell disaster the first time around. The Home Depot doorbell contraption we rigged up when Yehuda first came home was no longer a viable option. I pressured the case manager to work out a system well in advance. As the discharge date came closer, there was still no bell idea on the horizon. After numerous calls and emails, I finally got a response: There would not be a call bell in time, and, as it is "very dangerous for Rabbi Simes to be unable to communicate if there is an emergency, it is essential to never, ever leave him unattended!" Brilliant, thanks for your help. Thankfully, after a phone call from our lawyer, the case manager and the speech therapist quickly found a way to accommodate our needs.

The main obstacle the respirator presented was communication.

We had to find a way for Yehuda to speak to us. Aside from basic needs, he had so much wisdom to share. After all, "You are still you!" We were not going to give up on that, especially given Yehuda's success with his blog. He had become a whiz at Dragon voice typing. Sharing his story with others gave meaning to his days. He had come so far from the days in rehab when he cried to our mentors, "What will I do with my life now? What is the meaning of my life? I thought I had it all worked out. I wanted to make a difference, to impact children and their families, to share my knowledge with others. How will I be able to do that?"

Yehuda had found a new way—his computer was his tool. When he could not be in a classroom or giving a lecture, he was on his computer. It was almost like the good old days when I would have to remind him to space in and stop thinking about his students for a few minutes. My newer challenge was convincing him to save his blogging for after doing homework with the kids, or to remember to eat lunch. It might have looked different, but it was still the same.

Would we have to go back to the dark days of being unable to communicate?

We renewed our contact with the rehab center. They have a speech department that deals with augmentative communication. We knew we would be relying on another distribution center to find us a communication device and wanted to get the ball rolling. As I had seen in the case of the respirator and other equipment essentials, these things take time. Lots of time—too much time. If we were going to have to wait, we should at least start the clock ticking before he was discharged.

Yehuda's wheelchair, as well, needed modification. The rehab center suggested we wait until the wheelchair issues were sorted out before working on the communication device. The device would get attached to the wheelchair. I reiterated the need to begin NOW. We would *not* be waiting for the wheelchair to get sorted out. It had already been four years of continuous sorting out with the wheelchair. What I suggested was earth shattering. We could work on the communication device now. If we were to get a new wheelchair, we would—get this—unscrew the device from the wheelchair and...drumroll please...rescrew it to the new wheelchair. Presto! Change-o!

We did not get this far to be told "No"!

RABBI SIMES IS HOME!
November 3, 2014

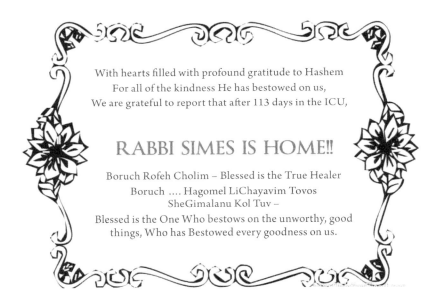

With hearts filled with profound gratitude to Hashem
For all of the kindness He has bestowed on us,
We are grateful to report that after 113 days in the ICU,

RABBI SIMES IS HOME!!

Boruch Rofeh Cholim – Blessed is the True Healer
Boruch .... Hagomel LiChayavim Tovos
SheGimalanu Kol Tuv –
Blessed is the One Who bestows on the unworthy, good
things, Who has Bestowed every goodness on us.

CHAPTER EIGHTEEN

Our New, New Normal

"THE SECOND TIME ABBA DIED" LED TO HIS LONGEST
hospital stay ever—113 days—nearly four months. He
was admitted in July and discharged in November. He
completely missed two seasons—there was no summer or fall for
Yehuda that year.

Those days were beyond harrowing. I felt like I was on a perpetual
hamster wheel, running and running in circles yet going nowhere. It
was a time of roller coasters and free fall. A time when there would be
incremental progress and improvement—inch up and up—and then
a wild drop down to the ground at colossal speed. We viewed even a
positive sign with trepidation, as we did not know how long it would
last. Our nerves were shot.

Finally, Yehuda came home and we slowly began to settle into
another "new normal." It reminded me of a conversation I once had
with a colleague. She had lived in a particular community for several
years due to her husband's job. While it had some positive qualities,
there were many drawbacks for her. When their stint in the community
ended, she was relieved to be moving "back home." I spoke to her after
her move back and she remarked, "It's unbelievable what a person can
get used to." I was the last person she had to explain that to.

Yehuda could no longer communicate verbally. He could not eat orally, and all the strength in his arms was gone. He could not even lift them, let alone drive his own power chair.

Communication was now our top priority. We worked tirelessly with the rehab center to get some kind—any kind!—of device for him. Until then, we resorted to using a letter board. This was a rectangular sheet of plexiglass containing quadrants with letters in them. Yehuda would gaze at a letter, one at a time. We would have to figure out which letters he was looking at and string them together to form words. It was draining for him, draining for me, and completely frustrating. This letter thing was not going to cut it.

Over the course of several months, Yehuda was set up with an eye-gaze computer. The technique was the same, but it was electronic, so it went faster and the results were quicker and more accurate. The program had a word-predict feature which significantly shortened the output time. The program could be individualized—we were able to program the computer with words and phrases that were important to Yehuda; my name, the kids' names, "Good Shabbos," wonderful—which was Yehuda's typical answer when anyone asked him how he was doing.

With lots of trial and error, a fair dose of frustration, and sheer determination, Yehuda became a whiz at that computer. Most people using that program use it for one-word utterances, such as pain, tired, hungry. Yehuda was "speaking" sentences and paragraphs, writing speeches and continuing his blog. He even figured out how to trick the computer to pronounce the words the way he wanted it to by spelling them wrong. He loved "hitting" the button that spoke his thoughts in a delightful British accent. There were several other voice options, but I drew the line at the child and female voices. Way too creepy.

It was invigorating to have my husband back and be able to really talk to him in a meaningful manner.

The only plus side to the trach was that Yehuda no longer needed the BiPAP machine. The respirator took care of those issues. For me, this meant that even after he was tucked in for the night, he could "talk." We acquired a special pole that attached to his bed for the computer.

The computer opened up a whole new world for him. Once again, he could contribute and share and teach, speak as a parent and a spouse.

The rehab center was so excited with his progress that they invited him to record a publicity piece for them, using the computer. Yehuda was thrilled to oblige; once again, he was Ottawa Rehab Centre's poster boy.

> I'm back (with a vengeance), thank G-d!
>
> Let me fill you in about my unfortunate lengthy absence (from our limited perspectives). As you know, my wife and I traveled on a journey of a lifetime to the Land of Israel. This incredible event took place in December 2013. Leading up to this endeavor, I worked and trained extremely hard for all the eventualities that would likely occur. This went on for several months before the trip... What occurred in Israel was memorable beyond words—except for a visit to the hospital with the wicked pneumonia.
>
> What transpired over the next several months was a cycle of hospitalizations in the ICU. Apparently, I had picked up a rare bug only found in the Middle East, especially in hospitals. This all culminated in an ICU stay of 113 days. I suffered from three major infections that almost cost me my life. These were a nasty case of MERS, Clostridium difficile (C. diff), and strep B in my bloodstream. This is so serious that one of these would likely do in an otherwise healthy individual. The doctors called my survival a miracle.
>
> This left me with a tracheostomy, dependent on a respirator to breathe. My new reality is that I cannot talk or eat.
>
> *From the Rolling Rabbi blog, "Hashem*
> *Still Wants Me Here!" March 13, 2015*

About four years ago, people often asked how it is that I never ask why I had to become a quadriplegic with a near loss of control over my body.

My answer was twofold. Firstly, I never got angry because to me, anger implies an object against whom you direct your anger. Now, objectively, whom would I be angry at, other than G-d?

Which leads me to my second point. If I would imagine to know why this catastrophe happened (from our limited perspectives), I would be G-d.

This all leads me to a major emotional inner motivator. I simply refuse to surrender to worthless despondence, useless depression, and purposeless anger. I just want to give myself the best shot of being happy with whatever Hashem throws my way. For the rabbis teach that only such an individual can be truly rich.

Now that I find myself in this new position, I have to ask the same question. I ask G-d *what* are my obligations in my world now? With my limited capabilities, how can I best serve Hashem?

In Hebrew this idea works neatly. I don't ask *lamah* [why], instead I ask *lemah* [what] (same Hebrew letters).

In short, be happy with what you have. (After all, it always could be worse!)

From the Rolling Rabbi blog, "I Don't
Ask Why, I Ask What," March 17, 2015

My close friend, Rabbi Lederman, asked me two insightful questions.

First off, how do I eat? Great question! Like a good Jew, I shall answer with a question. Who says I eat? I actually don't eat all day long. How's that for binge dieting?

Here is how I don't starve. I have a feeding peg that

leads into my abdomen. I get breakfast, lunch, supper, snacks, and coffee breaks in one shot. It drips straight into my belly. How convenient! A real time saver! And I love the fact that I no longer have to floss!

Now I would like to answer the second question.

How do I manage to blog? After all, when I could speak, I would use voice recognition software and I would speak through a microphone hooked up to my computer. Now what?

I finally got a dandy computer that mounts to my wheelchair. Here's how it works (when it works!). I simply (!) gaze with my eyeballs at letters or phrases and the computer vocalizes what I spell.

The top techies in the community and at a local university are collaborating to create a device that is more powerful and user friendly! May it be Hashem's will that they be successful!

From the Rolling Rabbi blog, "Be Happy
with Whatever You Have!" March 18, 2015

There was once a group of blind men, especially hand-picked to undergo a battery of treatments, with the ultimate objective of curing them of their blindness. They were brought to a specially outfitted mansion, retrofitted for their ultimate pleasure and benefit. In the mansion, they were supplied with a team of expert physicians, specializing in curing blindness. As well, the mansion contained balms and medicinal intervention to cure the patients.

However, the unfortunate blind men completely misunderstood the noble purpose of the specially equipped mansion. They chose to be self-absorbed in their sorry conditions. They actually ignored the doctors' useful instructions; as well, they adamantly refused to avail themselves of the necessary therapies. As a result of their [intransigence], they ended up colliding into obstacles and the very equipment that was intended to improve their lives. Those unfortunate souls fell on their faces...receiving bloody wounds and broken bones.

Because of their many woes, they cursed the designers of their imagined torture chamber. What terribly misunderstanding disabled souls! They mistakenly thought that the very equipment intended to heal them was instead designed to their detriment.

Aren't we similar to the blind men? And isn't Hashem similar to the designer of the mansion?

(Adapted from Chovos Halevavos)

From the Rolling Rabbi blog, "A Tale
of Blind Men," March 25, 2015

A thought.

Much like the men in the story, you would have to be blind not to notice that we are drowning in luxuries. It permeates us as it surrounds us! Each person ought to focus on the myriad of blessings that he's showered with.

In my case, here are but a few that I'm aware of. I'll start with the biggies:

I am blessed to be alive, escaping the likelihood of imminent death numerous times... Over the years, I left the land of the living, and was resuscitated by paramedics (when I checked out at home), and by doctors (when I checked out at the hospital)...

When the "accident" first occurred, and my spinal cord was crushed nearly completely right through, the lesion was at the very high level (C4, C5). In all likelihood, I should have been able to take shallow breaths for only a matter of a short few minutes; certainly not retain the ability to speak. In actuality, I breathed and spoke (screamed from massive pain) for about forty-five minutes before help arrived and they were able to extricate me from our van (using the "Jaws of Life")!

On Pesach, a couple of years ago, I suffered from a respiratory arrest. I am told that an ambulance arrived in short order, and the medics brought me back.

I also suffered a couple of major heart attacks in the hospital. I felt no chest pains or other classical symptoms of a heart attack. I just "happened" to be in the hospital for other reasons. In one case, I received four stents, and in the other, it took five full minutes to revive me. No brain damage!

Now for the small gifts.

I will limit myself to my present condition (honestly, with the onset of my quadriplegia, there is no end to the gifts).

I am blessed with this too-cool device which allows me to "simply" gaze at letters on a screen. The computer, like magic, then verbalizes that which I've typed. I can even choose the voice and accent! I chose "Peter," a British chap who sounds quite intelligent. This screen is mobile in that it can be installed onto my power chair. A friend who was in speech pathology told me that such technology was non-existent a mere fifteen years ago. It is difficult to imagine not being able to communicate with this technology (I know because I suffered through being soundless for quite a few months).

I also have a couple of fancy-delancey respirators. One comes along with me wherever I go. It is installed on the back of my power chair. My second respirator is stationary and is equipped with a humidifier. This one I use as I sleep. Both respirators have really cool settings, personalized to my breathing patterns. What a blessing!

I also have a hot-to-trot in/ex machine. I have this machine because I cannot clear my throat or cough. (You do that countless times every day, thank G-d.) In my case, secretions build up in my lungs. Much like a vacuum cleaner, the in/ex machine sucks my secretions out of my lungs. What a wonderful gift!

Once we become sensitive to the overabundant presents from Hashem, we will be much less likely to sweat the small stuff! No matter how hot of a climate you live in :)

From the Rolling Rabbi blog, "Addendum
to Last Post (A Tale...)," March 30, 2015

A sense of humor is no laughing matter!

We like to buy a variety of toys for our kids to play with at the Seder—things like squishy frogs and dark sunglasses for the plague of darkness. This year, my wife bought some cute fluffy toy matzah balls with functional legs that propel them across flat surfaces.

At least most of them worked in this way. There was one unfortunate matzah ball whose legs wouldn't work! I immediately declared, "He's just like me!" My wife dubbed it "the quadriplegic matzah ball"!

We cannot change my situation, but a level beyond acceptance is being able to laugh at it.

Truth be told, there were many instances that used to drive us crazy. For example, my caregivers would too often not show up. Now, we've reached a point where we matter-of-factly go along with it, and we make the necessary alternate arrangements.

In truth, I learned the importance of a sense of humor

from my great *rebbi*. He taught us, by example, the great benefit of laughter and being generally jolly.

I had the privilege of living in the Rosh Yeshivah's house for an unforgettable year. He was so happy that he commonly laughed or hummed an upbeat tune.

I had thought that he was incredibly happy, but I later found out that although that was true, there was an additional factor. Years later, a student who had studied in the yeshivah years earlier told me of an incident that changed my appreciation of my *rosh yeshivah*.

He related that the Rosh Yeshivah once stayed at his home in Dallas. He observed the Rosh Yeshivah strutting about the house as he hummed a cheery song. ...

"What made the Rosh Yeshivah so happy?" he asked.

The Rosh Yeshivah explained that he had just received a frantic phone call from a student in a far-flung community about a certain crisis he was going through. "The world is caving in!" he exclaimed.

The student asked the obvious question, "Then why is Rebbi so happy?"

The Rosh Yeshivah explained that otherwise he would go "crazy" with pain. It seems as if he was utilizing happiness as a protective device to prevent some level of emotional depression.

A second strategy the Rosh Yeshivah taught us was that laughter has the power to deflect even the most outrageous demands.

I myself try to perfect the strategy in the classroom. When my students would demand things I felt they didn't need, my response was to laugh out loud. I laughed sincerely, because I was able to find the humor in their unreasonable demands. For example, when they would ask for extra recess or free time, and they didn't need it, I just laughed. (On the other hand, when they did need it, I would award them with their now reasonable requests.)

Chag same'ach!

From the Rolling Rabbi blog, "The Quadriplegic Matzah Ball," April 2, 2015

In my prior post, I wrote about the importance of laughter. Because of the time crunch with the onset of Yom Tov, I neglected to mention an important point:

Some might wonder about the rationale of laughing at students' silly requests. After all, in their minds their requests are reasonable. ...

To my mind, a teacher has three options upon being confronted with outrageous demands. ...

1. The teacher might respond, rather loudly, something along the lines of, "What were you thinking? That is the most foolish request I have ever heard! My heavens, if you dare ask me something like that ever again, I will give you a punishment you will never forget! In fact, just for thinking such a *chutzpahdig* thing, the whole class just lost recess for an entire week!"

2. Just ignore them and their silly little question.

3. Laugh, because it's not rebellious nor is it worthy of a "dressing down." It's genuinely funny! I am demonstrating that I am not ruffled in the slightest! In fact, I find it humorous that they would come up with such a request from left field! I even find that my reaction will evoke muffled giggles from my students, despite themselves!

From the Rolling Rabbi blog, "Important Clarification to Last Post (The Quadriplegic Matzah Ball)," April 6, 2015

This year, we were determined to carry on the Seders in as normal a fashion as possible.

You all know, by now, that "normal" is a relative term—especially around here! We need to be constantly adapting to a "new normal." Things tend to fluctuate, so we have to be flexible.

I was driven to lead our family Seder like every other year, to the best of my present abilities... A plan was hatched. I programmed into my computer[1] (the same one I'm using now) the phrases and sentences I wanted to say. Things like *Kadesh, Urchatz* (with pauses between each so those assembled could repeat after my computer); the ten plagues (with pauses between each so those assembled could drip wine from their glasses as they recited the plagues along with my computer); various instructions; loose, engaging, and kid-friendly translations; and short *divrei Torah*.

I thus was able to be back in the saddle again! My family was so grateful and proud! I was tickled pink! It was certainly a unique experience. Different, to be sure, but somehow very much the same.

The lesson I derived was: Give Hashem your utmost with whatever resources you have at your disposal! You will most likely surprise yourself with the tremendous resources you have within you. All that's called for is a bit of creativity!

You and I can do it!

From the Rolling Rabbi blog, "Our Seders This Year," April 8, 2015

---

1.   According to the *psak* we received, Yehuda, who had the status of a *choleh she'yeish bo sakanah*, was allowed to use his computer on Shabbos and Yom Tov.

Every year, I long for the time I lived in Israel when I kept one day of Yom Tov. Now that I find myself far from our land, I grapple every year with how to make the second Seder fun and non-repetitive for the kids.

This year would be no different. So I devised a plan. Besides the things I had already saved on my computer, I programmed in new interactive stuff special for the second night.

From the Rolling Rabbi blog, "Our Second Seder," April 9, 2015

Being in a compromised state after a catastrophic accident, one might wonder how young children will react and adapt to their new reality of having a father whose appearance is radically different than before. For example, I no longer can give them bear hugs or pick them up and swing them through the air. Should we expect them to be in a state of confusion? Might they be angry? Perhaps they would be withdrawn or even alienated from their father? Well, in our case, our nine children—even the youngest ones—have shown remarkable resilience and a quick normalization process.

I would like to share with you a few examples which illustrate this.

A few days ago, my seven-year-old daughter was asked by her teacher to choose among a range of professions and to describe and illustrate the characteristics they possess. She immediately chose a nurse and drew things that she sees every day. We took the fact that she proceeded to do this so naturally as a sign that she has found comfort with her situation. The amazing thing is that she had to explain what the items were to the teacher.

I shall now show you the picture that she drew.

Nurse

Translation of what she wrote:

Cough assist

Suction

Trach tubes

Feed tubes

Band Aids

Bandages

She then proceeded to inform her teacher, "I think when I grow up, I will be a nurse. I already know most of it, and then I can help Abba!"

Now that's what I call being comfortable with her situation!

I have a four-year-old child who, when he was three, asked his friends who came by with an invitation to a bas mitzvah, "Is there an elevator? My Abba can come if there is one!"

My ten-year-old daughter went over to her teacher and mentioned that a girl in her class was not feeling well; could the teacher help her?

The teacher asked how she knew that the girl was sick. Did she tell her?

"No, I can just tell," she replied.

The teacher went over and asked if she was okay. The girl started crying; she was too shy to tell the teacher that she was unwell and wanted to go home.

The teacher was amazed! How did my daughter know?

This happened more than once. She was able to pick up nuances in her environment! This could only be because my young daughter has become super-sensitized to those around her. I think this is caused by her ever-watchful eye over her dear dad.

One of my eldest daughters had an interview for acceptance at a women's seminary in Israel. Apparently, the interviewer had heard about our story and was curious about how it affected my daughter. So the interviewer asked why she had neglected to mention anything about the accident in her essay. Her response was, "You asked me to write about myself, not about my father!" Clearly, she has a healthy sense that her identity is worthy in its own right, and it is totally separate from the accident that so deeply affected her.

The lesson is obvious. Although some adults act like children in all the wrong ways, there is one behavior that we should all mimic—and that's the behavior of flexibility and adaptability. Because getting stuck in one's ways can be dangerous when things "happen" to change in life.

From the Rolling Rabbi blog, "What We Can
Learn from Young Children," April 30, 2015

I have incredible news to share with you!

As you probably know, I am still regaining my strength after my extended hospitalization. It generally takes me a few days to recover for each day in the ICU. I am told this is typical for spinal-cord-injured people. I dreaded how long it would take to recover from a 113-day stay in the horrifying ICU.

Surprisingly, although I am a righty, and I had always been stronger in that arm, I returned from the hospital with more strength in my left arm! It was therefore determined by my physiotherapists that I should drive my power chair with my left hand. So the wheelchair wizards outfitted my power chair with a new driving switch for my left hand! They also completely removed my right hand rest, upon which sat my prior driving gear.

Incidentally, I now happily became more accessible to my young children on my right side! Now, my youngest son revels in climbing up on my lap without assistance!

My goal was to drive/dance at a good friend's wedding in late June. My physiotherapists said to go for it—but it would take extreme effort and patience to strengthen my left arm enough to meet my goal. I replied that I was no stranger to effort and patience!!

As two weeks passed with intensive strengthening exercises, which I did every hour, I sadly did not seem to progress. In fact, my physiotherapists told me I might have to resort to head controls to drive.

Today the wheelchair wizard returned to provide power to the joystick! My physiotherapists were present as well to assist.

The results were beyond belief! My physiotherapist, marveling at the results, said that I performed 70 percent better than they anticipated!

I was on the road again! I was actually driving on my own! I felt so free! I felt so independent!

From the Rolling Rabbi blog,
"I'm Driven!" May 5, 2015

As you all know, I was hospitalized this past summer in critical condition for an extended period of time. To be exact, they did not let me out for 113 days.

This proved to be a huge setback for me. Not only was I trached, leaving me unable to speak or eat food, but I also was left respirator-dependent, which comes with its own set of complications.

This being the case, one may wonder what my frame of mind is generally, being in this state, or specifically upon finally cutting loose from my hospital imprisonment. Well, if you possess such an inquiring mind, you've come to the right place! For herein you shall find the answers you so crave!

The first stage of my hospitalization exile, I could not tell you my state of mind. Because I was so weak and sick with raging infections, I was quite unaware of what was happening to me.

Gradually, I came back to my senses. It was then that I had to mentally and emotionally reconcile what I was (and still viewed myself) with what I had become (still uncomfortable with the man in the mirror). I found it a painful and heart-breaking process.

Actually, I could not cope with the prospect of not speaking or eating my wife's yummy food.

I knew one thing: I desperately wanted the trach out. I yearned for a return to what I knew as normalcy. I knew it would take incredible effort, but I told my doctors that I had successfully weaned off a trach and respirator in the past, shortly after the accident. I had been trached immediately following the accident. Through blood, sweat, and tears (just kidding about the sweat. Spinal-cord-injured individuals don't sweat!), I worked extremely hard to wean myself off the trach.

In fact, this was so ground-breaking that my world-class respirologist had me videotaped while I was still incarcerated in the ICU in order to show it to respirologists in his worldwide lectures... This improved my life immeasurably! I eventually gave inspirational lectures before large audiences in Ottawa and all over North America and Israel. I also Skyped with classes and groups around America. In addition, I was privileged to be interviewed on radio and in print. Plus, I was able to return to my passion of teaching young people, teenagers, and adults!

I actively sought out these opportunities in the hope that I could enrich the lives of others, thereby being *mekadesh Hashem* (sanctifying Hashem's Name). As well, I knew I had to do something positive with my new situation.

I felt so alive with meaning and fulfillment! I found purpose in my life! And I was so grateful and super motivated to carry on!

Now I found myself at ground zero, back to the dreadful trach and respirator. I wanted freedom from the machines, and I was sure I could do it based on my previous history. Before I was discharged from my latest ICU sojourn, I tearfully asked my doctors if I could do it again.

Their response? "You are an atypical patient"— meaning, it could be done!

Indeed, when I finally returned home, I tried incredibly hard to accomplish my goal. As a first step this involves going "cuff down" for long periods of time, eventually building up to "cuff down" for the whole day. Let me now explain what is meant by "cuff down."

There is a bulb connected to my trach in my throat which serves to hold the trach in place. "Cuff down" refers to being able to tolerate having the cuff down (that is, having the bulb deflated) so that, essentially, I am breathing on my own.

If you saw me blowing a whistle in an earlier post, that only could have happened because I was cuff down, so air could pass through my upper airway.

Indeed, I had sporadic success. Initially, I actually built up to three hours! But alas, as hard as I tried, the promising start was short lived. For an inexplicable reason, I started to produce large amounts of secretions from my lungs; they caused me to cough and sputter violently. This unfortunate turn of events precluded the possibility of continuing to meet my goal.

So I was stuck, having to use a highly frustrating letter board to communicate. The frustrating part is that in order to communicate I would have to gaze at the box that contained the letter of the word I wanted to say. This was accomplished by someone reading aloud all the letters until I nodded my head to indicate the letter I wanted.

Here is a photo of the letter board.

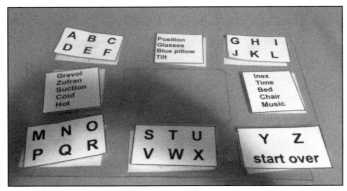

After some months of maddening efforts with the board, I finally got my too-hot-to-trot eyeball-gaze computer. This completely changed my life! It finally gave me a voice! In a very real sense, it gave me back my humanity!

Now, after ten months of being unable to speak, I find it extremely difficult to stop talking.

As a blessed plus, my personality and sense of humor comes through! And, what is most gratifying is being able to say "Thank you" or "Goodbye" to people even when the letter board is not available!

In the immortal words of Charles Dickens, "Never say never!"

From the Rolling Rabbi blog, "How I Felt
Upon Returning Home," May 8, 2015

I titled this post, "A Perk of Being a Quad Who's on a Respirator," and I can see you all wondering, "What is the perk of being in my situation? What is the Rolling Rabbi on?!"

Actually, I am thankfully off of all the powerful narcotics that reduced my unbearable pain but at the same time played with my mind! For example, one time early on I was sure I was hearing symphony music. I had my worried brother-in-law running around the rehab center trying to find the source of the phantom music. But at least my pain was somewhat under control!

So, what could possibly be a perk now that I've been hit with my present situation?

I find that I am closer to Hashem than ever before! I now pray like I never prayed before. I now cry to Hashem like I never cried before. I now connect to Hashem like never before.

Being trapped in this weakened body has caused all these benefits!

I feel the presence of Hashem so much during my day, especially during painful times.

I have no one to rely on besides Him!

I recall when I was a classroom teacher. Whenever I would enter the classroom, I would pause and say a short prayer. It went something like this: "I can't possibly teach this class without Your help. I'm so alone! Please let me succeed in my quest to teach Your children."

I should tell you that I am not a born teacher, being the shy guy that I am. I believe any success I may have had was due to my unquenchable thirst to get the job done right, and my prayers!

I discovered that the strongest prayers were when I stood outside a rowdy class. I really meant it then!

This is similar to the pouring out of my heart when I pray and cry now.

When I explained all of this to a friend, he pointed out that there is a *Ramban* which supports such an idea! This can be found in *Deuteronomy* 11:10.

He explains why the Land of Israel is not like the Land of Egypt. The explanation is that Egypt is a fruitful land with many streams and lakes, whereas Israel is a barren land, having to rely on rains from Heaven. He seems to go on to say that Israel in essence is insecure, and by its very nature must rely on heartfelt prayer.

This has poignant meaning in our days. We know that we are sorely lacking in security in Israel. Whom do we have to rely on other than Hashem?

The Ramban actually relates this to sick people. They are so insecure and in need of Hashem's mercy that they can be expected to turn to Hashem with full hearts.

It is apparent to me that this applies to anyone who faces challenges. They ought to create a close connection to Hashem. They are in such a precarious condition that it is natural to turn to Hashem.

I hope you take this powerful lesson to heart, for who among us does not face tremendous challenges?

From the Rolling Rabbi blog, "A Perk of Being a Quad Who's on a Respirator," May 17, 2015

It is difficult to put into words my good fortune of being enveloped within a loving family and community ever since the accident. I was made aware by a reader in New York how fortunate I truly am! I was cheered on by adoring members of my family and community throughout my journey. This includes both the ups and downs.

Sadly, there are cases where exclusionary tactics are employed against disabled individuals. This makes me shudder with wondering where I would be if I had not benefited from such loving care and concern.

Within days of the accident, three initiatives took place.

A massive prayer rally was held at the local Jewish Community Center. We were informed that there was standing room only. What a boost we felt in the hospital at Syracuse! All colors and shades of Ottawa's community showed up. We felt that this alone should be a merit for my recovery!

Also, my students ran a fundraising project which included a car wash at the school parking lot. This project raised a tremendous amount of money. Especially considering this aggressive project was conceived of and implemented by my grade school students! A feeling of love and togetherness swept over us!

Then there was a Shabbos-observance project. This was successfully spearheaded by my close friend and partner at Torah High! This initiative encouraged people to increase their Shabbos observance... Again, we felt that if we could be the conduit of so much good, something positive would come from it!

This care and concern continues to this day. The myriad of visitors and well-wishers testify to the togetherness of our remarkable community!

I truly feel that I have a powerful task force on my side!

From the Rolling Rabbi blog, "My Life-Saving Inclusion," May 27, 2015

My good friend Rabbi Lederman wonders about whether or not I had ever wished that I had died at the scene of the "accident." What a thought-provoking question!

I suppose there might be room for such an inquiry. After all, in one unforgiving instant, my entire life was turned upside down. Up until that moment I had felt on top of the world. And for good reason! I earned a very high profile in the Ottawa Jewish community. The community adored me as much as I adored them! Chief among my beloved community were the many hundreds of my students whom I truly love. I was selected as a Grinspoon–Steinhardt Award winner for the top Jewish educators across North America. Most importantly, we were changing lives Jewishly as much as *we* were being changed for the better!

Then, poof! It all disappeared. Or so it may have seemed.

This is besides the obvious loss of control over my body. My body no longer behaved the way I wanted it to. And we must not leave out my constant companion of physical pain.

The past five years have been an exercise in gains, losses, and regrowth. I suffered numerous quad-related hospitalizations. Because of this, I was separated from my family for about a year of this time.

Now a whole new situation hit me. I can no longer speak or eat delicious food. I can no longer deliver uplifting lectures to small and large crowds.

So, yes, the question is a valid one. Did I ever wish that I could have saved myself all the physical and emotional turmoil by being taken on the spot?

Allow me to make myself super abundantly clear: I never ever entertained such a thought! It never even entered my mind before quickly dismissing it!

Why, you may ask? Because I embrace my life, however it looks or feels!

I wake up every morning hearing the birds sing. I immediately hear my youngest children frolicking and carrying on. Then the older ones pitter-patter down for breakfast. I hear their spoons clanging in their cereal bowls.

The point is, they behave like normal and well-adjusted kids. I wonder what the scene might have looked like had I not been here.

I still have the same responsibility to be here for my family. And I am so grateful that I am!

I have always viewed my life's mission to use whatever resources I had at my disposal to be *mekadesh Hashem*. I am so grateful that I can still do that!

I have always loved nature. I am so grateful that

I can still partake of Hashem's stunning luxuries that surround us!

I especially get inspired when I can touch people's lives. I am so grateful that I have opportunities, almost daily, to do so!

I must make mention of this blog. Sharing my thoughts and feelings with you, my loyal readers, and hearing your comments, helps brighten my day. And for that I am so grateful!

For all these reasons and more I am most grateful to be here!

From the Rolling Rabbi blog, "Did I Ever Wish
I Had Died at the 'Accident'?" June 7, 2015

A close friend of my family asked about my background and how it influenced who I am today.

I suppose that I cannot be definitive about the influences of the past, but I can comment on what changed...

I spent many years immersed in *mussar* study while I was in yeshivah. As well, I worked hard on my *rebbi's shmuessen.*

All that I had thought I knew, I quickly found out after the accident that I had no clue!

Now, I want to be absolutely clear that I really did know all about *emunah* and *bitachon* (faith and trust in Hashem). When it really counted, however, I found myself at ground zero. I had to relearn that which I had taken for granted.

My fresh new book of choice became *Chovos Halevavos.* Fortunately, I had placed sticky flags at places of interest in the book before the accident. The accident rendered my hands and fingers useless.

My life-saving chapter became the chapter on

bitachon. I suddenly came to the realization that I understood life on a whole deeper plane! What I had thought was important no longer mattered to me... I guess I am saying that my past studies gave me a strong foundation with which to work, but I viewed life through a different lens.

Never before had I appreciated swallowing or taking a breath as I do now. When I regained the ability to move my arms a bit, I discovered the tremendous blessing of movement. When I got sensation back, I realized the gift of feeling. This came in handy to know when an arm or a leg got caught in a doorway. And this new sensitivity spilled over to things I had not lost.

Now I realized the blessing of sight and hearing as never before. I became super-sensitized to the myriad of gifts that Hashem has gifted our bodies with. Now I can add eating and speaking. I suppose it's time for a T-shirt that says, "Eating and speaking are overrated."

In addition, my experience has reinforced the powerful truth that Hashem has endowed us with incredible inner strength to accomplish unbelievable feats when a situation calls for it. We are all familiar with stories where regular people went beyond their capabilities when in crisis mode. The explanation is that these super-human abilities lay dormant within them until they detonated with terrific force when called for!

My *rebbi* used to relate that when he was a young man, he once told his father that he felt like a hypocrite when saying the Shema prayer. The Shema says that we must be ready to give up our lives when the situation calls for it. My *rebbi* sighed that he could not honestly say those words. He was not ready to sacrifice his life for Hashem.

His father reassured him that, true, he could not do so

now, but when the time came, he would suddenly find the strength! He explained to him that one is endowed with untapped strength. This unknown strength will rush to the surface when the motivation is great.

The trick is to live life with inspired motivation so that we can tap into our true strengths and abilities!

From the Rolling Rabbi blog, "How I Got to Where I Am Today," June 14, 2015

Let's talk about giving up your life when the situation calls for it. Although this is our most precious commodity, we are sometimes thrust into unfortunate situations when it is called for.

I am not only talking about giving up one's life instead of committing the three cardinal sins of murder, idol worship, and immorality. I am talking about each one of us in our regular lives.

Allow me to explain.

The Jewish People, fresh out of Egypt, after witnessing all the wonders there, stood at the banks of the Red Sea. They were effectively trapped on all sides. The mighty Egyptian army threatened them from behind. The raging sea was looming in front of them. Ferocious animals were licking their chops on either side of them.

The Jewish People did the only thing they could. They prayed to Hashem.

Surprisingly, the Divine command was to go forward right into the sea!

At this point, the Jews were frozen with fear. To make matters worse, the Midrash describes how the tribes argued with one another, saying that they would never enter the stormy sea first.

Suddenly Nachshon, the son of Aminadav, from the

tribe of Yehuda, without a moment's delay, jumped right into the forbidding sea!

Nachshon was greatly rewarded for this selfless act.

Rabbi Chaim Shmuelevitz asks a most disturbing question.

We generally focus on Nachshon's great act. But where were the tribes? Why were none of the other Jews willing and ready to sacrifice their lives for the sake of Hashem? There was a direct command to enter the sea!

Are we not familiar with the stories of entire communities giving up their lives when the hour called for it? Throughout the blood-soaked and tear-drenched pages of our history, even simple Jews sacrificed their lives when they had no choice! So why didn't the Jewish People, who must have been on a lofty level after living through the exodus from Egypt, have the strength of conviction to do the same? The answer offered by Rabbi Shmuelevitz had a tremendous effect on me.

He answers that the test facing the Jews of the desert was qualitatively different than the tests facing the Jews through the ages. Had the Jews of the desert been faced with the identical test of the Jews through the ages, they would have jumped into the sea without a moment's delay. The test of the Jews of the ages was to sacrifice their lives for the sake of Heaven; to give themselves up in order to die. But the test of the Jews of the desert was to give themselves up in order to live. They had to look at the raging sea as if it was dry land. They had to view the stormy waters as if therein was their salvation.

The former test of the ages was already trail-blazed by Avraham when he went into the fiery furnace, and at the binding of Yitzchak. Those great actions were set into the spiritual DNA of all the Jews throughout the generations who had the strength to sacrifice their lives in order to die.

But the generation of the desert was hit with a brand-new test. This test was the ultimate challenge, one that no generation ever faced. They were faced with an unbearable test of faith to look at the raging river of seeming certain death, and see tranquility.

I identify so much with this explanation, because in my life I have to find a way to look at the danger that surrounds me daily, and see only tranquility!

...We would do well to utilize this coping technique. Instead of drowning in our troubles, we have the ability to float upon tranquil waters!

From the Rolling Rabbi blog, "Sacrificing Your Most Precious Commodity in a Whole New Way!" June 16, 2015

Yesterday I made an agonizing but correct choice.

As you probably are aware, I have been working on strengthening my arm so I could drive my power chair! Let me tell you that this has been an exercise with much blood, sweat, and tears. Unfortunately, this process has yielded limited positive results.

Just last week, I told my physiotherapist, with a determined and tear-soaked face, that "I will never give up!" There was silence after my outburst. I've said those words so many times during the past five years to stimulate success! I later found out that my wife left the room in tears. The reason for this will become clear soon.

My outburst came on the heels of a discussion about alternatives to driving with my hand, such as head controls to maneuver the chair. Considering the proficiency with which I had driven before my hospitalization, I felt I could get back to that place. As well, I viewed not driving as a loss of my independence. Please understand that my independence is very precious to me!!

Following a few more failed attempts, I found myself at a crossroad. Should I keep pursuing my dream, no matter how long it would take, or was there a compelling reason to forgo my dream? If you know me, the reason to forgo would have to be pretty compelling! After much soul-searching and serious discussion with my wife, we decided to forgo our dream.

The reason for this was because we discovered the true priority in my life. After nearly dying last summer, I attained a sharper focus on what life is all about. If I am in this world, I want to live my life to the fullest! That might mean sacrificing a personal goal for a better outcome.

I want to spend time with my family on outings just like we used to! I want to fully participate in my family's lives and not have to stay home and miss out! If I spend the warm Ottawa months practicing to drive on my own, I will necessarily miss out on a meaningful period of my children's lives.

This is my priority!

But I must realistically admit that it comes at a great personal price. I cherish any independence that I can muster! Life has become a huge loss of my independence. So anything that I can do on my own is so precious for me! Therefore, it pains me emotionally to not drive myself.

The clincher is that my power chair weighs four hundred pounds, and my family and caregivers actually have had to push this monstrous chair around the house so long as I could not drive it myself.

In short, I took a look at the high price I'd be paying by my extended learning curve and I decided that life is too short. As well, I did not want to be a burden on others.

In all of our lives, we will find ourselves at a crossroad that necessitates making a tough choice. We can do the convenient or desired thing, or we can choose the right thing.

Let's hope that we have the wherewithal to make the right choices for us and our families!

From the Rolling Rabbi blog, "My Tough Decision," June 26, 2015

CHAPTER NINETEEN

Changes

I N THE FALL OF 2015, YEHUDA BEGAN HAVING TROUBLE WITH the computer. It was not responding as well as it had before. His eye gaze was not as accurate as it had been. His processing time was slowing down. We were getting frustrated again. We kept going down to the rehab center to tune things up. They even made house calls. The computer was being temperamental; sometimes it worked really well, other times it barely worked at all.

Mommy's Stroke and Passing

Around that same time, my mother suffered a basilar stroke. She was intubated and in a coma, with zero chance of recovery. I made arrangements for round-the-clock care for Yehuda, sent the children to friends, and flew down to New York. As Rosh Hashanah was approaching, and I could not remain away from Yehuda any longer, I tearfully and fearfully went home to Ottawa.

I was able to leave one more time for twenty-four hours to visit my mom. That was the last time I saw her. She passed away six weeks after the stroke. It was a devastating blow to all of us. My mother was the pulse of our family. She was only sixty-four years old. We were all so close to her. We were reeling.

Once again, I had to leave Yehuda behind to be able to attend my mother's funeral and sit *shivah* for her. Yehuda tried so many times to reach out to me, but his computer was on the blink. I tried to stay patient while listening on the phone to his computer-generated voice and clicks of the keyboard as he tried to type the words he wanted to say.

I lost my mother, and I had a feeling I was losing my husband as well—two of the most important people in my life. My life was crumbling around me.

Shmuly and Asna Begin Dating

Life is an emotional spectrum. On one extreme we faced illness and death; on the other, imminent joy. Our son Shmuly was seriously dating a girl with whom he had been set up in the summer, and the week after the *shivah* for my mother ended, our daughter Asna started dating a boy with whom she had been set up.

Those few months from September to December were a microcosm of my life, a juggle between emotions that ran the gamut from grief to ecstasy. The fact that a human is capable of feeling such extreme emotions at the same time is mind-boggling.

I missed my mother terribly, but I was so busy caring for Yehuda that I did not have time to mourn. I was on autopilot.

As Shmuly's engagement became imminent, I was determined for Yehuda to be able to communicate with his daughter-in-law-to-be. He had so looked forward to watching our children grow up, marry, and have children of their own. He wanted to be able to walk our children down the aisle. When researching wheelchairs, he had his eye on a really unique one that could, with the push of a button, rise to a higher position so the seated individual is as tall as the people surrounding him.

Prior to Thanksgiving weekend, I dragged Yehuda to the rehab center once again. They just *had* to figure out what was wrong with the computer. The staff tinkered around for a while, made some changes, and sent us home. We hoped for the best.

Motza'ei Shabbos, November 28th, Shmuly proposed to Margalit, daughter of Mayer and Gail Mattuck, and we had an impromptu engagement party. (Actually, I had been baking for weeks prior, stocking up the freezer for such an occasion!) It was an open-house celebration for the entire community.

Yehuda was thrilled, but sadly, the computer did not work well. He could only respond with smiles to Margalit and all the well-wishers. As disappointed as we were, we had to be glad that Yehuda was actually at the engagement party. Not so trivial a feat, considering everything he had been through.

Two weeks later, Ari, son of Eli and Esther Hertz, proposed to Asna. We were on a high. Our two eldest were engaged to the sweetest, kindest, most refined, beautiful human beings—you can trust me on that. I am not biased at all.

We planned another open-house engagement party for a weekend shortly after. It gave me enough time to restock my freezer.

Baking had been and continues to be an outlet for me—to express excitement, frustration, and to feel like I have a sense of control over a situation. It is predictable and provides instant gratification—not to mention comfort with a glass of milk. It speaks to the nourishing, nurturing side of me and is my way of showing people that I care about them and they are important to me. Over time, I came up with a catchy name for my hobby—"Shaifala Sweet Treats" ("Shai" being the first letters of my name). I hired a graphic designer to create a logo which I then had printed on labels and ribbon to add a personalized touch. My sister Fraidel bought me a practical gift—a blue spatula with the words "Keep calm bake on" written on it. It is hanging in my kitchen. I do not actually use it.

Just before the planned party, Yehuda ended up in the hospital again. This time, not only could he not communicate at the celebration, he was not even able to attend! As a show of solidarity, a close friend tearfully told us that if Yehuda was unable to attend the party, neither could he. It would be too painful for him to be part of the festivities without Yehuda.

We invited Ari for a second weekend. This time, we hoped, he would get to spend time with Yehuda, unlike at the engagement party.

According to our plans, it was to be a busy and full weekend. That Thursday evening was our daughter Chan's bas mitzvah celebration. After the party, our wedding caterer, David Smith, was coming with his staff for a wedding dinner sampling. They were bringing samples of food, table linens, cutlery, dishes, glassware—even flowers! Although he usually hosts these trial runs at his office or home, David came up with the idea to have the event at our house so that Yehuda could be included. We were eagerly anticipating a jam-packed, fun-filled weekend.

Wednesday afternoon, Asna and I were out at the Rideau Shopping Centre, spending time together and doing some pre-wedding shopping. As we were sifting through the racks and choosing some beautiful things, my cell phone rang. The caregiver was calling with bad news. Yehuda had turned blue and was having difficulty breathing. The paramedics were on the way.

Frantic with worry, we ran through the huge mall, trying to get to the parking lot. Unfamiliar with the layout, we were running around in circles and not reaching the correct exit. As we raced to our car, we prayed we would reach Yehuda in time. At the lot's exit, the bar refused to rise although we had paid for parking. I frantically pushed the call button on the machine. *Help! Open the gate! Medical emergency! My husband isn't breathing!*

We raced to the hospital and rushed into the emergency room. The staff recognized me and immediately pointed me in the right direction. I ran into the room. Yehuda looked up and smiled. Not funny! I shook with relief to see him alive and breathing.

The doctors determined that the cause of the event was likely a mucus plug that had traveled and blocked his airway and then traveled away. As Yehuda was unable to cough on his own, he was not able to move it independently. We were told that this would likely happen again. Yehuda was admitted for several days of observation.

Once again, we were thrown into a whirlwind of emotions and activity. We went from utter panic to flooding relief within the span of an hour. Yet, the show had to go on. Chan's party was less than twenty-four hours away. We prepared the house and got everything ready. The girls would be arriving straight from school at 4:30 p.m. on Thursday. Our Chai Lifeline coordinator had arranged a beautiful event and would be coming in from Montreal with a dance teacher to lead dancing, a custom-made cake, and other treats.

On Thursday afternoon, as I drove to school to pick up Chan and her friends, I got a call from the coordinator. She was running a little behind schedule. All the fears and emotions of the last twenty-four hours overcame me. "I can't do this alone!" I panicked. "My husband nearly died again yesterday. Now is not the time for me to be planning and running a party!" She reassured me that everything would work out.

The party was at its peak, the girls were having a blast—when in walked Ari. I briefly filled him in on what was happening, and explained that I was busy with the girls. "No problem," he amiably replied. "I just wanted to say hello before heading over to my hosts." As the girls were being picked up, David's crew arrived to set up the dinner. After enjoying some mouthwatering dishes and admiring the beautiful décor, we escorted the caterer out the door. And then I collapsed on the couch.

My brain was spinning. I felt like a pinball in a pinball machine—boom, boom, bang, bang, hit to this side, hit to that side, go up, go down. Swing here, swing there—and keep on going.

"After the Weddings"

The wedding dates were set—March 31st for Asna and Ari, and May 9th for Shmuly and Margalit—six weeks apart, with the eight days of Pesach in between. Our only goal was keeping Yehuda alive and well enough to be physically present at those weddings.

This was a huge paradigm shift for me. In the early days post-accident, I was focused on progress and improvement, never willing to rest at our level of success, only seeking to push forward and work toward more. At this point, progress was not a reality. The goal was stability and maintaining the status quo. So long as Yehuda was healthy enough to be at home, we were satisfied. His therapies continued, yet the focus was on maintaining the strength he had left. We put the computer issue on hold; it was becoming way too frustrating, without results. In addition, I was so busy with wedding plans and delegating tasks that I simply did not have energy to devote to it.

In addition, we were having caregiver issues yet again. Our live-in caregiver, Christina, was working out very well, but she was legally only allowed to work forty hours a week. Yehuda needed additional hours of caregiving, and this became a source of frustration. We had hired a woman who, based on her interview, seemed capable. She was vivacious and said all the right things. In actuality, however, dealing with her was a nightmare. One morning, she pounded on my bedroom door in a complete panic. I was terrified—I thought Yehuda had died. As I burst into his room, I saw that he was alive. I looked from Yehuda to her, back and forth, trying to figure out what was going on. She pointed upward—there was a spider on the ceiling. She was arachnophobic and was having a full-fledged panic attack. I could not have this woman taking care of Yehuda; it was insane. On the other hand, I physically could not add anything more to my plate. To fire her and have to go through the search yet again, to interview someone yet again, to train someone yet again—who would most likely not show up yet again—was not going to happen. We were forced to keep her. We were in survival mode.

My refrain to any request or task I was asked to take on became "After the weddings."

Our daughter Chan wanted to go to sleepaway camp for the first time that upcoming summer. When she asked, I answered with my usual, "Can't talk about it now, we will have to research camps. What are they like? What are the costs? I just can't do that right now."

"Well, when can you?"

"After the weddings."

"But Mommy, that will be too late. Camp registration will already be closed by then. There won't be any slots left."

"Well, then, I guess the answer is no. I'm sorry, maybe next summer."

As the weeks progressed, Yehuda was indeed admitted to the hospital again. The staff was very up-to-date with our lives and were thrilled about the upcoming weddings. We explained to them that their job was to keep Yehuda well enough to attend them.

We avoided taking Yehuda out to public places as much as possible, especially since it was winter. We were also scrupulous about who was allowed to enter our home. Anyone with any hint of a cold was not welcome. We had bottles of hand sanitizer placed strategically throughout the house.

It was countdown to "W1" day. It was time to resort to our successful "daddy bag" plan. Together with the caregivers, I made a very detailed list of everything Yehuda might need on those evenings. We had to anticipate any scenario. We brought up the trunk we had taken with us to Israel to begin collecting items. We made a detailed schedule to be followed to enable Yehuda to play his significant role as best he could, keeping in mind that this plan was for both weddings but would be fine-tuned after the first one.

Nearly six years back, when word of the accident and its ramifications had spread, we were showered with blessings. Chief among them was, "May Yehuda recover and be able to walk his children to the *chuppah* and dance with them at their weddings!" People meant well, but it was a painful wish. Barring a miracle, he would not be able to walk down the aisle on his own two feet. But we held true to our motto: "It may look different, but it's still the same." We sought out ways to make that wish a reality.

I reached out to Rabbi Michael Goldstein, executive director of Congregation Machzikei Hadas, where the weddings would be held.

A prominent member of the congregation, Claire-Jehanne Dubouloz Wilner, was a professor of occupational therapy at the School of Rehabilitative Sciences at the University of Ottawa. We all met at the shul to see what we could do to make it logistically possible for Yehuda to take his children to the *chuppah*.

We faced two sets of obstacles. The *chuppah* was to be held in the sanctuary. Several steps led down from the entrance of the sanctuary to the aisle, at the end of which was another set of steps leading up to the platform where the ceremony would be performed. We would have to get Yehuda down the steps, down the aisle, and up another set of steps. Claire and her students took all kinds of measurements. Rabbi Goldstein pointed out that the platform was actually accessible via a ramp at the back of the platform. Technically, Yehuda could be up and waiting on the platform and not "walk" down the aisle. That was not good enough for me.

The stairs leading to the aisle were steep and did not allow for safe placement of a ramp. The next idea was to get a portable lift, an elevator-type device, which could be prepared in advance. Prior to the *chuppah*, Yehuda would be brought into the sanctuary, go onto the platform via the ramp, take the lift down to the aisle, be rolled up the aisle, and wait at the bottom of the stairs for Asna and me (and, at the second wedding, for Shmuly and me). The plan seemed simple enough. We knew that our guests would be more than understanding if the proceedings took a few extra minutes.

Ari and Asna's Wedding

My brother-in-law Michael would be Yehuda's personal caregiver throughout the wedding. Caregivers would be present at all times if backup help was needed. My father would push Yehuda down the aisle to escort Asna and me to the ceremony.

Our excitement mounted—plans were falling into place and Yehuda was feeling well enough.

One of the most sentimental and emotional parts of a *chasunah* is when the *chassan*, flanked by his father and the *kallah's* father, comes to veil the *kallah* at the *badeken*. There was not a dry eye in the room as Ari, his father, and Yehuda approached Asna. Emotions ran high; deepest happiness and relief that we had lived to see this day. Traditionally, the *kallah's* father raises his hands to bless her. Yehuda could neither raise his hands nor communicate. Asna stepped off her bridal chair to be closer to Yehuda. I raised my husband's hands above our daughter's head and allowed for a few moments of silent prayer. We were all praying at that point—for the health and happiness of the young couple and for Yehuda.

The sanctuary was silent as our guests shared in the drama of the moment. It was indeed a night to remember and cherish forever. We looked forward to the same in a few weeks' time.

Pesach with the New Couple

The pressure to keep Yehuda healthy was intensifying. Pesach preparations took a strong second place in escalating pressure levels. Pesach, while a joyous Yom Tov, often gets a bad rap from housewives across the globe. It does not have to be that way. I made a conscious effort throughout the years to make the preparations as joyous and exciting as the Yom Tov itself. As I had seen in all areas of life, when children are involved and can take ownership of their tasks and responsibilities, they rise to the occasion.

Pesach that year was pleasant as we hosted the new couple. Ari introduced us to some of the *minhagim* his family followed at their Seder. Shmuly viewed the Seder through the eyes of a *chassan*; this would be his last Pesach as a single man.

It was different than our Seder the previous year. Then Yehuda was still efficient at the computer. He prepared for days in advance to be able to run the Seder and to make the experience an interactive one. He prepared several songs and games that he had my brother-in-law Avromi program into the computer for him. Once saved onto the computer, "all" Yehuda had to do was gaze at the correct button and instructions for the family would follow. It was a tremendous hit with all of us as we laughed and played along.

These Sedarim were different from the first Pesach at home following Yehuda's discharge from the rehab center. Then, I helped Yehuda don his *kittel* and wheeled him to his place at the head of the table. He looked like royalty. On Pesach, we remember that we were once slaves in Mitzrayim but are now free. Yehuda, too, was "enslaved" and on his way to freedom. As we sang and chanted the songs of the Haggadah, we reached a *pasuk* that I found most meaningful. It speaks of how Yehuda, the progenitor of his *shevet*, created an awareness of Hashem among those around him. I suggested that the *pasuk* best represented our Yehuda, as he made people aware of the miracles Hashem performed for him.

All too soon, Pesach was over. Seven days until "W2" day!

Shmuly's *Aufruf*

Typically, a wedding is held in the *kallah's* hometown. Margalit and her parents were extremely understanding that despite Yehuda's inability to travel, it was important for him to participate in Shmuly's wedding. They immediately assumed that the wedding would take place in Ottawa, not Vancouver. I did not even have to ask.

The wedding was scheduled for a Monday evening. The weekend prior was the traditional *aufruf* Shabbos. A group of forty to fifty friends and family members came to us for Shabbos. It was lively and busy, the kind of energy I thrive on. Several family members spoke at the family Shabbos dinner, including, to my surprise, the *chassan* himself. In an emotional delivery, Shmuly thanked Yehuda and me for all we had done for him over the years. He made special mention of the efforts and strength it took for me to keep the family safe—both physically and emotionally—after the accident, and said that Yehuda's strength would always be a source of inspiration to him.

The next morning, we had the rabbi stall the Torah reading so we could get Yehuda to shul on time for the *aufruf*. The congregation broke out into joyous song as they showered Shmuly with candies.

After *davening*, our family and friends went down to the social hall for a festive Shabbos *seudah*. Yehuda seemed to be a little bit off. I kept an eye on him and hoped for the best. When lunch was over, we all went back home. I hoped that after a nap, he would be more like himself. Perhaps the early morning, combined with the excitement and the crowd, were too overwhelming. But deep down I knew this was wishful thinking on my part. As Yehuda was being put to bed, he began to have trouble breathing. I quickly did what I was trained to do in such a situation. It seemed to help a bit, but I did not like what I saw. Once again, paramedics were on the way.

We raced to the hospital where he immediately began treatment. I reminded everyone on staff that Shmuly's wedding was in forty-eight hours. They had forty-eight hours to put Yehuda back together so that he would be at the wedding. They reassured me that by hook or by crook, he was going to that wedding. The team leader/charge nurse went so far as to say that he would get there no matter what, even if it meant she would have to leave the unit to chaperone him and monitor his safety.

Once Yehuda was safely settled in the ICU, I began my forty-five-minute walk back home. I wanted to reassure Shmuly that we were still on target; Abba will be coming to the wedding. Just a "usual" scare. He had seen the ambulance rush by and was obviously concerned. Based on the doctor's report that afternoon, we were not concerned at all. Well, okay, a little bit.

Motza'ei Shabbos, some family members went to check on Yehuda. They were not able to visit, as the nurses were providing care. In the morning, I called the ICU to check on how his night had gone. The nurse gently informed me that for now he was stable and doing okay. However, overnight there had been some complications, even instability. The doctor had tried to contact me but was unable to reach me. That was when I realized that my cell phone had been left at the hospital. While I slept, blissfully unaware, Yehuda was not doing well at all. In a way, I was grateful that I had had no idea. I desperately needed that night's sleep in preparation for the wedding.

I went to the hospital to assess the situation. At the time, Yehuda was on a respirator, receiving high levels of oxygen. The settings on his respirator needed to be adjusted, but that in and of itself was not a deterrent to his going to the wedding. Neither was the fact that he was on oxygen, as we had seen when attending my niece's wedding in Israel. The issue was the level of oxygen Yehuda needed. How much time would he be out of the hospital? How quickly would he drain an oxygen tank? The ability to have enough tanks on hand would be one of the factors that would determine the safety of a release.

The staff and I began to plan for different scenarios. If Yehuda's oxygen needs were reduced, he would be able to go. Which were the "most important" parts of the wedding for him to attend? How much time would that take? How would he get there, and with whom? The doctors and nurses began checking their schedules to see who was available when; they were willing to juggle shifts if necessary. We were greatly warmed by their empathy and support. They loved Yehuda and they loved our family and were willing to move mountains to make this happen. But the one thing no one was willing to compromise on was his safety. Nothing would be done to put his welfare in jeopardy.

By the end of the day, it became obvious that Yehuda would not be able to leave the hospital. The hospital staff said that his overall health was so precarious that it was way too risky. If we were to take him out against medical advice, something very dangerous might happen to him.

Our second-to-biggest fear had come true. It was a devastating blow, but there was no way around it. We would not do anything to endanger Yehuda. I shuddered at the thought of having to break the news to Shmuly and the rest of the family.

My heart broke for Shmuly and the raw emotion he expressed. I wished I could turn back the clock and take it all away, but I could not.

His siblings erupted in shouts of disbelief. They refused to accept that there was no way we could get Abba to the wedding.

No, there was no way to get Yehuda to the wedding—but he had to be able to see the wedding. We made plans to have two people in charge of Facetiming the entire event. One person would stay with Yehuda, and Rabbi Goldstein would video from the wedding. It was the best we could do under the circumstances.

Shmuly and Margalit's Wedding

The morning of his wedding, Shmuly went to spend some quality time with his father on his way to shul. I stopped by with the rest of the family en route to getting our hair and makeup done.

Yehuda looked awful. Not only was he on a high level of oxygen, I noticed that he was now getting even more assistance on the respirator than he'd been getting before.[1] As he breathed, his nostrils flared— never a good sign. He slept through our visit. I wondered if he would get to watch the wedding at all. I left strict instructions with the staff as to whom to call in the event of a crisis, all the while praying there would not be an emergency during the wedding.

We arrived at the shul in plenty of time. Other than immediate family, we had not told anyone that Yehuda would not be attending. They would figure it out soon enough.

Margalit's father and mine escorted Shmuly to veil Margalit. The tears were just as copious as at Asna's wedding, only this time they were of a different nature. The walk down the aisle was somber as more tears were shed for the man who had lost so much, had fought so hard, had triumphed over adversity, yet could not attend the wedding of his firstborn son. The idle lift at the base of the platform was a stark

---

1. The respirator would do the work of breathing for him. It was usually able to provide enough support to sustain him on room air without supplemental oxygen. However, when his lungs would collapse or fill with fluid, for example, room air was not enough and they would have to include oxygen support.

reminder that Yehuda had been there mere weeks before but could not be there tonight.

At the end of the *chuppah*, Shmuly stomped on the glass and we erupted in happy tears and joyous singing. We put aside our pain and disappointment and celebrated. It was a lively and joyous wedding. One who was unaware of the circumstances would never have been able to tell that someone very important was missing.

Numerous friends had traveled to Ottawa to celebrate with us. When they realized what was going on, they took turns sneaking out of the wedding to go "dance" with Yehuda at his hospital bedside. In the midst of the dancing, we were surprised to note that Shmuly's *rebbi* from Vancouver, with whom he was very close, had arrived. We had not known he was coming; in fact, he had sent his regrets. Now he explained that Shmuly's friends had called him as soon as they heard that Yehuda would not be attending the wedding. They pooled together the funds to pay for a last-minute flight to Ottawa. It was incredibly heartwarming. We felt cared for and supported, and danced well into the night.

On the way home, still dressed in our wedding finery, I stopped off at the hospital with all the children. The staff was eager to hear about the wedding, as they had seen parts of it on Facetime. Yehuda was sleeping. He had been awake for the entire wedding and enjoyed every minute of it. I noticed that the settings on his respirator were closer to normal and his oxygen levels were significantly lower than they had been in the morning. He looked as peaceful as a sleeping baby. I could only wonder if he was dreaming about the wedding.

After the wedding, his condition stabilized enough to allow for him to be discharged—though "stable" is a relative term. We lived life, not wondering *if* something would happen, but wondering *when* it would happen.

The Decline

Without realizing that there was a term for what we were doing, we often resorted to gallows humor. Living on the edge, staring death in the eye day after day, takes a toll. In a staring contest, there is only one winner—and we prayed it would be us.

I often teased Yehuda that in reality he must be a cat. If cats have nine lives, he certainly did too. After all, not counting the near-misses—of which there were many—he had already died twice!

How many times can one watch one's loved one die and be brought back to life? Any time there was a crisis, I heard a voice in the back of my head whispering, "Maybe this is it for real." And then he would pull through. My heart would race with the anguish of having nearly lost him, then calm down and wait for the next crisis. My mind planned his funeral many times; I had ideas for what we would include on his *matzeivah*. In moments of panic, these thoughts and feelings would bubble to the surface, only to be squelched when the crisis passed.

By December of 2016, Yehuda's decline was becoming obvious. Desperate as I was for him to have a means of communication, my gut told me it was time to give up. We had tried several last-ditch attempts, but they took too much energy and perseverance, of which Yehuda had practically none. We had finally made slight headway using a personalized innovative system that several techy friends were creating. In addition, we had heard about a company in New York that works with adaptive technology for the visually impaired. I even ordered a new computer system and had it shipped for us to Ogdensburg, New York. I optimistically made the one-hour journey across the border to pick it up and explore the options. Ironically, we were able to install a siddur on it. It was a dream of Yehuda's to be able to *daven* on his own, without relying on someone to turn the pages for him when he became too weak to do so on his own. With a "simple" gaze of the eye, he could scroll down to the passages that he wanted to pray. But by November/December 2016, that "simple" gaze at the right location for even the shortest duration of time was impossible.

I had to come to terms with the fact that I must let go. Why pressure and frustrate him? I knew that more than anything, he would want to please me and use his every last bit of strength to hang on—and I could see that he had zero strength. It was another step in the grieving process. Deep down in my heart, I knew where this was headed.

Medically, there were other signs. We were warned by the doctors that as his condition deteriorated, his breathing difficulties would become more frequent and his body would become immune to even the strongest medications, which we were saving to be used as a last resort. We did not want to bring in the "top guns" until absolutely necessary, because once we did, there would be no recourse left.

As Chanukah approached, an unsettling feeling took strong hold. Our daughter Bayla was in seminary in Israel for the year. We sent her off in September with a prayer in our hearts that we would not have to call her home for an emergency. We were in frequent contact and she always knew when her father was in or out of the hospital and, in general, all of the goings-on of his condition. I was starting to feel the need to bring her home while he was still "okay." On the one hand, I did not want to alarm her. On the other, I wanted her to spend time with her father while she still could. I spent several nights in bed tossing the idea around. Should I discuss the situation first with her principal and get official permission, or discuss it with Bayla directly?

As it turns out, Bayla brought up the topic in conversation. When she had been in high school in Rochester, if there was a concern about Yehuda's condition, she came home. Should she not come home now as well? When she heard I had been contemplating the same idea, she became understandably alarmed. I reassured her that I was not hiding anything from her. I was of the belief that she would never regret spending time with her father and hopefully she would have many chances to do so. We really could not guarantee how much time he had left. We did not want to live with the regret of "could have, should have." Within hours, permission was granted, we purchased a ticket, and Bayla was on her way home. It was a decision for which she is extremely grateful.

The same weekend Bayla arrived, my sister Ahuva came with her husband, Avromi, and newborn daughter. Baby Rochel (named for my mother) came to meet her Uncle Yehuda, whose first international journey post-accident was to New York City for her parents' wedding. We gently placed Rochel into Yehuda's arms. We watched for his smile and rejoiced. In my heart, I thought of the grandchildren we were hoping for and wondered if he would live long enough to see any.

Over the next several weeks, Yehuda was on a very strict regimen of IV meds. Several toxic drugs coursed through his veins to keep his lungs clear. The potential toxicity necessitated very specific blood draws at very specific times. A visiting nurse would come to our home and draw the blood. In turn, I would rush to deliver it to the lab in time. The whole process was approved by the doctors and was cleared as an exception to the "rules." Generally, a patient had to be brought to a specific lab for this process. Due to the precariousness of Yehuda's condition, it was done on an outpatient basis.

Hurried and harried, I arrived at the lab. To my dismay—but not shock, as by now I had become accustomed to glitches—the receptionist refused to accept the sample. Blood drawn outside the lab goes to a different lab, she insisted. As calmly as possible, more firmly than possible, I explained the situation. "This is a timed blood sample given authorization to be spun here. Please start spinning it and then do your research." As I had anticipated, the authorization had not been passed down to the receiving office. Next issue: Was I aware that the form I included as a requisition was for an outside lab, not the hospital lab, as it did not have the correct logo on it? Once again, firmly and calmly, I replied, "Frankly, I don't care which picture, if any, is on the requisition. The doctor gave the order, it was authorized and approved. We are slowly maxing out the allotted time frame for proper analysis." The nurse agreed to spin the blood as a new requisition was submitted to the doctor for completion. Triumphantly, the nurse emerged from the back office with the new signed form. Trusting no one, I asked to see it. Once again, as I had suspected, something was wrong. Only two boxes were checked off instead of the three results we needed. "Oops!"

Oops? Are you kidding me? We are talking about meds that could kill my husband if the dose level is too high in his bloodstream! She insisted I was wrong, only two were necessary, whereupon I showed her the original requisition. She made her way back to the doctor's office.

This regimen was continued for several weeks, thankfully without further incident. We waited with bated breath to see how long this could continue. At one point, there was a discrepancy between the blood results and the timing of the IV drips. Further doses were put on hold. More anxious waiting, as we were unsure of how Yehuda's body would react without the medication. It did not take long to find out.

Once again, we needed to call the paramedics. As they transported Yehuda out of our house, I had a premonition that this would be his final hospital stay, his final illness, after which he would not return home.

After defying death on multiple occasions, Yehuda had the odds stacked very highly against him. We were at the point of no return. We knew that now there was only one expected outcome. It was just a matter of time. Once again, we were called to come say our final goodbyes. The respirator was set to the highest setting possible. Nothing more could be done.

The End

When we entered the room, we all called out, "Abba!" Yehuda opened his eyes. He had not done that in days. He looked around the room at all of us. A huge smile filled his face and then he closed his eyes. We said, "Yay! Abba, do it again! Do it again!" He did. We tried for a third time. He could not open his eyes, but he smiled.

On the Friday before Yehuda passed, the nurses all came in to hug us and wish us well. Some asked permission to just sit with us. The look in their eyes expressed their fear that he would no longer be there when they returned on Monday.

At around 10:00 a.m. Tuesday morning, February 7, 2017/11 Shevat 5777, the nurse slowly pointed to the monitor. Softly, gently, she indicated to us that there was a change in his heart rate. It was slowly dropping. Shmuly noticed that it seemed that every time I stepped away, Abba's numbers would drop a little more. I came close. The numbers rose. I stepped back. They went down. Close. Up. Away. Down. It was time to stand back. Within moments, the monitor beeped no more.

As much as you think you are prepared for the end, you are not. Nothing can prepare you for the end. No amount of close calls, declining health, or unresponsiveness can brace you for the harsh reality. It hit fast and hard.

I had to notify the family of the devastating news. I sent a simple text:

That's all.
I'm sorry.
BDE

Final Goodbyes

Preparations had to be expedited for the funeral to take place as soon as possible. I asked Rabbi Finkelstein and Eliezer to take care of the arrangements and made only two requests: It must be an honorable ceremony befitting Yehuda's stature and there must be two services, one in Ottawa and one in New York. There had to be a way to allow for the multitudes of family, friends, and supporters to pay their final respects.

Having to cross the border involved many technicalities, and the ominous weather report did not bode well. A major snowstorm was gearing up to hit Ottawa Tuesday night and was predicted to reach New York Wednesday night. We wanted to ensure that the funeral would be held as soon as possible. All the plans would have to unfold in a narrow time frame.

The Ottawa funeral was set for 9:00 p.m. at Congregation Beth Tikvah Ottawa, the shul where we were members and where we had *davened* for the past fifteen years. Yehuda's body would then be transported through the night. The second funeral was scheduled for Wednesday at noon, in Queens, and livestreaming would be provided for those unable to attend in person.

In true Simes form, a full-blown blizzard was expected Tuesday evening and was due to continue through the night. Even our deepest grief could not prevent us from appreciating the irony. Wherever Yehuda went, the weather refused to cooperate—whether it was Hurricane Sandy in NYC or the snowstorm of the millennium in Israel. Now this—a blizzard! Even by Ottawa standards, this was no ordinary snowstorm.

The snow began as predicted. Ottawa is no stranger to the white stuff, but this was something else! Heavy drifts began to pile up everywhere as hundreds of friends and family members arrived. The weather could not place a damper on the love, admiration, and respect that were displayed that evening for a man who had served as a beacon of light, faith, and resilience amid adversity; for a dedicated teacher, friend, and community leader; for a beloved husband, father, brother, son-in-law, uncle, and cousin. Just as he was unstoppable (in his own words, when asked, "When will you stop? When will you give up?" he emphatically replied, "Never!"), so too, the outpouring of grief was unstoppable by the weather.

As speaker after speaker extolled Yehuda's virtues, our feelings of loss hit harder. The attendees were respectfully asked to give us our space as we departed the synagogue. We had to leave to the airport for our flight to New York at 4:00 a.m.

Sixteen of us filed into the airport. Security officials greeted us with a cheery "good morning," assuming we were off on a family holiday. We exchanged glances. *Not quite.* Who would have thought we were on our way to a funeral? There were children aged six and up among us! Death is not supposed to affect children.

In New York, as in Ottawa, throngs of people arrived to pay their last respects. People flew in from cities around the United States and from Israel. The funeral home was packed—standing room only—and people spilled into adjacent hallways and foyers. Numerous *roshei yeshivah*, *rabbanim*, family members, colleagues, and friends offered *hespedim*. Each speaker confirmed what we all knew: Yehuda was a *mentch*, a scholar, a friend, a confidant, a mentor, a comforting support. The fact that he was critically injured only enhanced his inherent qualities. He connected with all those whose lives he touched—in shul, in the community, at work—and was held in high esteem by everyone, regardless of their religious background. The assembled mourners were reminded that we had had the unique privilege to share our lives with a one-of-a-kind, irreplaceable human being who was true to himself and to what he represented.

En route to the cemetery, the *levayah* detoured past Yeshiva Chofetz Chaim. The entire *hanhalah* and student body—four to five hundred people—came out and followed the hearse on foot for several blocks, respectfully escorting Yehuda on this leg of his final journey. *Chazal* teach that the high caliber of those accompanying one on one's final journey is validation that the deceased was a meritorious individual. People commented that this was the funeral of a *gadol*, a truly righteous person.

It was unseasonably warm—60° F—when we arrived at Beth David Cemetery in Elmont, New York. Over the horizon, the sun was just beginning to set as Yehuda was laid to rest and we said our final goodbyes.

We returned to Queens to begin the week of *shivah*. The plan was to sit *shivah* in Queens on Wednesday and Thursday and fly back to Ottawa Thursday night to complete the seven days. Not surprisingly, the snowy weather pattern followed us from Ottawa to New York. Our flights were either canceled or rescheduled. The changes seemed completely random; minor children were rescheduled, adults were canceled—we saw no pattern at all. More than sixteen people were due to fly home for the *shivah*.[2] Obviously, we had to either reschedule or cancel everyone as a group. We had to find alternate means to get all of us back in time for Shabbos. We chartered a bus to drive us back to Ottawa through the night on Thursday. Neighbors prepared snacks and drinks for all of us and obtained family-friendly Jewish videos to keep everyone comfortable for the minimum eight-hour trip.

Recently, I had occasion to travel with my family on a chartered bus to Great Adventures on a Chol Hamoed trip sponsored by Misaskim.[3] As I battled nausea while an outdated black-and-white video in Yiddish (a language I do not understand) blared in the background, I texted Fraidel: "Why do I feel as if I'm on the way home from a funeral?"

---

2.   We brought more people home with us than had left Ottawa. Rachel and her family, Fraidel, and the *shomer* who drove down with Yehuda all came back with us.

3.   This wonderful organization was there for us during the *shivah*, providing low chairs and other necessities and even sending gifts and toys for the younger children. Nochi was so excited that we were now part of two organizations that give treats—Chai Lifeline and Misaskim. Oh, the perks…

CHAPTER TWENTY

Yehuda's Legacy

A FEW PROGRAMS AND EVENTS CRYSTALLIZED FOR US Yehuda's legacy.

Benoseha

We always anticipated visits from family and friends from out of town. The support it demonstrated was a booster shot in our arms, affording us the encouragement we so desperately needed to go on. We lived from visit to visit.

During one such visit with our friends Rabbi Yaakov and Rivky Trop, an interesting topic came up. Nochi had started kindergarten that fall. I was thinking aloud, "Now that all of my children are in school, maybe I should go back to school also!" The idea was ludicrous. Where in my day would I find extra time to attend classes, let alone study for exams or write reports? Besides, for the last twenty-odd years I had been doing what I loved to do without a master's degree. Would it be worth spending $40,000 for a seemingly worthless piece of paper?

I had a hard time falling asleep that night. I kept replaying the conversation in my mind—and I had a brainstorm! Instead of looking for something new to do, what if I just did more of what I loved doing? What if *I* started an advanced class? There were learning programs and opportunities available in our community. I thought the time was ripe to take it up a notch, for there to be a higher-level Chumash class.

My mind raced. If I were to start, it would need a name. What should it be called? I reflected back on the tumultuous 113 days Yehuda had spent in the ICU the previous year, leaving him respirator-dependent. He needed all the *tefillos* and *zechusim* we could possibly garner for him. What if the learning would be dedicated as a merit for his well-being? A *pasuk* from *Tehillim* (48:12) came to mind: *Tagelnah bnos Yehuda*— "The daughters of Yehuda should rejoice." Well, Yehuda had daughters (and sons!) and I wanted them to rejoice. I blended the words in my head…*Bnos Yehuda*…it became *Benoseha*—"her daughters." Who was "her"? Linguistically, "Torah" is a feminine word. Thus, by learning and acquiring Torah, the women would become the daughters of the Torah. Satisfied, I promptly fell asleep.

As soon as Shabbos concluded, I contacted a journalist friend, Zev Singer, to write an article about my planned program for *The Ottawa Jewish Bulletin*. I designed a flyer to be included as an ad in the upcoming edition of the newspaper and to post around town.

Yehuda was very supportive and encouraging. Each time I became nervous and said, "What was I thinking? No way! I'm changing my mind!" Yehuda set me straight.

The night of the first class arrived. Elisheva manned the door, collected names, contact information, and payment. Chan distributed specially designed purple folders with the *Benoseha* logo, containing the relevant source material. All in all, over twenty-five women gathered around my dining room table. I was blown away; this was some turnout! The positive feedback was motivation to continue. In fact, one attendee came over to me with tears in her eyes and confided, "I have been thirsting to learn like this for so long!"

The program continues online, garnering *zechusim* for Yehuda one word at a time.

Hachnasas Sefer Torah

Six months after Yehuda passed away, a delegation from our shul approached me with an interesting idea. A major fundraiser was needed to bring in funds. Knowing how beloved Yehuda was to our community and beyond, and aware of his love and devotion to Torah, they suggested: What better way to perpetuate his memory and legacy than by commissioning the writing of a *sefer Torah* in his merit? Would I be on board with such an idea?

It did not take me long to decide. Commissioning a new *sefer Torah* was well beyond my personal financial capability. This would be a dream come true; a win-win situation for both the shul and me. I made one stipulation: The campaign had to be run in a manner that would bring honor to Hashem and to Yehuda's memory. We agreed that the shul would deal with the fundraising campaign and the purchase of the *sefer Torah* and I would have sole discretion of the program and how the *sefer Torah* would be transported to Ottawa.

When I shared the idea with my children, they were deliriously enthusiastic. Yitzchak, who was eleven at the time, had the most emotional reaction of all. "That's going to be the Torah I read from on my bar mitzvah!"

The campaign began in earnest. I provided a mailing list and a letter to be distributed, and left the committee to decide where to purchase the Torah and how to finance it.

I went to work planning the program. I contacted the Ontario Provincial Police to inquire about permits and other legalities and found out I would have to do several things; choose a date, officially notify the police department of the intent to have a parade, provide a detailed map of the parade route, ensure that there would be safety measures put in place to protect pedestrians, and notify the neighbors along the route about the upcoming event in both English and French.

Sunday, May 27th, was chosen as the big day.[1] When I looked at the

---

1.   I was warned of a potential major glitch: The annual Ottawa Race Weekend is held the last weekend of May. This two-day running event includes seven races and over 40,000 participants. As the city would be using the majority of its security personnel to cover this event, there might not be enough security for ours. Fortunately, we were not affected.

Hebrew date, tears came to my eyes. It was 13 Sivan, just six days after Shavuos, five days after Yehuda's Hebrew birthday. The *parshah* we would read just the day before was *Naso*, Yehuda's bar mitzvah *parshah*! It felt like a kiss from Hashem. We chose the date with Ottawa weather in mind, but Hashem already had a plan.

There were so many details to handle! How would the Torah get to Ottawa? It needed to be personally transported. Would we have to pay customs or taxes at the border? With some research, we discovered that religious books and artifacts were exempt from customs. Just to be on the safe side, we printed out the law to have on hand should any trouble arise. Our friends the Glazers were coming to us for Shavuos and they would bring the treasure with them.

I contacted the famed Korn's *hachnasas sefer Torah* truck company to request one of its gorgeously decorated floats, along with music and a sound system, to accompany the parade. Unfortunately, their trucks were not available for our date. Undeterred, I called Yo Aisenstark, the Montreal musician who performed at Shmuly's and Asna's weddings. Could he help? He could! He would need a Ford 150 pickup truck with a driver. He would be *on* the truck playing the music, and he could not be driving at the same time. It would be complicated to rent the vehicle in Montreal and drive it to Ottawa. The two-hour travel time would add to the rental fee. We realized we would have to locate a truck in Ottawa proper. But this was easier said than done. Not every rental agency dealt with this model.

Someone reminded me that Yigal Hadad drove a Ford 150. Yigal is an accomplished contractor who designed the modifications and additions for our new home. He and his family are close friends of ours, and Yehuda taught his children. He was always available for us— to put up our sukkah every year, figure out the cause of the elevator's nonstop beeping, or change LED lights that were out of my reach. Yigal agreed to lend his truck and be the driver.

I was determined that the event would be forever etched in everyone's minds—men, women, and especially children. Special crowns were ordered for the kids, along with bursting party bags filled with sugary loot. I did not want even one child to cry on that special day so I over-ordered, just to be sure. And then I ordered more. Bamboo torches were added to the list, and huge banners for both our home and the shul were rented.

Religious affairs are never complete without food. David Smith graciously donated a beautiful spread with his signature style, taste, and décor. It was truly fit for a king.

The plan was for the final letters of the *sefer Torah* to be completed by family members at our dining room table. Then the Torah, held lovingly under a *chuppah*, would be marched to the shul. The shul's six *sifrei Torah* would be carried out to greet the newest *sefer Torah* and escort it to its new home. We had to make some decisions: Who would hold the four posts of the *chuppah* and carry out the six Torahs? These were not decisions to be taken lightly. This was a chance to include, thank, and recognize friends who had gone above and beyond in their love and care for Yehuda, and who had "purchased" letters, words, *pesukim*, *perakim*, and *parshiyos* in our new *sefer Torah*.

As the day circled on my calendar drew closer, my nerves became jittery. Would everything work out? Would the weather cooperate? Would people come?

The day dawned clear, sunny, and unseasonably warm. So warm, in fact, that someone had to be dispatched to buy water bottles to have on hand for the participants.

Rabbi Eleazar Durden, the *sofer*, set up his ink, quills, and various equipment. Family members who had traveled in from near and far gathered to fill in the outlined letters with special black ink. When the last letter was complete, everyone burst into song and dance.

With tears coursing down my face, I closed my eyes to capture the emotions in my mind and heart. It felt like an auspicious time for *tefillah*, much like Shabbos candle-lighting or standing under the *chuppah*. I felt an aura of spirituality pervade the room, like when

Yehuda reached his hand to his eyes the first time for Shema. Now, my lips murmured in supplication to Hashem, *Guard me and my children, keep us safe, let Yehuda's memory be a blessing for us. Know that throughout it all, we trusted You, we believed in You. Please shower us with Your goodness and kindness.*

Escorting the *sefer Torah* out of our home.

Ari and Yitzchak dancing in honor of the *sefer Torah* being held by Shmuly.

Shmuly cradled the *sefer Torah* in his arms like a beloved newborn. The front door was thrown open to the sight of over four hundred people and the sound of joyful music. As the procession circled the block, more and more people joined. The 160-meter (.1 mile) walk to the shul took forty-five minutes as we extended the distance by looping around the block.

When the crowd reached the parking lot, each member of Yehuda's *Tefillin* Brigade danced out of the shul carrying a *sefer Torah*. The dancing was like that on Simchas Torah, and

Yitzchak with the *sefer Torah*.

only ended when all the scrolls were tenderly placed into the *aron kodesh*.

It was time for the next part of the program. Words of inspiration were delivered by Rabbi Finkelstein, Rabbi Bulka, Shmuly, Ari, and Rabbi Shaps. A collective gasp met Shmuly's announcement that he would be reading the very same *dvar Torah* Yehuda had read at his bar mitzvah thirty-seven years prior. You could hear a pin drop as Shmuly spoke. Yehuda referred to the law of whether or not one fulfills the mitzvah of *tefillin* if the *tefillin* are wrapped on him by someone else. How could Yehuda have known that one day he *would* fulfill the mitzvah in that manner?

A slide show depicting Yehuda's life both before and after the accident was shown to the backdrop of personal accounts from family, colleagues, friends, and students, all narrated by Rabbi David Rotenberg. The day was documented on video and in photos. To our surprised delight, the still photographer, Mr. Issie Scarowsky, presented us with a gorgeous panoramic print of me and my children taken with the Torah. It hangs proudly above my Shabbos candlesticks.

The day surpassed our wildest expectations and was a beautiful tribute to Yehuda's too-short but meaningful life.

"Out of the Mouths of Babes"

In the summer of 2016, our community was shaken by news of a tragic car accident. Our neighbor, Mr. Michael Linderman, was killed in a head-on crash. A brilliant scientist, he worked for the Michael J. Fox Foundation doing research on Parkinson's disease. The accident happened in Canton, New York, on a road we often traveled to pick up our daughters from where they got off the bus on their way home from school in Rochester.

At first, my friends were afraid to tell me the news. They knew it would be a big blow and cause me to reflect back on our accident and what could have happened. I, in turn, hesitated to tell my children. Yet I knew that I could not hide it from them.

Elisheva was devastated. "Oh, Mommy!" she cried. "Why did he have to die? Couldn't he at least have been a quadriplegic?"

My brain froze. *Are you serious? Do you have any idea what you are saying? A quadriplegic, of all things? Do you have any idea at all what the life of a quadriplegic is like? G-d spared him that pain!*

But then I realized that yes, she does know what the life of a quadriplegic is like. She does know what it means to the family. Thank G-d! Our efforts had paid off. She internalized what Yehuda and I had hoped to imbue. Yes, the life of a quadriplegic is far from easy. It is not a life we would wish upon anyone. Yet it is a life, and one worth living. As long as there is breath, there is life. We suffered so much, and despite the pain—or, more likely, because of it—we came to a deeper appreciation of the value of life, the value of family, and the value of good times. We experienced everything in a heightened and deepened state. The lows were very low, but the highs were celebrated in their purest form.

Some years later, Yitzchak came home from summer camp, disturbed after hearing of a complex family situation of a fellow camper. As I heard the story, my mind was racing: How and what to respond? But Yitzchak looked at me nonchalantly and said, "He is much worse off than me. Even though Abba died, I know that he loved me." Out of the mouths of babes. I assured him that indeed Abba loved him very much and I was grateful that he knew.

We are grateful for every milestone we were able to share with Yehuda. Every day that he woke up in the morning, we declared that it had been a good night. Every night that he went to sleep (preferably in his own bed and not in the hospital), we declared it to be a good day.

Yehuda had received numerous "second chances" at life. He embraced them all and lived life to its fullest. As Bayla said with such mature insight after his passing, "Mommy, Abba was only forty-nine years old. His years were short, but his days were long."

From the Grave

My summer project after Yehuda's passing was to work on the text for his *matzeivah*. I was off from teaching and wanted to use that extra headspace to come up with a meaningful, relevant, and appropriate text that would do him justice. There were some ideas going through my head that needed to be sorted and organized. I wanted to capture his essence in many areas. I was very afraid of the task before me. Even once I had the text, it took time for me to put it in the order I felt was appropriate.

Yehuda's *matzeivah*.

In commemoration of his first *yahrtzeit*, the family and I gathered at the cemetery to say Tehillim and *Keil Malei Rachamim*. When Judy saw the inscription on the headstone, she shared a story with us.

Several summers earlier, she had come to Ottawa for a visit with Nahum and some of their children. Their son, Elishama, had interviewed his Uncle Yehuda as part of a school assignment. One of the questions he posed—one that I never asked Yehuda myself—was, "What do you want written on your *matzeivah*?" Yehuda answered, "*Eved Hashem*—servant of Hashem."

Upon hearing this, I completely broke down. Judy said, "Look what you wrote—'*Ani avdecha ben amasecha*—I am Your servant, son of Your maidservant'—and it's the very first line!" I was looking for reassurance from others that I chose his epitaph accurately, but in reality, I needed validation from him—and he gave it to me. *Sifsosav dovevos bakever*—"his lips are murmuring in the grave."

The Black Box

"Ma," Shmuly asked, "when is the last time you looked through Abba's box?"

Shmuly was referring to Yehuda's black file box that is stuffed with assorted index cards from before the accident. Each handwritten card contains pieces of information Yehuda collected—pearls of wisdom he found insightful, inspiring, or thought-provoking, and just random tidbits of Jewish thought. These were the ideas he had incorporated into lessons at the supper table and in the classroom.

"The black index-card box? I can't remember? Not in ages. Why?"

"I was looking through it today. There are two cards I think you would be very interested to see. I left them for you on your pillow."

I hurried up to my room and shut the door, eager to see the messages waiting for me. I sat down on the bed and slowly read the fronts and backs of each card.

The first card was titled "Body/Soul." Yehuda had paraphrased *Chovos Halevavos*, "Gate of Serving Hashem" (89):

The soul (the real you) gets absolutely no pleasure from the benefits of this world, nor does it get pain from the lack of benefits in this world. Only the body does. For example, a placenta has no value for itself—only for the fetus. When the fetus is complete it is no longer necessary, so it "dies." Another example, the egg of a chicken. When a chicken is developed, the egg falls away. So too, when YOU are developed (the soul) the body has no more use. It falls away.

My heart skipped a beat as I recalled Yehuda's challenges. He had developed his soul to the point that his body was no longer necessary.

The second card was titled "WYSIWYG (what you see is what you get)—*Olam Haba.*"

So too—us. How we are when we leave the world is how we will be in the next world. But in this world—can't really see me—just see the exterior shell—but don't really know. Next world is WYSIWYG. When die—I emerge. I step out. I will clearly be seen—all thoughts, etc. No more hiding.

When I read the cards from the box, I realized that Yehuda had lived knowing these lessons all along. We learned it from him. Yehuda, you did not hide from us. We were able to see very clearly who you really were. You did not have an exterior shell to hide behind. Once your body no longer functioned as it should, YOU emerged. YOU stepped out. YOU left this world in a state of perfection.

CHAPTER TWENTY-ONE

Embracing Our New Reality

Feeling Again

I HAVE A MAGNET ON MY FRIDGE—I THINK IT IS BRILLIANT: "Incredible as it seems, my life is based on a true story."

After Yehuda's death, I often pondered an ironic and tragic thought: *My husband died. Why did my life get easier, in a way, to deal with?* All the managing, arranging, dealing with people and their moods just disappeared without a physical trace. No longer would I have to worry that a caregiver would not show up, that medications would be administered wrong, that tests needing to be performed at specific times would miss their deadlines. Nobody was calling to ask me where supplies were. Nobody was calling to inform me that Yehuda was hanging from the ceiling on his track lift, as they had forgotten to charge the remote...

The Pesach after Yehuda's passing, Fraidel, Eliezer, and I were sitting at the table, talking. I mentioned that it was the first time in over six years that I was able to feel again. The body armor was off. No longer was I waiting for the next shoe to drop.

What Now?

Right after Yehuda passed away, people asked me if I would be moving back to New York. I answered honestly that at this point, I had no such intentions. We had just been hit with a huge blow; this was not the time to be making any big changes. We had to adjust to life without Yehuda in the safety and security of our own home. We had to create another new normal. We had to relearn how to be spontaneous, to be able to make plans that would be emergency-free. To not wait for the phone to ring, to get used to the silence without the background hum of medical equipment, and the bustling in and out of various caregivers and therapists.

The seasons flowed by; winter, spring, summer. By the fall of 2017, we had settled into a semblance of routine. My two married couples were living in Queens and the next three girls were boarding by the Glazers. There were more of us "there" than "here." Home was getting too quiet. I kept myself distracted by hosting the extended Vinitsky clan for Sukkos. Asna and Ari missed out on the fun, but for a good cause—I was eagerly anticipating the imminent arrival of my very first grandchild.

I'm a *Bubby*!

As soon as Sukkos was over and the last carload of guests had pulled away, I worked like a woman on a mission to get the house back in tip-top shape. I knew that as soon as Asna called with news to report, I would be in the car and off to New York. I could not leave the house in shambles.

Thursday morning, October 19th, Asna called. "You should probably start thinking about planning to be in Queens for Shabbos…" I made a mental calculation of how long it would take to drive and what I would need to pack. Somehow, I got the kids off to school and myself to work. Antsy as could be, I somehow got through the morning. I came home and quickly prepared food for Shabbos to take with us to share with whichever friend or relative we were going to surprise with a last-minute Shabbos visit. I packed myself and made a packing list for the kids. By the late afternoon, Asna was absolutely certain that I must be in Queens for Shabbos. When the kids came home from school, I told them that we were surprising everyone and going to New York for Shabbos. Armed with coffee, a charged cellphone, and a prayer on my lips, we set off.

I managed to maintain a safe driving speed, all the while willing my phone to ring. Brockville, Ontario, one hour away from home, was where I lost cellphone reception. Half an hour left to the border—still no call. Luckily, there were no lines by the border. I pulled up to the customs agent, who promptly asked for our IDs and the purpose of our visit. As I whipped out our passports, I shrieked, "To see my new grandchild! I'm about to become a grandma!"

"Anything to declare? Gifts?"

"Clothes for the baby!"

He rolled his eyes as he waved me through. As we drove onto US territory, my phone finally rang.

"Mazel tov! It's a girl! A girl!"

It was now after nightfall, officially Rosh Chodesh Cheshvan, my mother's second *yahrtzeit*! How befitting. I laughed. I cried. I bounced up and down in my seat as I digested the news. I WAS A *BUBBY*! I had to spread the news! Good news travels fast, and the phone kept on ringing. Everyone assumed that it was too late for me to come to Queens for Shabbos. They all laughed hysterically when they heard that I was already on the road.

I managed to drive halfway before we needed to pull into a motel. With only four hours left to drive, there was sufficient time to continue in the morning.

A morning phone call confirmed our hunch—the new princess was named Rochel Leah, after my mother. There was now a tug at my heart drawing me to New York.

New York, New York

The next fall found me sending Chan off to high school, joining her siblings in Queens.

Shmuly and Margalit shared some exciting news with me. I should start considering the option of spending the upcoming Pesach in Queens. Busy times indeed; Yitzchak's bar mitzvah would be just three weeks before Pesach. There was a lot to plan.

We made numerous trips to New York. It was getting easier for me to travel down with the "at-home kids" than for the "New York kids" to take off time from work or school to come to Ottawa.

On the day of Yehuda's second *yahrtzeit*, we once again gathered at the cemetery. That night, Malka and Yosaif, son of Rabbi David and Dina Slotkin, announced their engagement! Her *chassan*, whose full name is Yosaif Yehuda, "added" a Yehuda to our family.

Yosaif was fortunate enough to have been at Yeshiva Chofetz Chaim in Yerushalayim when Yehuda spoke. It was comforting to know that Yehuda had "met" Yosaif. Their wedding was planned for just weeks before Yitzchak's bar mitzvah, a little over one month before Pesach. There was a lot to prepare…and there were more tugs at my heart drawing me to New York.

Over the next few months, I made several more trips to New York, the planned location for the wedding. Amidst the hustle and bustle of planning, we talked about the differences of each of the three children's weddings. Stark contrasts marked the three, yet there was also tremendous joy. After basking in the glow of Malka and Yosaif's beautiful wedding, we returned to Ottawa for Shabbos *sheva brachos*.

A meaningful Shabbos bar mitzvah for Yitzchak was next and celebrated in Ottawa. He proudly—and flawlessly—read from the *sefer Torah* dedicated in memory of Yehuda. The affair was the perfect combination of including Yehuda but without overshadowing the joy of the moment. Yitzchak eloquently delivered the same *dvar Torah* that Yehuda had prepared with Shmuly for Shmuly's bar mitzvah. I did not cook a single item on the menu this time, unless you count all the baked goods for dessert and a *tefillin*-themed, personalized fondant cake.

On April 3rd, just five days after the bar mitzvah, Shmuly called to prepare me to expect a very special phone call. It was only a matter of time. All afternoon, I willed the phone to ring. Finally, in the early evening, the eagerly anticipated call came.

"Mazel tov! It's a boy!!"

A boy, a boy, a boy! I could not believe my ears. My heart was full of intense joy and gratitude to Hashem. I was now a *bubby* to two! There was no doubt in anyone's mind as to what this baby's name would be. The exciting news traveled far and wide.

Once again, I packed everyone up and made the trip down to New York for the *bris*. I was jittery as could be, filled with nervous energy, anticipation, and a hodge-podge of emotions. The intensity increased as the morning of the *bris* approached. I stood off to the side, deep in thought, and prayed for the future of this tiny infant.

As Ari called out his name—Yehuda Pinchas—I burst into tears, shoulders shaking, my emotions overflowing. Yehuda Pinchas Simes, a name synonymous with greatness, dedication, perseverance, and faith in the face of strong adversity.[1]

We traveled home to Ottawa for what would turn out to be one of the last times. Within days, we were back in New York to celebrate Pesach with our extended family.

A few days after our return home, we traveled *again* to New York. An already momentous occasion, Yehuda Pinchas's *pidyon haben* was even more special as it was the first time this ceremony was performed in our family.

---

1. There were two others already named for Yehuda. My sister, Elisheva, gave birth to a boy about one month after Yehuda passed away, and named him Yehuda. Osnat and Shay named their baby boy Ori Yehuda. Yehuda was a light unto the world, and they hoped their son would grow up to be just like him. About a year after Shmuly's baby Yehuda Pinchas was born, Malka gave birth to a boy, and he is named Pinchas.

We Answer the Call

We could no longer ignore it: New York was calling my name loud and clear! It was time for Operation Family Reunification. As much as I would have wanted, I could not postpone sharing our decision with our friends in Ottawa. It was important that they hear the news from me, before it "hit the streets." Over the course of seventeen years, our Ottawa friends had been together with us through thick and thin. When I told them, they were disappointed but not shocked. Thankfully, they supported our decision and understood the need for our family to be together. That July, we moved to Queens, New York.

The school year began, and Elisheva went off to seminary in Israel. I was able to drive her to the airport for her group flight—I was not able to do that for Malka and Bayla. Chan started tenth grade. It was the first time in ten years that I did not have a daughter boarding in another city. Bayla, having just recently gotten engaged to Simcha, son of Yosi and Tova Greenfield, had been able to date from our own home. My heart felt whole again. My family was together.

"Like Olive Saplings around Your Table"

In December of 2019, I celebrated my forty-seventh birthday. As it approached, I had mixed feelings. Forty-seven is not necessarily a milestone birthday, but it felt like one to me. I had been through a lot in the past nine and a half years. In six months, it would be a full decade since the accident. It saddened me and I was in a contemplative mood for a few days.

One evening, I said to myself, *Shaindel, no self-pity now. On with it! Celebrate—you're turning forty-seven—rock it!* I sent a group text to my children announcing that I would be throwing myself a birthday bash on a Shabbos in a few weeks' time. Unbeknownst to me, there was another group text going around from which I was intentionally excluded. My children were conspiring to plan a grand birthday dinner for me. When they saw my text, they were thrown into a quandary. Do they tell me what they were planning and take over? Do they drop the idea and let me take over? Smart kids, these kids of mine; they know what is good for them. They dropped the element of surprise, filled me in on the plans, and took over from there. They shopped, prepared, cooked, and baked two multi-course meals with all the trimmings—down to the color-coordinated table décor—no dishes for me to wash.

I let my mind wander to the events that led me to be sitting at my dining room table, here in Queens.

As I sat at the table gazing at my family and taking in the scene, my heart was bursting with pride and gratitude. I could not help but marvel. I thought I had nine children; surrounding me I saw children, teens, adults, couples—healthy, happy, successful human beings—some with children of their own, chatting away, carefree and happy.

I thought about how far we had come. In the past nine and a half years, there were many growing pains, but we also experienced intense highs. Graduations, a bar mitzvah, engagements, marriages, and births. A piece of us is missing, a piece that can never be replaced, the piece that made us who we are. We will treasure that piece always, as we take Yehuda's memory with us into the years to come.

Afterword

I HAVE ALWAYS LOVED BUTTERFLIES. THE SHEER BEAUTY AND magnificence of these small creatures, the dainty flap of their wings in flight, never cease to amaze me. An up-close encounter with hundreds of butterflies is one of my fondest memories.

It was our third year in Ottawa. A friend casually mentioned a butterfly exhibit on display at Carleton University. I was enchanted by the prospect of experiencing it. On the day of the event, I eagerly prepared my daughters' clothes. They would wear their matching dresses with images of butterflies on the front.

We walked into the netted room. Everywhere we turned, we saw flitting, fluttering butterflies. As I held my seven-month-old daughter, a butterfly landed on her. It was the sweetest sight you could imagine. Fortunately, we captured the moment forever on camera.

To me, butterflies are symbolic of life. Butterflies do not start out as their beautiful selves. They begin as caterpillars and must undergo metamorphosis. They are encapsulated in a cocoon before emerging from their transformation.

Chan at the Butterfly Exhibit, Carleton University, Sukkos 2004.

Over the years, my children have asked for various pets. I explained to them that I do not take care of animals, I take care of children. One summer, I magnanimously allowed them to keep a caterpillar that we found on a nature hike. There was one catch. It had to stay on the deck in a shoebox; it could *not* come into the house. We watched it spin a cocoon and took turns guessing what color butterfly it would become. Alas, our dear pet did not survive the frigid Ottawa winter.

When I think of our own journey, I prefer to think about the butterflies that do survive the process. I think of the cocoons we have had to build—spinning round and round, adjusting to new circumstances time and time again. At first, events were referred to as "before" and "after" the accident. "Before the accident" was "normal." "After" was not! But it did become normal. No matter how "not normal" our circumstances were, we were forced to grow and change and mold ourselves to fit our new situation. It was a constant growth process in which we would barely get used to the new stage of normal before being tested with another trying situation.

I look at those trials as the silk of the cocoon. Spin and spin so that we can grow and become better human beings. I think of the lessons we have learned, the character traits I have worked on, and I realize: I am not the same person I was nine years ago. I am not the same person I was five years ago. Or even last year. This is a good thing. I am growing and I am becoming. For, after all, that is my purpose in this world; to become the best me I can be.

There was a time I used to think, "I did not sign up for this." But now I know the truth. I did.

I really did.